Capitalism and the New Political Unconscious

Political Theory and Contemporary Philosophy

Political Theory and Contemporary Philosophy encourages a sustained dialogue between the most important intellectual currents in recent European philosophy—including phenomenology, deconstruction, hermeneutics—and key political theories and concepts, both classical and modern. In doing so, it not only sheds new light on today's shifting political realities but also explores the previously neglected consequences of the two disciplines.

Series editor: Michael Marder

Other volumes in the series include:
The Fascism of Ambiguity: A Conceptual Essay, Marcia Sá Cavalcante Schuback (translated by Rodrigo Maltez Novaes)
Ethics Under Capital: MacIntyre, Communication, and the Culture Wars, Jason Hannan
Politics in the Times of Indignation: The Crisis of Representative Democracy, Daniel Innerarity (translated by Sandra Kingery)
The Sacred and the Political: Explorations on Mimesis, Violence and Religion, edited by Elisabetta Brighi and Antonio Cerella
Medialogies: Inflationary Media and the Crisis of Reality, David R. Castillo and William Egginton
Democracy and Its Others, Jeffrey H. Epstein
The Democracy of Knowledge, Daniel Innerarity (translated by Sandra Kingery)
The Voice of Conscience: A Political Genealogy of Western Ethical Experience, Mika Ojakangas
The Politics of Nihilism, edited by Nitzan Lebovic and Roy Ben-Shai
On Hegel's Philosophy of Right, Martin Heidegger, edited by Peter Trawny, Marcia Sá Cavalcante Schuback and Michael Marder (translated by Andrew J. Mitchell)
Deconstructing Zionism, Michael Marder and Santiago Zabala
Heidegger on Hegel's Philosophy of Right, Marcia Sá Cavalcante Schuback, Michael Marder and Peter Trawny
The Metaphysics of Terror, Rasmus Ugilt
The Negative Revolution, Artemy Magun
The Voice of Conscience, Mika Ojakangas
Contemporary Democracy and the Sacred, Jon Wittrock

Capitalism and the New Political Unconscious

A Philosophy of Immanence

Edited by Riccardo Panattoni and Fabio Vighi

BLOOMSBURY ACADEMIC
LONDON • NEW YORK • OXFORD • NEW DELHI • SYDNEY

BLOOMSBURY ACADEMIC
Bloomsbury Publishing Plc
50 Bedford Square, London, WC1B 3DP, UK
1385 Broadway, New York, NY 10018, USA
29 Earlsfort Terrace, Dublin 2, Ireland

BLOOMSBURY, BLOOMSBURY ACADEMIC and the Diana logo are trademarks of
Bloomsbury Publishing Plc

First published in Great Britain 2023
This paperback edition published 2024

Copyright © Riccardo Panattoni, Fabio Vighi and Contributors, 2023

Riccardo Panattoni and Fabio Vighi have asserted their right under the Copyright, Designs and Patents Act, 1988, to be identified as Editors of this work.

For legal purposes the Acknowledgement on p. ix constitutes an extension of this copyright page.

All rights reserved. No part of this publication may be reproduced or transmitted in any form or by any means, electronic or mechanical, including photocopying, recording, or any information storage or retrieval system, without prior permission in writing from the publishers.

Bloomsbury Publishing Plc does not have any control over, or responsibility for, any third-party websites referred to or in this book. All internet addresses given in this book were correct at the time of going to press. The author and publisher regret any inconvenience caused if addresses have changed or sites have ceased to exist, but can accept no responsibility for any such changes.

A catalogue record for this book is available from the British Library.

A catalog record for this book is available from the Library of Congress.

ISBN: HB: 978-1-3502-4024-7
PB: 978-1-3502-4029-2
ePDF: 978-1-3502-4026-1
eBook: 978-1-3502-4027-8

Series: Political Theory and Contemporary Philosophy

Typeset by RefineCatch Limited, Bungay, Suffolk

To find out more about our authors and books visit www.bloomsbury.com and sign up for our newsletters.

Contents

List of Contributors   vi
Acknowledgement   ix

Introduction   *Riccardo Panattoni and Fabio Vighi*   1

Part 1   Institutions

1   On Institutions   *Roberto Esposito*   9

2   For a Clinical Theory of the Institution   *Massimo Recalcati*   21

3   Instituting Power   *Riccardo Panattoni*   35

4   Vox Populi, Vox Dei: On the Vocal Substance of the Present
    Federico Leoni   47

Part 2   Ideology

5   Neo-plebs and Elites in the Global World   *Matteo Vegetti*   65

6   On the Theatricality and Historicity of the Political   *Gregor Moder*   87

7   A Critique of Biopolitics   *Maurizio Lazzarato*   105

8   Profit, Knowledge and *Jouissance*: Lacan and the Logic of Action
    Matteo Bonazzi   119

Part 3   Capitalism

9   Jansenist Morality and the Compulsion of Capitalism   *Samo Tomšič*   135

10   Capitalism and Law: From Servitude to Freedom   *Todd McGowan*   165

11   *Matrix Resurrections*, or *Jouissance* as a Political Factor   *Slavoj Žižek*   183

12   The Perfect Crime? Baudrillard, Covid-19 and Capitalist Virulence
    Fabio Vighi   195

Index   217

List of Contributors

Matteo Bonazzi is a researcher in Moral Philosophy at the Department of Human Sciences, University of Verona, where he is scientific coordinator of the Tiresia Research Centre for Philosophy and Psychoanalysis. He is a psychotherapist and psychoanalyst (member of the Lacanian School of Psychoanalysis and the World Association of Psychoanalysis) and managing editor of the Journal *PHI/PSY. Journal of Philosophy and Psychoanalysis* (ETS). In addition to various essays, he is the author of *Il Libro e la scrittura. Tra Hegel e Derrida* (2004); *Scrivere la contingenza. Esperienza, linguaggio, scrittura in Jacques* Lacan (2009); *El lugar político del inconsciente contemporáneo* (2012); *Il teatro del desiderio. Jacques Lacan, da Platone e Spinoza* (2022).

Roberto Esposito is Professor of Theoretical Philosophy at the Scuola Normale Superiore of Pisa, Italy. He is the author of several books including *Communitas: The Origin and Destiny of Community* (2004), *Bios: Biopolitics and Philosophy* (2008), *Immunitas: The Protection and Negation of Life* (2011), *Living Thought: The Origins and Actuality of Italian Philosophy* (2012), *Two: The Machine of Political Theology and the Place of Thought* (2015), *Politics and Negation: for an Affirmative Philosophy* (2019). On the topic of institutions he has recently published *Instituting Thought: Three Paradigms of Political Ontology* (2021) and *Institution* (2022).

Maurizio Lazzarato is a sociologist and philosopher. In the 1970s, he was an activist in the workers' movement (Autonomia Operaia) in Italy. He was also a founding member of the journal *Multitudes*. He is a researcher at Matisse/CNRS, Pantheon-Sorbonne (University Paris I), and a member of the International College of Philosophy in Paris. Among his publications are *The Making of the Indebted Man* (2012), *Signs and Machines* (2014), *Governing by Debt* (2015), *Experimental Politics: Work, Welfare, and Creativity in the Neoliberal Age* (2017) and *Capital Hates Everyone: Fascism or Revolution* (2021).

Federico Leoni teaches Philosophical Anthropology at the University of Verona, where he directs (with Riccardo Panattoni) the Tiresia Research Centre for Philosophy and Psychoanalysis. He co-edits the international journal *Chiasmi*, writes in various Italian and European scientific journals, collaborates with 'il manifesto', 'Alias', and 'Doppiozero'. He edited *Sade, Masoch. Two ethics of immanence* ('aut aut', 2019). His books include *Habeas corpus. Sei genealogie del corpo occidentale* (2008); *L'idiota e la lettera. Saggi sul* Flaubert *di Sartre* (2013); *Jacques Lacan. L'economia dell'assoluto* (2016); *Jacques Lacan, una scienza di fantasmi* (2019); *Bergson. Segni di vita* (2021); *L'immagine-scatola. Joseph Cornell, Masashi Echigo, Robin Meier* (2022).

Todd McGowan is Professor of English and Film at the University of Vermont, USA, where he teaches film, psychoanalysis and critical theory. He is also the author of several books in these areas, including *Universality and Identity Politics* (2020), *Emancipation After Hegel* (2019), *Capitalism and Desire* (2016) and *The Real Gaze: Film Theory after Lacan* (2007). He is the series editor of 'Film Theory in Practice' (Bloomsbury), and co-series editor (with Slavoj Žižek and Adrian Johnston) of 'Diaeresis' (Northwestern University Press). He is also the host of the podcast *Why Theory* (with Ryan Engley).

Gregor Moder is a Senior Research Associate at the Department of Philosophy of the Faculty of Arts, University of Ljubljana. In 2019, he won a 3-year research grant for a project on the theatricality of power, and he visited Princeton in 2020 as a Fulbright scholar to pursue this question in the writings of Foucault, Hegel and Shakespeare. His recent works include *Hegel and Spinoza: Substance and Negativity* (Northwestern University Press, 2017) and an edited volume on the *Object of Comedy* (Palgrave Macmillan, 2020). He co-founded Aufhebung: International Hegelian Association in Ljubljana and served as its first director (2014–20).

Riccardo Panattoni teaches ethics and psychoanalysis at the University of Verona, where he also directs the Department of Human Sciences, as well as, together with Federico Leoni, the Tiresia Research Centre for Philosophy and Psychoanalysis. With Federico Leoni, he is the editor of 'Le parole della psicoanalisi' (Orthotes) and 'PHI/PSY. Journal of Philosophy and Psychoanalysis' (ETS). Among his latest publications are *Giorgio Agamben. La vita che prende forma* (2018), *Altitudo. Perché l'essere umano desidera elevarsi?* (2019) and *Kim Ki-duk* (2019).

Massimo Recalcati, one of Italy's best-known psychoanalysts, teaches at the University of Verona and the University of Pavia. He directs IRPA (Institute for Research in Applied Psychoanalysis) and founded Jonas (Psychoanalytic Clinical Center for New Symptoms) in 2003. He writes regularly on the Italian daily newspapers 'La Repubblica' and 'La Stampa'. He is the author of numerous books, translated into several languages, including *L'uomo senza inconscio* (2010), *L'ora di lezione* (2014), *Il complesso di Telemaco* (2014), *Cosa resta del padre?* (2017), *I tabù del mondo* (2017), *La notte del Getsemani* (2019), *Il gesto di Caino* (2020), *Ritorno a Jean-Paul Sartre. Esistenza, infanzia e desiderio* (2021), *La tentazione del muro* (2021), *Il grido di Giobbe* (2021), and a two-volume monograph on Jacques Lacan (2012 and 2015).

Samo Tomšič is an interim Professor of Philosophy at the University of Fine Arts Hamburg, as well as a research associate at the Humboldt University Berlin. His research areas comprise political philosophy, critical epistemology and psychoanalytic theory. Recent publications include *The Capitalist Unconscious: Marx and Lacan* (2015) and *The Labour of Enjoyment. Toward a Critique of Libidinal Economy* (2019/2021).

Matteo Vegetti is Professor of Theories of Space at the University of Applied Sciences and Arts of Southern Switzerland. He also teaches at the Academy of Architecture in Mendrisio (USI) and at the University of Bergamo. His main works include *La fine della storia* (2000), *Lessico socio-filosofico della città* (2002); *Hegel e i confini dell'Occidente* (2004), *Filosofie della metropoli* (edited, 2009), *L'invenzione del globo* (2017).

Fabio Vighi is Professor of Critical Theory and Italian at Cardiff University, UK. His recent books include *Unworkable: Delusion of an Imploding Civilization* (2022), *Crisi di valore: Lacan, Marx e il crepuscolo della società del lavoro* (2018), *Critical Theory and the Crisis of Contemporary Capitalism* (2015, with Heiko Feldner), *Critical Theory and Film: Rethinking Ideology through Film Noir* (2012) and *On Žižek's Dialectics: Surplus, Subtraction, Sublimation* (2010).

Slavoj Žižek is a philosopher, cultural theorist and public intellectual. He is international director of the Birkbeck Institute for the Humanities at the University of London, visiting professor at New York University and a senior researcher at the University of Ljubljana's Department of Philosophy. His breakthrough work was 1989's *The Sublime Object of Ideology*, his first book in English, which was decisive in the introduction of the Ljubljana School's thought to English-speaking audiences. Since then has written over 50 books, translated in multiple languages, the latest of which is *Surplus-Enjoyment: A Guide for The Non-Perplexed* (2022).

Acknowledgement

Special thanks to Michael Marder, curator of *The Philosophical Salon* (online channel of the *Los Angeles Review of Books*), for allowing us to publish, in chapters 11 and 12, some revised sections of short pieces previously appeared in his online magazine.

Introduction

Riccardo Panattoni and Fabio Vighi

Jacques Lacan once stated that 'the unconscious is politics'.[1] This volume takes Lacan's claim seriously by exploring the idea that contemporary politics is undergoing a radical redefinition of its role in connection with the functioning of our institutions and their exercise of power within the context of contemporary capitalism. The book interrogates the assumption that today's power structures tend to function by exploiting unmediated forms of unconscious performance rather than provide transcendental conditions for the articulation of political meanings and social structures. Today, political apparatuses would seem to work by making the unconscious speak, and by displaying it in policies, speeches, tweets, images, gestures – in short, through political and institutional language. It is as if today's political power does not need symbolic or ideological frameworks any longer, but instead relies on its ability to tap into the people's disavowed modes of enjoyment. Far from demonstrating a shift to a post-ideological age, however, this transformation would seem to establish an altogether novel apparatus of power based on propaganda techniques and the uninterrupted coordination of consent.

The unconscious we interrogate in this book emerges in contemporary politics' communication and praxis, such as the automated bureaucratization of its policies and strategies, or in bodily and social media performances whose fundamental political target is the direct activation of the audience's libidinal response. By exploring contemporary power structures, the twelve chapters in this book, divided into three interrelated sections, aim not only to develop new perspectives in ideology critique, but also to stimulate critical thinking around political potentialities which are yet to be envisioned. Ultimately, the book asks whether a psychoanalysis and philosophy of immanence can be integral to the articulation of an alternative understanding of the political, one that is more attuned to grasping what appears to be the paradigm shift under way in contemporary capitalism. In short, when politics appears completely subjugated to the economic drive (the blind, anonymous and unconscious modus operandi of contemporary hyper-financialized capitalism), what are the chances that it might reinvent itself *beyond* its traditional transcendental role?

The volume begins with a text by Roberto Esposito, who reflects on the role of institutions vis-à-vis the Covid-19 pandemic. Esposito argues that through their very presence, institutions have managed to contain the spreading of a virus that would have otherwise ravaged entire populations. However, institutions have at the same time revealed an undeniable limit, which, rather than prompting us to attack them, should encourage us to improve them. While much has been said about the need to repair the damage caused in recent years by the neoliberal restructuring of public health, Esposito argues that such discussion should be extended to all the public institutions, from education to public administration. Through a survey of the relationship between institutions and movements, Esposito reflects on his concept of 'institutive praxis' [*prassi istituente*], understood as the process of *instituting* – of establishing something new.

Next, Massimo Recalcati's contribution, 'For a Clinical Theory of the Institution', makes use of Jacques Lacan's theory of the four discourses to offer some criteria for the assessment of the formal and normative consistency of institutions. The basic premise of Recalcati's text is that, at an institutional level, consistency does not coincide with the dominance of one discourse over others, but with the specific capacity to make distinct discourses flow and, as it were, breathe together. The necessary condition for the plural circulation of discourses is identified in their dependence on a fundamental void, which as such proves to be crucial also for 'institutional leadership'. The essay ends with a brief exploration of the main symptomatic formations that, in relation to the four discourses, could potentially corrupt the institutional machine: bureaucratization, indecisiveness, ideology and also, in connection with the fixity of the analytic discourse as theorized by Lacan, the risk of hindering the emergence of sociality as such (the social bond).

Endorsing a philosophical perspective of pure immanence, Riccardo Panattoni's chapter on 'Instituting Power' explores the 'disjunctive unity' of *destituent* power, as popularized by Giorgio Agamben, and *constituent* power. By emphasizing the intensity of the that disjunctive unity, Panattoni argues that it functions as the inaugural moment of what Roberto Esposito calls 'institutive power' (*potere istituente*). In order to explore the significance of institutive power starting from its intensity, the essay develops a comparative analysis of how power is conceptualized in the works of Giorgio Agamben, Roberto Esposito and Gilles Deleuze.

Federico Leoni's essay 'Vox Populi, Vox Dei' is a discussion of the status of the voice that starts from its psychoanalytic definition and develops its political significance. Leoni focuses on the voice as theorised by Jacques Lacan (voice as object cause of desire) in order to interrogate its meaning in connection with the crisis of contemporary democratic institutions. Specifically, the essay discusses the archaic notion of 'the people's voice' which, at a time when representative democracy is under pressure, would seem to constitute a 'purely expressive' form of politics.

Next, in Massimo Vegetti's contribution, 'Neo-plebs and Elites in the Global World', neoliberalism is discussed as an ideology that has progressively deconstructed the traditional class organization of society, promoting new forms of wealth (such as those of financial capitalism) and social marginalization. The concept of neo-plebs, which is central to Vegetti's investigation, refers to the latter: it corresponds to the 'social waste' of the contemporary mode of production – a 'social excess' that the processes of delocalization and automation have made irreversibly worthless. Vegetti defines and contextualizes the concept of neo-plebs starting from Hegel, who sees in the modern plebs a sort of enigma, since they seem extraneous to any social dialectic, and are thus also alien to the historicity of Spirit. In dialogue with authors such as Geiger, Foucault and Derrida, Vegetti demonstrates the relevance of the neo-plebs for understanding today's world, attempting to delineate the physiognomy of new social bonds and new governmental technologies.

The aim of Gregor Moder's essay, 'On the Theatricality and Historicity of the Political', is to explore the difference between the theatricality of 'polite everyday interactions and exchanges' and that of 'a staged Real'. By distinguishing between the two notions, one is able to separate the two theories of performativity in Slavoj Žižek's political thought. In addition to the analysis of the tension between these two theories, Moder explores their relevance through Hegel's understanding of historicity. He argues that if we take the two staple Hegelian concepts relating to performativity – the ceremonial monarch and historical repetition – the latter is perhaps better suited to Žižek's political theory precisely because it provides it with a historical dimension.

In the next piece, 'A Critique of Biopolitics', Maurizio Lazzarato argues that biopolitics is no longer able to function as Michel Foucault described it. On the one hand, most of its functions are taken over by the modern enterprise and its managerial structure, as the coronavirus crisis has shown; on the other hand, political movements throughout the twentieth century have operated in the opposite manner to the biopolitical logic of translating historical processes into biological ones. Today's public health sectors are not governed through the biopolitical logic of 'taking care of the population,' nor by equally generic 'necropolitics' (biopolitics of death, or eugenics). Rather, they are ruled by a meticulous, pervasive, rational (in its madness) and violent (in its performance) mode of production driven by profit and rent.

In 'Profit, Knowledge and *Jouissance*: Lacan and the Logic of Action', Matteo Bonazzi contends that, unlike Foucault (who tends to connect knowledge and power), Lacan's key focus rests on the (non-)relationship between knowledge and enjoyment (as derived from the analytic experience). Starting from this assumption, a possible understanding of two strategies of economic enjoyment emerges: the capitalist and the psychoanalytic one. Through the comparison of these two strategies, or discourses, Bonazzi investigates both the exit from capitalism prophesied by Lacan in *Television* and the Lacanian argument on the homology between surplus-value and surplus-enjoyment. Finally, Lacan's reference to China and the economic impact of its discursive strategy is questioned as another way of engaging the notion of profit within the subjective horizon of the *parlêtre* (speaking being).

Samo Tomšič's 'Jansenist Morality and the Capitalist Compulsion' begins with Jacques Lacan's *Seminar XVI* and his much-discussed claim that Marx's analysis of surplus-value and Freud's theory of enjoyment must be read in a homologous way. Tomšič, however, focuses on the next major claim of that seminar, which involves the step from Marx to Pascal. As well as engaging in an extensive discussion of Pascal's wager, Lacan eventually suggests that Pascal can be seen as the founder of capitalist morality, thus seemingly inverting Max Weber's thesis: it is not the protestant (work) ethic that underpins capitalism, but a much more problematic link between the play of speculation and the production of surplus-value. Against this background, Tomšič shows how Lacan's attempt to bring together Pascal, Marx and Freud illuminates the system of compulsions that capitalism succeeded in installing as a social link. The hard-line neoliberal – the libertarian – who blindly pursues the perpetuation of capitalism beyond democratic frameworks and environmental limits, should then be seen as the ultimate successor of Pascal's converted libertine. The big question, however, remains the same: by what means can psychoanalysis and Marxist politics break the vicious circle in which capitalist subjectivity is embedded?

Todd McGowan's 'Capitalism and Law: from Servitude to Freedom' discusses the authority of the state vs the authority of capital. He argues that while the legal apparatus of the state is visible and self-evident, the true master of modern life is capital, whose authority relies on presenting itself as liberation. In other words, McGowan contends that the capitalist economy is the site of servitude in modernity, while the state, despite functioning through coerced obedience, is the site of (potential) freedom – as asserted by Hegel. Arguing against biopolitical thinkers like Foucault and Agamben, and taking on Marx's view of the state, McGowan insists that the fundamental problem with the power of capitalist economy is that we cannot confront it as authority. Conversely, when we antagonize the state we miss how its role is precisely to obscure the primacy of capital in forming the social order.

Slavoj Žižek's essay, '*Matrix Resurrections*, or *Jouissance* as a Political Factor', begins with the analysis of *Matrix Resurrections* (2021) against the background of the original *Matrix* film. From there, he launches into a dialectical discussion of what the Lacanian symbolic order represents in relation to capital, delving also into the complex relationship between virtual reality and the Real. Finally, while interrogating the link between humans and machines in the context of today's highly automated capitalist order, Žižek claims that there can be no relationship between knowledge and the apocalypse – as exemplified in today's world plagued by pandemics and potential nuclear wars. The (Hegelian) truth of a 'knowledge about the apocalypse' should thus be turned around: it is knowledge itself that is by definition catastrophic, i.e., traversed by its impossibility.

In the final essay of the book, 'The Perfect Crime? Baudrillard, Covid-19 and Capitalist Virulence', Fabio Vighi explores the Covid-19 health emergency through Jean Baudrillard's notions of simulation and hyperreality, which he discusses at length. Specifically, Vighi argues that what is at stake in contemporary 'emergency capitalism' is the reproduction of a socio-economic order that, having destroyed its substance (value-productive labour), must now conceal at all costs the fact that real economic growth is vanishing. Since the 2007–08 economic crisis (and particularly since 2019) the monetary simulation of real growth requires an endless flow of 'global emergencies,' whose function is both to justify monetary expansion and to install a new authoritarian paradigm. Vighi argues that at the heart of our predicament lies the ruthless evolutionary logic of a capitalist system that, to prolong its lifespan, is ready to sacrifice its liberal-democratic framework and embrace a hyper-financialized regime supported by corporate-owned science and technology, media propaganda and a continuous flow of disaster narratives.

Note

1 Lesson of 10 May 1967, Seminar XIV, 'The Logic of Fantasy' (unpublished).

Part One

Institutions

1

On Institutions

Roberto Esposito

1

If I were to indicate the task we are faced with, while we are still waging war against the Covid-19 pandemic, I would say that it is to rethink the institution, in its most intense sense of *an institution of life*. After months in which human life has been threatened, and even overwhelmed, by death, our common endeavour can only be to establish it anew – to establish life anew, or even, to use Dante's term, to establish a *Vita Nova*.

After all, what is our life but a constant institution of new relationships and meanings? Recalling St Augustine, Hannah Arendt wrote that humans themselves are a beginning, because their first action is that of being born, thus giving birth to something that did not exist before. Therefore, it is not possible for human beings to stop instituting life. Even in the toughest times, like the ones we have gone through and are still currently experiencing, humans never lose their inclination towards starting over, setting off for a journey which concerns everyone.

All this is only possible through institutions, by modifying those already in place and establishing new ones. Of course, while each may have an individual life plan, no one can be totally indifferent to the surrounding society and its institutional organization. From this perspective, life and institutions are tied together in an indissoluble knot. Just as there is no life without institutions, so institutions incorporate people's lives within them and are made vital as a consequence.

Ultimately, institutions themselves are living organisms which are born, develop and occasionally perish. Not unlike the individuals, they are part of the flow of history, by which they are affected and which they affect in turn. In fact, it can be said that institutions are at the intersection of life and history, allowing for succession and generational replacement. Indeed, the function of institutions is not only to secure coexistence within a certain territory for a certain number of human beings, but also to provide continuity in transformation, by ensuring the transmission of the past generation's life onto the life of the generations to come.

Against this background, if we look at what is currently happening to us, we see that institutions have often been criticized for the way they responded to the present challenges. What is more impressive, though, is that the controversy came from different and sometimes opposite standpoints. Institutions were blamed on one side for their excessive reaction, and, on the other side, for their lack of decision-making. They were accused by some of unlawfully limiting individual freedoms and attacked by others for being unable to govern individual and collective behaviour with a firm hand.

I am not doubting the legitimacy and, in some cases, the validity of these criticisms. But, to preserve balance in judgement, we must stave off excessive generalizations and try to distinguish and articulate the different levels of the current discourse. Undoubtedly, some mistakes were made by the regional, national and international institutions in the effort to contain the spread of the disease – one could even argue that the negative aspects prevailed over the positive ones.

It is impossible to forgive the inadequacies, the shortcomings and delays which, in Italy, characterized the immediate reaction to the spread of the virus, causing irreparable harm not only on a social level but, especially in some areas of the country, also in terms of health. In addition to this lack of decisiveness, excessive interference occurred too, with severe social, economic and political costs.

The shifting of the border between legislative and executive power to the advantage of the latter, driven by the at times arbitrary and unnecessary use of the Emergency Ordinance, reached the point of threatening the democratic stability of Western political systems, which appeared to be troubled by their inevitable incapacity to rival the effectiveness of the draconian measures put in place by authoritarian regimes.

Having said that, we should also interrogate the role of institutions in reverse. That is, we should not ask ourselves how the institutions behaved towards us, but, on the contrary, how would we have withstood the virus attack without them. What would have happened, here and elsewhere, had there been no institutional framework to guide our behaviour?

From this point of view, we must acknowledge that, even though it is not immune from errors and omissions, the contribution of institutions appears to be our only available resource, at least during the most aggressive phases of the Covid-19 pandemic. I am not just referring to regional and national administrations, but to all the institutions available in the areas affected by the virus – from social organizations to professional associations and NGOs – which provided the last line of defence against the pandemic.

Only thanks to them could the pandemic be stopped from spreading undisturbed and ravage the whole country. Moreover, the fact that the institutions have revealed their undeniable limits should prompt us to try to amend them, rather than attacking them. Much has been said about the need to repair damage caused in recent years by the restructuring of public health. But the discussion should be extended to all public institutions, from education to public administration.

This is not only about the actual practices, but also about the philosophy of institutions in terms of their relationship with history. Institutions are valuable only if they are able to determine transformation. They should be considered in terms of becoming, rather than something petrified in time. The only institutions that can aspire to be trusted are the ones who are able to transform themselves according to the citizens' needs. Far from being in opposition, institutions and movements constitute the two complementary sides of social development. The difficulty in acknowledging this dialectic is generated by a double fallacy: on the one hand, the tendency to identify institutions with the state; on the other hand, the tendency to consider them as something static, rather than dynamic.

Conversely, as posited by the juridical theory of 'institutionalism', which has its roots in Italy, there are institutions which are beyond the state, and also anti-state institutions, such as organized protest movements or resistance movements. However, even in this case the relationship between institutions and movements must be considered as open and dialectical. Whilst movements can gain political relevance only by gradually institutionalizing themselves, institutions must prove themselves capable of movement and mobilization towards specific goals, in order to meet the demands that are directed to them.

To grasp the richest meaning of the word 'institution', our focus should shift from the noun to the verb, from the institution as something which is already formed, to the process of *instituting*, which literally means to establish something new. Of course, not just starting from scratch, but drawing on a pre-existing institutional framework which is inevitably destined to be altered. The institution – or better, the *institutive* praxis [*prassi istituente*] – is precisely what links the past to the future through the present moment.

For many years, this encounter between institutions and history has been overshadowed both in theory and practice. In particular, I am referring to the 1960s and 1970s, when a rigid separation between institutions and movements imposed itself. In the debates taking place in those years, institutions and movements were separated into two apparently irreconcilable polarities, in stark contrast with each other.

On the one hand, there was a re-proposition of a conservative type of institution, averse to any kind of change; on the other, a multiplication of anti-institutional movements devoid of any plan for political institutionalization. This divergence resulted in an increasingly marked gap between politics and society. The self-referential institutional mindset, unable to speak to the social world, was confronted by a wave of fragmented social protests, incapable of joining together to create a political front.

All this led to a twofold counterproductive outcome. The self-serving lack of openness of the institutions triggered a radical anti-institutional wave, which in turn exacerbated the institutions' rigidity. Any mediation was excluded a priori, so that conservative institutions and anti-institutional practices were reinforced mutually, thereby hindering any political process of renovation. It is striking that, albeit with different intentions, both right-wing and left-wing intellectuals ended up sharing the same static and conservative understanding of institutions – the former aiming to preserve them as they are, the latter to critique them and, ideally, dismantle them. In this way, the potential for a radical transformation of the existing institutional logic was stifled.

If we compare the writings of leftist intellectuals like Jean-Paul Sartre, Herbert Marcuse and Michel Foucault with those of right-wing intellectuals like Carl Schmitt and Arnold Gehlen, they seem to converge on a key point: albeit with opposite purposes, none of them understands institutions in terms of transformation. It appears as if the only possible approach is either to accept the existing institutions or abandon them to their fate. Thus, each side fed into the other in a vicious circle, since the conservative interpretation of institutions provoked an extremely anti-institutional reaction from those who contested their legitimacy. Many leftists felt that, if institutions were reactionary in themselves, then there was nothing left to do but to fight them head-on, without making any distinction.

The armed struggle of the 1970s (not only in Italy) was the extreme outcome of this vision, stuck in its inability to correlate institutions and history. The comeback of explicitly anarchist views is based on the same understanding, which alternates revolutionary claims with the abandonment of institutions.

What connects these contrasting positions is a claim for immediacy against institutional mediation. After all, what we call populism is nothing but the will to bypass institutions; and before that, the failure to understand their meaning.

2

Not until the 1980s was the interest towards institutions restored. Yet already in previous decades there were cultural movements – particularly French phenomenology, German anthropology and Italian juridical institutionalism – which revitalized the theory of institutions in many different ways, which cannot be examined here. What united these cultural strands, despite their many differences, was the idea that institutions are not superimposed on society like bastions defending existing powers, but are themselves the fruit of a social dynamic that continually modifies them. They are the intermediate space between society, law and politics that allows and channels social change within certain limits.

Rediscovering Institutions is the title of a book by James March and Johan Olsen. Published in 1989, it marks a symbolic watershed with respect to the previous thirty years, which had been characterized on the one hand by an underestimation, and on the other by a rejection, of institutional logic. It therefore opened a new phase in international reflection on the subject.

It is no coincidence that it was published on the same year as the fall of the Berlin Wall, reflecting the profound changes it brought about not only politically but also culturally. Until then, methodological individualism and Marxist culture, although opposed, had found themselves allied in an attempt to de-institutionalize politics. Both ended up not recognizing the role of institutions – for the liberal culture, institutions are oppressive with respect to individual choices; for the Marxist culture, they are ultimately determined by economic events.

For a long time, institutions were considered mere containers of individual and collective behaviour rather than decisive political subjects. Social class, economic models and technological transformations were regarded as determining factors of political dynamics much more than institutional practice. Then, at a certain point in the 1980s, the scenario changed: institutions began to appear more and more relevant in defining, orienting and transforming political agendas. And, in turn, political agendas had to take account of institutions, recognizing their importance with an intensity that has led some to speak of a 'new discovery'.

But what is decisive is the fact that, contrary to what one might think, this rediscovery of institutions was not followed by a strengthening of sovereign states, but by a reduction in their centrality. It is true that the state can be interpreted, not without reason, as the first and most comprehensive of institutions. The great modern philosophical-political tradition, from Hobbes to Hegel, has theorized this primacy, making the state the culmination of the historical process.

Nevertheless, although taken for granted by many, this primacy was questioned by the globalization process, whose escalation intensified in the late 80s as a consequence of the resolution of the Cold War and the end of the opposition between the two conflicting political and military blocs. The reunification of Germany and the acceleration of the European unification process, through the adoption of the euro, marked a profound change in international relations.

Today, we are well aware of the contradictions and inequities of the globalization processes – often successfully challenged by resistance and nationalist tendencies. Islamic fundamentalism has definitely buried the *belle époque* of globalization, together with its 'end of history' ideology. Nor can we rule out a lasting conflict between the West – already internally divided between Atlantic and European interests – and China. But even in this case, the conflict is for the moment confined to the economic terrain, within a world unified by global finance and information technology, which appear to be irreversible processes in the long term.

Indeed, it is highly unlikely that, in the long run, anything will stop, or even reverse, the decline of the modern order, which for at least five centuries was based on the full autonomy of sovereign states as the sole holders of the political decision-making. This does not mean that we can go back to the period before the sovereign state. It does not mean that we can return to pre-modern or even neo-medieval conditions. History, as is well known, does not go backwards.

Rather, what lies ahead is an international order centred upon the hegemony of a few continental-size powers, such as the United States, Russia and China. It is still an open question if the European Union will have enough political strength to compete with them. However, it seems unlikely that single European states will be able to play an autonomous role within the global scenario.

Even what is improperly defined as *sovereignty* appears to be a form of resistance to ongoing processes rather than a phenomenon capable of intercepting the future. It is true that the geo-political situation is evolving very rapidly. It may well be that the terrible pandemic crisis will produce, in the short term, forms of phobic closure within national borders. But the very possibility of countering the virus with structural measures, in medical and economic terms, requires a network of connections of at least continental, if not global, dimensions.

In the midst of this dynamic, institutions seem to have a crucial function in several respects. They can play a role both inside and outside the states, through forms of institutional cooperation which break the boundaries of the sovereign logic. The European Union itself, despite its limitations, is an extraordinarily relevant institutional creation. Conceived during the Second World War, it is the demonstration of an *institutive* ability that intensifies during the most dramatic moments, like the ones we are experiencing today.

This is further proof of how, in certain situations, an entire institutional process can be set in motion that was unimaginable only a few years earlier. The problem is always that of giving institutional logic a creative force that goes beyond the static definition of an institution. Institutions can play a fundamental role in the historical dynamic if, instead of limiting themselves to consolidating existing powers, they manage to govern the transformations under way, indeed becoming their primary channel.

This is only possible on condition that, rather than trying in vain to stop innovations and even ongoing political conflicts, they become the terrain for their deployment. Against the idea that the role of institutions is to neutralize conflicts, we must recognize the relationship between institution and conflict, already emphasized by Machiavelli when he argued that the social conflict in Rome between nobility and populace was the driving force behind the power of the Roman Republic.

3

Today we are witnessing a veritable proliferation of institutions that are independent of the national legal systems and located on a sub-, supra- or transnational horizon. In an increasing number of areas – from trade to health, from technology to communications – national laws are being expanded, or overridden, by conventions that make law itself a shifting, ever-changing mosaic.

Since states have lost the exclusivity of legislation, new institutional actors are increasingly taking over the creation of rules, giving rise to legal procedures that cut across the traditional bipolarity between the public and private sectors. Of course, the drive in this direction comes from the economy, since it has totally disengaged from national legislations, rather adapting them to its own purposes.

However, the legal vacuums opened up by the financial markets have been filled by other types of organization, not only external to states, but sometimes even in open competition with them, such as non-governmental organizations. Oriented not towards profit but rather towards generally humanitarian ends, they constitute one of the most interesting experiments in innovative institutive praxis. Although they are formally private organizations, they pursue public goals, submitting written rules to demands, needs and questions that are irreducible to the often rigid language of the state. Situated at the crossroads between law, ethics and politics, NGOs do not respond to (and indeed often force) the laws of states, referring instead to a sort of global civil society, indefinable in legal terms, but in fact operating in emergency situations such as war, migration, famine and epidemics.

Of course, in the chaotic scene of globalization, alongside institutions of this kind there are other bodies. They also are non-governmental, but expressing specific economic interests, such as the International Monetary Fund or the World Trade Organization, not to mention lobbies and corporations of an even more opaque nature. It goes without saying that these institutions are not equivalent: sometimes they favour vested interests, sometimes disadvantaged social groups. What is important is not only to distinguish between them, but to take a stand for one against the other, inserting explicitly political motives into arrangements that are only apparently technical.

Today it is increasingly difficult to separate law and politics. The European Union itself, born of an act of political will but constructed through legal treaties, is a mixed institution, the object of a bitter clash between different overlapping and juxtaposed levels of sovereignty that lead us to a post-state horizon. Of course, once the necessarily state-like character of institutions is contested, it would be difficult to exclude the state from the list. What we need to beware of is the bipolar scheme that sets state order against global order, or even sovereignty against government, without realizing that these are not only inextricably intertwined, but historically inscribed within each other.

On the other hand, as economic historians know, it is impossible to separate the birth and development of capitalism from the state as its container – which admittedly capital expands to the point of deforming it, but never breaking it. Who else but the state has produced, since the late 1970s, the structural conditions for the primacy of the economy, by diminishing or suspending its control over the organization of the labour market?

Neo-liberalism, in all its forms, including German ordo-liberalism, also stems from a political choice of states, particularly Atlantic and Central European ones, soon followed by almost all the others. Even the phenomenon of denationalization originated within the nation-states – as did the opposite attempts at out-of-date renationalization that we have been witnessing in recent years.

On the other hand, states can also be an important area of conflict between opposing interests. If in the last half century they seem to have lost part of their function, in the previous thirty years, the so-called glorious ones of the construction of Welfare societies (between the 1950s and 1970s), they constituted a fundamental terrain of class conflict. Even recently, in Latin America, Spain, Greece and elsewhere, the government of those countries has been the subject of a political battle between opposing social forces that has resulted in highly innovative constituent processes. This means that state institutions, and the state itself as an institution, can be used in different and conflicting ways – as a site for the accumulation of economic power by dominant groups, but also for the modification of power relations in favour of the disadvantaged.

It is true that many of these constitutional experiments within nation-states have failed or regressed in the face of internal and external pressures. From North Africa to Brazil, they have even given rise to a series of authoritarian backlashes, in the same years that Greece was bowing to the diktat of the Troika. This shows that, although still in operation, national sovereignty does not have the strength to victoriously counter the operations of capital.

This makes what some define as 'left-wing sovereignty' very problematic. The latter is often combined with populist rhetoric inclined to mythologize a homogeneity of the people that ends up neutralizing social conflict. In short, even without leaving the scene, the state does not have the strength to challenge transnational economic powers if it does not play at their same level, linking up with a wider network of non-state institutions.

Obviously, not every state or government is equal in terms of enabling political transformation. But the latter is bound to stall, or regress, if closed within the confines of sovereign states. Over the long period of Western history, institutional capacity has experienced different fortunes. Once the communal age was ended by the constitution of absolute states, only at times, and for rare moments, did the instituting paradigm resurface in modern history. After the eighteenth-century revolutions, its resurgence is only recognizable at the end of the Second World War.

The first resurgence occurred when a number of constitutions were written (including the Italian one) and the foundations of the European Union were laid in Ventotene. The second resurgence took place in the following thirty years, when parties and workers' unions played a literally constituent role that changed the balance of power in many European countries. Parties and trade unions worked by connecting the spheres of politics, economy and society – making labour and civil rights a political issue and politics a social issue. Today that glorious season is behind us, like the entire twentieth century, and it has not left heirs worthy of the name. But this is precisely why a new *institutive* commitment is required, which follows two different but converging lines.

The first line runs through the relationship between public and private institutions, opening up a space for what have been called 'the common good'. This term should not only be understood as referring to specific goods, but also to the cooperative form taken by new *institutive* processes through associations, organizations and networks designed to widen the circle of social inclusion in every sphere. The second line, which has yet to be activated, should link political organizations in different countries – in our case, mainly in the European area – united by common civil, social and environmental goals. Here too, rather than existing institutions – parties, trade unions, parliamentary groups – it is a question of establishing new bodies capable of taking over from the exhausted twentieth-century political groups – liberal, popular, socialist – that still sit in the European Parliament.

None of them seems able to deal with the challenges that lie ahead of us. Here too, the pandemic represents a decisive testing ground, not only for national and transnational institutions, but more importantly for the *institutive* thought which is flourishing in several epicentres of the contemporary intellectual scene. Moreover, what is being proposed on the level of theory has already been widely anticipated in historical reality by the proliferation of institutional arrangements that are external, and sometimes alternative, to the state order. From the economy to law and politics, the order centred on the nation-state enters into a dialectic of conflict with other institutions, public and private, global and local.

Far from being neutralized, political conflict is situated at the heart of the *institutive* praxis in a form that does not allow us to imagine a return to the old scenario of nation-states. Not even the pandemic, which threatens to produce new confinements, will be able, in the long term, to halt this process of universalization – as both the worldwide spread of the virus and the convergence of responses to it, starting with the search for a vaccine, clearly attest.

The truth is that we have entered a biopolitical dimension, irreducible to the sovereign paradigm. Its proliferation is marked by the increasing centrality assigned to living bodies; the classification of the population in sections based on age, gender, state of health; the strong correlation between politics and medicine. All these signs point in the same direction, which is rich in opportunities, but also in risks.

In this respect too, alongside and through individual choices, the function of institutions will be decisive in the society to come, on condition that they are able to address life in an affirmative manner, re-establishing the bond between institutions and movements that seems to have been interrupted. The need to institute life comes to the forefront once again, in the double sense of vitalizing institutions and restoring to life those *institutive* traits that push it beyond mere biological matter.

Translation from Italian by Francesca Campoli

2

For a Clinical Theory of the Institution

Massimo Recalcati

The question I consider crucial in this contribution is the question of the 'general health' of an institution. When does an institution fall ill? When does it breathe well and is generative? When does it produce symptoms that invalidate its functioning in different ways, and when is it able to make its dynamic force prevail over symptomatic inertia? In short, when does the death-drive prevail in an institution, rather than the life-drive?

My reflection consists of a very personal take on the theory of the four discourses that Jacques Lacan expounds in the first part of *Seminar XVII* (The Other Side of Psychoanalysis) and its application to the institutional field. With his discourse theory, the French psychoanalyst proposed a structuralist reduction of the hermeneutic multiplicity of discourses to four: master, hysteric, university and analyst. The notion of discourse defines the fundamental modes of social bonding. If with his psychology of the masses Freud had conceived the social bond as established by a constitutive alienation from the leader, structured on the basis of a principle of vertical identification (mass identification), in his theory of the four discourses Lacan shows that the social bond has different articulations, not always reducible to the phenomenon of mass association. It is therefore necessary to provide a preliminary definition, albeit in extreme synthesis, of the content of each individual discourse. I will do this very freely by interpreting Lacanian doctrine autonomously.

Master

The discourse of the master is the discourse of identification, the one that more than any other is linked to Freud's investigation into the power of identification over the social bond. This discourse structures the social bond on the basis of an idealizing identification with the charisma of the master. Not accidentally, in the algorithmic construction of this discourse Lacan places S1 in the position of the agent – that is, of the signifier deciding the basic orientation of the discourse, understood as a guide, a master-signifier. The grip of this signifier tends to be firm and univocal; it generates teams, tending to exclude otherness and produce homogeneity. Identification with the leader promotes – as Freud also pointed out in his psychology of the masses – a horizontal identification that assimilates the group's multitude into the same vertical identification. Everything that defines singular otherness is removed: in the algorithmic formulation of the discourse of the master, the small object a – index of the absolute singularity of desire – occupies the position of waste. In an institution governed by the discourse of the master there is no room for criticism, difference, the Jew, the woman.

Lacan conceptualizes the discourse of the master as a kind of matrix of all other discourses, the foundation of every possible discourse. This means that the master's is the discourse that grounds the possibility of the institutional field as such. Without the removal of the small object a – of the absolute and unconditional character of singular desire – there would be no institution at all. This is a major Freudian theme. The discourse of civilization can only be based on an original loss of *jouissance*, or, as Freud openly theorizes, on a 'renunciation drive'. In this sense, the discourse of the master is homologous to the symbolic dimension of the Law. This is a general definition that Lacan gives of every human institution whose primary task would be to put the brakes on *jouissance*. Without the law, it would not be possible to stem the anarchic drive of *jouissance*. The absolute and unconditional character of desire needs boundaries and limits. Every human institution is only possible against the background of a constitutive loss of *jouissance*. For this reason, in *Seminar XVII* Lacan recalls the profound homology between the Name of the Father (as a symbol of the Law) and castration (as a necessary loss of *jouissance*). Human life is humanized only as it transits through the institution of language. The latter demands the separation of the subject from any totalizing version of *jouissance*, and the prohibition of incest is the symbol of such separation. The discourse of the master is the discourse of the exclusion of the animal and, at the same time, the humanization of life in its necessarily alienated form. The master-signifier acts as that which, by negating life, separates existence from its immediacy, the body from *jouissance*. This is why Lacan reminds us that the master-signifier, while representing the subject for another signifier, negativizes its very being by making it unrepresentable. The discourse of the master, in other words, prohibits an unlimited, unrestrained, incestuous, castration-free *jouissance*. It prohibits the deadly *jouissance* of the Thing. This is, in fact, a common experience for those who live in institutions: an unregulated institution is one that does not know how to curb *jouissance*, failing to let the Law exist as the guardian of the impossible. This means that the discourse of the master is not simply alternative to the discourse of (unconscious) desire. On the contrary, the latter springs precisely from that discourse. This is what Paul of Tarsus also recalls in his Letter to the Romans: only thanks to the Law can sin and transgression exist. For this reason, Lacan can, in a way that may surprise us, define the discourse of the master as that which creates the conditions for the existence of the unconscious.

The main function of this discourse, however, is that of structuring an idealized identification that is at the heart of very meaning of identity. A flag, for example, is a master-signifier for the people who recognize in it the ideal symbol of their history and identity. And the word of a father, a teacher or a leader can also function in this way. Nevertheless, the role of the master-signifier does not stop at identity structuring, since it also implies the formalization of an ordered hierarchy that derives from the normative action of this same signifier. In more direct terms: there would be no institutional organization without a master-signifier. This is what anti-institutional movements miss: without the exclusion of the small object *a*, there is no structuring of a shared identity, no institutional field. On the one hand, it demands its symbolic rehabilitation in the face of the rising tide of anti-establishment criticism; without putting a stop to the erratic enjoyment of the multitude, communal life is unlivable – there is no institution without the discourse of the master, i.e. without the Law. On the other hand, it tends to cement an idealizing identification with the charisma of the leader while also generating phenomena of paranoid identity ossification. Internal and external otherness is experienced as a potential threat to the institutional stability of the whole. This is the symptom of the discourse of the master, to which I will return.

Hysteric

The discourse of the hysteric is the radical alternative to the master's. If in the latter truth is identified with power, in the hysterical discourse it assumes the dignity of a cause that orients desire. The hysterical discourse does not promote the master's identification with truth, but rather its incessant questioning, thus the very dynamism of truth, as Lacan wittily puts it. For this reason, in its algorithmic articulation, in the place of agency we find the signifier of the division of the subject, the barred subject $, indicating precisely that the orientation of the hysterical discourse is determined by the passion for the search for truth and the warning of its lack. Not, however, of an abstract, universal, ontological truth, but of a truth that cannot be separated from life. For this reason, as Lacan states, the hysterical discourse inscribes the truth in the symptom, attributing to the symptom 'a value of truth'.

At the forefront, we no longer find the idealising identification with the master-signifier and its pragmatic efficacy in guaranteeing institutional functioning, but a non-coincidence, a displacement. We do not find not identity but dis-identification, differentiation rather than uniformity. In fact, while the discourse of the master favours the coincidence of knowledge and truth, the discourse of the hysteric establishes a rift between them: truth is not the property of knowledge, but is rather an excess irreducible to any defined form of knowledge. 'There is nothing that can define me' is what a hysterical patient told me, revealing the fundamental vocation of her discourse.

Nevertheless, the knowledge that the hysterical discourse activates is not the dead encyclopaedic knowledge of the university discourse, nor the knowledge of the charismatic truth embodied in the sacred enunciation of the master. Instead, it is a knowledge that tends towards the truth, a knowledge that is in love with the truth. The knowledge without truth, without any relation to the absolute singularity of desire; the knowledge as abstraction, as the dissociation of singular and universal; the numerological, quantitative, impersonal knowledge that we will find at the heart of the university discourse, does not interest the hysteric at all. While the discourse of the master promotes a solid identity, the result of an idealising identification, that of the hysteric activates the unfulfilled search for truth. For this reason, Lacan tends to make science coincide with this discourse in its most dynamic movement of its search. From this point of view, the hysterical discourse is essential to the good functioning of the institution in that it counteracts every rigidifying consolidation, every paranoid hardening of identity, every masterly reduction of knowledge to power. In this sense, the soul of the hysterical discourse can be identified with the permanent dimension of criticism and self-criticism. It challenges the anonymous, conformist, paranoid and authoritarian rigidities that can arise from the discourse of the master.

University

The third discourse is that of the university. In his algorithmic formalization, Lacan places the reproduction of knowledge (S2) in the position of the agent. This is anonymous knowledge, a serial battery of desubjectivized utterances which are not supported by any singular enunciation. The knowledge of the university attempts to replace the charisma of the father with an apologetics of numbers. Its knowledge is grey and bureaucratic; it is the knowledge of repeated quotations. This knowledge, unlike the knowledge demanded by the hysterical discourse, has no relationship with truth. It is a sad knowledge without truth. If hysterical knowledge is fully absorbed in the endless search for truth, the knowledge of the university is closed in on itself, lifeless, dead, without momentum. It is the antiquated knowledge of philology without criticism, without strength and without desire. Its symbol is that of classification: the alphabetical accumulation of knowledge.

As we have seen, to this disembodied knowledge the hysteric opposes the knowledge of the symptom, which is the place of a painful incarnation where truth speaks in the suffering of the body. In the university degradation of knowledge, as in the scientistic degradation of science, what is at stake appears to be the exclusion of the subject. The university discourse excludes subjectification, interpretation, criticism, the vital eroticism of transference, the small object *a* that causes desire. Its ideal of knowledge is based solely on the uniform repetition of the same, which gives rise to 'established knowledge' – i.e., consolidated ignorance. For this reason, the university discourse is not required to generate knowledge, but only to preserve it. At the same time, as with any discourse, we must also enhance the dynamic side of university discourse. There is no institution without repetition. Repetition defines the necessary time of every institution. Just think of the automaton that governs school life: without repetition – *automaton* – there is no encounter with difference – *Tyche* – difference being nothing but a twist in repetition rather than an (impossible) avoidance of repetition. The purely charismatic presence of the master's enunciation must be able to be positively countered by the discourse of the university. The esoteric, inspired attitude of the master's *supposition* of knowledge must be tested by the *exposition* and *transmission* of knowledge. It is no coincidence that didactic repetition is an indispensable form of knowledge transmission in the highest sense of the term. In the discourse of the university, public exposition must take the place of private supposition. In order to produce new knowledge, capable of breaking through the uniform framework of repetition in which university discourse is inscribed, it is necessary to pass through this very repetition.

Analyst

The fourth discourse, finally, is that of the analyst. We have left it for last – following Lacan – because this discourse is a sort of degree zero of every other discourse. It is the unspeakable core included in every discourse, which as such is always wordless. It is no coincidence that here Lacan places the small object *a* in the position of the agent, the one who gives the basic direction to the discourse. In his algebra, object a as agent indicates the absolutely singular character of the object that is the cause of desire. This object decouples the plane of the universal, to which the discourse of the master would like to reduce the institutional field, by permanently de-totalizing any illusion of totality. The task of the discourse of the analyst is to point out that there is at least one element – the small object *a* – which resists assimilation to any universalizing procedure where the absolute difference of singular desire is integrated within a homogenous and normative plane. The discourse of the analyst reminds the master that every discourse is flawed. In this respect, it stands for the continuous subversion of the discourse of the master. The agent is not the idealizing identification (S1), but the dissolution of all identification, existence 'alone and without excuse', as Sartre would put it.

This discourse, then, does not drown singularity in universality, but exalts singularity as absolute, as a traumatic hole in the field of the universal. It is the Kiekegaardian loneliness that creeps into every discourse. However, while the hysterical discourse promotes singularity in the form of a knowledge that is not separated from truth (without ever coinciding with it), the analyst introduces singularity as *absolute difference* in order to displace any authoritarian or totalitarian tendency inherent in the discourse of the master. If the latter demands an inescapable quota of alienation and identification, the discourse of the analyst appears instead as anti-hypnotic; it reverses identification back into dis-identification. In this sense, it preserves the anarchic principle of singularity and desire – its excess with respect to the Law – which we can summarise with the determining position attributed to the small object *a*. What matters here is the discontinuity that this discourse introduces within the hypnotic identificatory mechanism that qualifies the discourse of the master and the psychology of the masses. While the latter sacrifices the singular to the universal (desire to the Law), the discourse of the analyst shows the irreducible heterogeneity that characterises the nature of the singular (desire) in relation to every universal (Law). By doing this, it works against identification (master), but also against vacuous hysteria (hysteric) as well as against abstract universalism (university).

The discourse of the analyst captures the negative point (the lacking substance) of all other discourses (identification, hysteria, universalization). Nevertheless, one cannot fail to notice the limits of this discourse if transferred to the level of institutional life. Without a basic level of identification and belonging there can be no human community. It is perhaps for this reason that the history of psychoanalysis highlights the difficulty of psychoanalysts fully to identify with the institutions that is supposed to represent them. In order to build a common place or share an institutional field, it is necessary to temper the principle of 'absolute difference' that constitutes the first instance of the discourse of the analyst. Without this tempering, the discourse of the analyst becomes an insurmountable obstacle to any form of symbolic mediation, since the absolute unconditionality of desire rejects any affirmative form of the Law. However, the analyst poses a fundamental problem for the institutional field: how to construct a common structure against the backdrop of the anarchic multiplicity of absolute differences. For Jean-Luc Nancy, this is the fundamental problem affecting the social bond: how is it possible to share the unsharable; how can we make the unsharable, in its impossibility, the condition of sharing?

Circulating discourses

The thesis I am proposing is that an institution breathes well and is generative when it is able to circulate the discourses that constitute it, when it is not rigidly identified with a single discourse but is able to circulate the plurality of the four discourses. Discursive fixation is generated by the univocal prevalence of one discourse over the others and the consequent unilateral unbalancing of the prevailing discourse. In fact, we should always distinguish two faces of a discourse; a dynamic face, and an inertial face. We have already noted this with regard to the discourse of the master, which is both an indispensable condition for creating an institutional field – no institutional life is possible without a rehabilitation of the discourse of the master – and a tendency toward the paranoid stiffening of its identity. When an institution falls ill, it is because the inertial side of the prevailing discourse annihilates the generative side. More broadly – and this is my basic thesis – this happens when there is a kind of stagnation, jamming, or discursive congealing instead of dynamic rotation between discourses. It follows that there is institutional illness when the institution identifies itself with a single discourse; when its ability to make discourses circulate among themselves is lost. It is not by chance that in *Seminar XVII* Lacan defines love as a 'change of discourse'. As such, every change or passing of discourse implies a subversion of the subject, an encounter and experience of transformation. On the other hand, the presence of hatred is always an indication of the tendency of the institution to fixate on a single discourse and (in particular, but not only) that of the master. Hatred is the most eloquent manifestation of discursive ossification. It prevents love as a 'change of discourse'. It is not by chance that, for Wilfred Bion, hatred is hatred of the void, of the not-thing, that is, for what should allow for rotation among discourses.

The central vacuum

An institution becomes ill when instead of the self-correcting circulation of discourses it crystallizes the hegemony of a single discourse that generates specific symptoms: identity paranoia (discursive fixation on the master's discourse); hyper-specialist bureaucratization (discursive fixation on the university's discourse); sterile inconclusiveness (discursive fixation on the hysteric's discourse), impossibility of any link (discursive fixation on the analyst's discourse).

An institution expands its field and becomes generative when it knows how to preserve the circulation of discourses, when it does not crystallize its identification with a single discourse. It is, as we have seen, the necessity to allow love as a 'discursive shift'. If the institution does not keep alive the force of Eros – the desire that should animate it – its existence risks sinking into inhibited mortification as the result of a despotic Law that overrides desire, or into the chaos of an acephalous magma resulting from a desire disconnected from the Law. In both cases – Law without desire or desire without Law – we would be faced with the domain of the death drive (*Todestrieb*). If the All-One of *jouissance* – its 'absolute difference' – is blind and noncompliant with the bond, the bond itself is empty, devoid of drive consistency. This is why Lacan defines love – the 'passage of discourse' – as the only possibility of making the *jouissance* of the One converge with the desire of the Other.

For discourses to circulate and fertilize the institutional field, there must be a central vacuum that acts as the pivot point of discursive rotation. The function of so-called leadership must be rethought starting from the inescapable centrality of this void. It is not a question of filling but of guarding the void. It has nothing to do, therefore, with the top-down managerial representation of that function. The filling of the central void is always an indication of an authoritarian-totalitarian distortion of the institutional mechanism. The risk of reading the function of leadership as an authoritarian guide committed to closing gaps rather than preserving their existence is a feature of groups and institutions supported by discursive fixation on the master's ideological discourse. Preserving the central void is instead the indispensable condition for the circular fluidification of discourses. It is a kind of unary trait devoid of idealization. This is the crucial problem of the irreducible discrepancy between the central void and *jouissance*'s tendency towards discursive fixation. In Lacanian algebra it is the relationship between $S(\cancel{A})$ and the small object *a*. How can the void be preserved without reviving the temptation of the father-master, but without, at the same time, reducing the void to a merely formal option? How can we make possible a link with the Other that is not based on the centrality of the Ideal, but is capable of taking into account the drive and territorial localizations of *jouissance*?

Keeping the central void open is not an abstractly transcendental function, but an ethical act. The circulation of discourse is not meta-discursive, but the effect that arises from an ethical positioning of those who have responsibility for giving direction to the institution. It is a matter of preserving the empty box that allows discursive rotation, the shift from one discourse to another. The authoritarian turn of any institution consists in reducing the empty to the full. It happens when the leader fills the central void with his own person, instead of presiding over it. That is why a healthy institution is one whose founder dissolves in his own act, takes care of his own deconstruction, knows, as Nietzsche would say, how to choose to set at the right time. If the void remains open, allowing circulation between discourses, it is because there is no reduction of the power of desire to the pure exercise of power. Rather, this very exercise is subordinate to keeping that power alive. This is why the institutions that breathe best are those where their founder or leader knows the 'art of sunset', of his own deposition.

Institutional subjectivity can therefore be diagnosed by following the general principle of discursive circulation or fixation. If each discourse has two faces – one propulsive, the other inertial; one plastic, the other fixed – and the rotation between discourses activates the propulsive side of each discourse by stemming the inertial one, discursive fixation is, on the contrary, determined as a stiffening of the inertial face of the discourse. In this specific case, we can speak of the institutional symptom as the result of a discursive fixation that prevents rotation between discourses. This is my thesis: institutional sickness is always related to the prevalence of discursive fixation over circulation between discourses. When this circulation is activated, however, it signals the affirmative convergence between the institutional field (Law) and that of the subject (desire). This convergence makes sure that desire is not identified with an object or an ideal institutional stance. In fact, desire must not be confused, with its imaginary relationship with the object, which is always frustrated and unsatisfied. Rather, desire must be thought of as a dynamic force, an affirmative expression of power in action. Keeping an institution in tune with desire means keeping alive the drive of desire, its dynamism, its generative transcendence. This point is also precisely isolated by Deleuze when he conceives of the institution not so much as 'putting the brakes on *jouissance*' (as Lacan would have put it), but as a 'positive model of action', a drive to expand its field, a force of de-territorialization.

Discursive fixations

Let us now try to briefly isolate the prevailing symptoms that afflict the life of an institution. There are indeed typical symptoms generated by the different discursive fixations. Let us first examine the discursive fixation at the university discourse. What happens there? Knowledge fills the central void that makes the rotation of discourses possible. It is a knowledge that has, as we have seen, the characteristic of being devoid of singular enunciation. It is a dead, recycled, bureaucratic knowledge, without creativity or invention. The S2 that governs the discourse of the university indicates the repetition of knowledge: knowledge as the site of a deadly repetition that subtracts space from the creative gesture. Desire, as a result, is not only extinguished and alienated, but is experienced as a destabilising threat to be normalized. The transmission of knowledge here takes place without the eroticism of transference. This is the formal, dehumanizing, impersonal, grey, administrative character of the university discourse. Its most specific symptom is that of bureaucratization: hierarchies, roles, titles, the distribution of tasks, the harnessing of individual initiatives, quantitative evaluation procedures, the fetishistic cult of figures. Concern for the specialized efficiency of the institutional machine discourages invention by animating obsessive and sometimes openly paranoid hostility towards its possibility. But if the equivalence between knowledge and value, or between knowledge and power, is valid for the university discourse (the decisive factor being not the relationship between knowledge and truth, but its possession) we must nevertheless remember, against the university discourse, that knowledge is never a property because its value depends on its circulation. But this circulation is what the university discourse actually tends to hinder by extinguishing the erotic desire for knowledge under the weight of an already constituted knowledge.

Let us now examine the second discursive fixation, the hysterical one. This is the reverse of the university fixation. While in the university the central void is filled with a hyper-specialized knowledge devoid of desire, here the central void is not filled with any knowledge but is attacked in the name of a truth that rejects all knowledge, that is, that considers all forms of knowledge inadequate to define itself as truth. The knowledge that the hysterical discourse seeks is never available, it never coincides with what is produced. Rather – and this is the propelling side of this discourse – it promotes knowledge as a quest, as a desire to know. It is the sublime gesture made by Socrates in Plato's *Symposium* in front of Agathon: the teacher does not possess knowledge, but is empty, animated by the desire to know. It is the dynamism of the hysterical discourse that every institution should highlight. Nonetheless, the hysterical discursive fixation of the institutional field consists in making the search for knowledge a motive for permanent and potentially self-dissolving criticism of the existence of the institution itself, whose knowledge would always be inadequate vis-à-vis the authentic spirit of the search, vis-à-vis the indefinable truth as transcendence irreducible to all knowledge. Anything that takes on the character of a defined production of knowledge is viewed with suspicion; any affirmative discourse is considered collusive with power. Only perpetual negation remains consistent with the spirit of the hysterical discourse. But this negation is not dialectical, it knows no self-overcoming, but rather becomes rigidly oppositional. It is the price that must be paid to preserve the purity of criticism in the face of the compromise that every institution must establish with reality. If in its clinical-psychopathological version the hysteric reveals her desire as perpetually unsatisfied – incapable of finding a point of mediation with the Law – this dissatisfaction is the same that is reproduced in the institutional field with a discursive fixation of the hysterical type. This field becomes that of a permanent and unproductive dispute with the discourse of the master: the claim of freedom against discipline, of the singular point of view against shared decisions, the always active suspicion of an institutional degeneration, of the deviation from the purity of the line, the refusal of every organisational principle, the prevalence of the anarchy of desire over the conservative immobilism of the Law, improvisation against programming, confusion and dispersion against every hierarchical stiffening of titles and roles.

But the major and clinically distinctive symptom of the hysterical discourse is the inconclusiveness of a sterile desire opposed to the Law. A desire that does not find support in the Law but which only experiences the Law as an antagonist is destined to generate empty transcendence. In this sense, the hysterical discourse is truly the mirror image of the university discourse. While the latter would like to subject desire to merely quantitative and institutionalized procedures, the hysterical one affirms a desire that is resolutely opposed to the institution, radically anti-institutional. It affirms desire as separated from the Law. If the discourse of the university favours the anonymous and universalistic repetition of knowledge by oppressing the erotic flicker of desire, the hysterical discourse affirms desire against all forms of knowledge in the name of a truth that differs from any realisation. In this sense, the hysterical discourse tends towards the impotence of a utopia, just as the university discourse tends towards its own lifeless self-preservation.

The pathology of discursive fixation on the master's discourse characterizes all authoritarian institutions. The symptomatic bond it generates reproduces euphoric identificatory compactness and the rejection of critical thought, which is typical of the masses studied by Le Bon and Freud; the same masses that Bion defined as 'mindless'. The drive is perverted and exalted by an idealizing vertical identification with the leader. Fanaticism, sectarianism, the systematic practice of censorship, the paranoid inclination that interprets every internal or external otherness as a permanent threat to one's identity have as their counterpart the strengthening of the sense of belonging. The institution dominated by the master's discourse appears firmly oriented. A classic example is that of ideology. What is ideology if not a discourse that loses plasticity, that tends to exclude other discourses, that presents itself as the ultimate discourse that closes – rather than rotates – other discourses? It is not by chance that Althusser in his *Three Notes on the Theory of Discourses* defines ideological discourse as centred on itself, with a single focus. The discursive fixation of the master's discourse tends structurally towards ideological illness. If in the hysterical discourse desire prevails over the Law, in this case it is the Law that dissociates itself from desire by subjugating it. In his reflections on the psychology of the masses, Freud deciphered the discursive fixation on the master's discourse as the cause of the totalitarian degeneration of the masses in the twentieth century: rigid and conformist identification, collectivism, fanaticism, paranoia towards the enemy (especially the internal one).

The last discursive fixation is on the analyst's discourse. This discourse introduces into the discursive rotation the crucial element of non-identification or non-homogeneity. The analyst's discourse has as its pivot point the small object *a* that in Lacanian algebra indicates what no social bond is able to make common; it is the subject as 'absolute difference': incomparable, indefinable, not sharable. When a discourse is fixed around this element, it makes any form of sociality impossible. It is not by chance that psychoanalysts find it extremely difficult to be together, to share a point of identification. If in fact the analyst's discourse moves in principle against any form of identification, thus consigning the subject to his/her own absolute difference, it is difficult, if not impossible, for this same discourse to promote any form of community. However, if there is no ideal institution, there can only be an institution that tends to unite desire and the Law rather than treating them as opposites.

3

Instituting Power

Riccardo Panattoni

Falling into the Political

Every time philosophy is questioned about its effective capacity to influence political action a point of crisis becomes visible. A sort of constitutive obstacle seems to materialize, as if searching for an immediate translatability of the political sphere entailed a loss of the status within which philosophical discourse is established. Clearly philosophy is able to discuss the political, but as soon as it subsumes it under its own criteria, it forces it to become the object of its own theoretical assumptions. For this reason, it is necessary to understand how thought can be developed between the instituting and the constituent criterion of power [*potenza*].[1] Indeed philosophy must always remain alert to the possibility of its political precipitate.

It is in the context of this unavoidable tension that philosophy is repeatedly called upon to express itself – from within the irreconcilable contrast between its tendency to include the political in its own narrative, and the need to place the political outside the philosophical field in order to be able to access it directly. The issue is, after all, always the same: philosophy is inherently established through speech, public speech. This speech, however, is peculiar, in that no one is necessarily obliged to listen to it. The risk and fascination of philosophy lie precisely in this undecidable contrast: its words are always destined to appear as words spoken in vain. This is why the political sphere, its public dimension, resonates as the fundamental phantasy underlying all philosophical thinking and summons it to measure itself against its own crisis point, its own unavoidable tendency to dissolution.

Indeed, at the structural juncture in which philosophical speech is upheld to invoke direct adherence to political acts (i.e., when it is required to perform by adhering perfectly to the criteria of the latter), it is as if its articulation were somewhat distorted, not least because it is not possible to say that the politicization of philosophical discourse necessarily implies an intensification of the political reflection. On the contrary, the more philosophical language is made to serve such a function, the more it loses its antagonistic drive. It becomes oriented towards a pure force of acceleration, in an attempt to fully adhere to its precipitate in history, engaged by the need to provide an answer to the immediate future. Here, however, lies the reason for referring to what we might call, following Deleuze,[2] the disjunctive synthesis between the *destituent* force of thought,[3] and the instituting power of the political, in order to retain the necessary inoperativity that philosophical reflection is called upon to instill with respect to any pure actualization of history.

It is possible to read the preface of Hannah Arendt's *Between Past and Future* in this sense.[4] Arendt highlights how René Char joined the Resistance – during the Second World War – as if he were sucked into politics with the force of a vacuum. The totally unexpected defeat of France emptied the political scene of the country, and the poet, who had never been directly involved in political events or in the country's public sphere, found himself implicated without any forewarning. According to Arendt this was against his conscious inclination: the void was such that the poet was left speechless, and his resolution could be translated only into pure action. A completely different situation from the one Heidegger found himself in when, in 1933, reading a speech when elected to Rector of the University of Freiburg, he joined the National Socialist Movement. The German philosopher structured his inaugural speech believing he could interpret historical events – i.e., the novelty represented by the advent of National Socialism – through his own philosophical categories. This led him to openly shift towards what, quoting Carl Schmitt, we may call Political Romanticism.[5] He was convinced, in other words, that if the National Socialist Movement had followed his philosophical arguments it would have acquired its proper political form; that is, it would have become able to respond adequately to its historical destiny: to bring the German people to the metaphysical heights from where it would be possible to hear the voice of being. In this case we are not dealing with the experience of a historical void, but with something so full it overflowed, pouring over the edges. This story has nothing to do with the event described by René Char. No one is left speechless; on the contrary, it is clear that the philosopher believed he would be able to voice the event of being, so the destiny of appropriation could unfold in all its articulations.

We may say that Heidegger's political ontology is the exact opposite of the aphorism with which René Char described his experience of the historical moment (mentioned by Arendt in her Preface): 'Our inheritance was left to us by no testament.' On the contrary, Heidegger intends to directly link the inheritance of the German people to the testament left by Greek philosophy, to inscribe the destiny of Nazi Germany in the mark left by the ancient Hellenic tradition, creating a bridge able to connect the two metaphysical peoples *par excellence*, one looking to the past, the other to the future. For this reason, Heidegger not only made the dramatic political error of joining the National Socialist Movement, but he also failed to address the connection between his own philosophical assumptions and the attempt to view them as useful in giving shape to the political possibility emerging in that particular historical juncture: precisely what Paul Celan asked of the German philosopher and was denied. This responsibility becomes radical when Heidegger starts to believe that the lasting connection with the legacy of Greek philosophy, with its tradition, could become one with the future represented by the novelty of the National Socialist Movement. Also for this reason, it is not particularly important to criticize the impolitic turn of his philosophy following this failure. What is more important is to consider the very impolitic nature of his philosophical position, the intrinsic possibility of such a sudden outcome in the context of this historical event. His is a transcendent position with respect to historical reality: Heidegger seems to observe everything from a perspective that is external to the same reality his discourse articulates – once again attributing a decisive role to the symbolic and performative nature of language.

Also, Deleuze's participation in the movement of 1968 (leaving aside the indisputable and incomparable differences in the historical and political context with respect to Heidegger's participation in the National Socialist Movement) represents the moment a precipitate is formed in the actuality of a historical present. In this case too we may speak of the acceleration of the expressive force of a voice that tends to propagate and disperse in the multitude of its own becoming. Here there is no vacuum, no suspension of speech: rather, once again, a fullness, an intensification that goes beyond any specific and contingent particularity. This horizon is in many ways exclusively affirmative, it is an activation captured inside a pure plane of immanence, where each singular life seems to be engaged in the dissolving act of a continuous generative process. Even though the effectiveness of this continuous constituent power is actually always (that is, every time in an exact manner, and thanks to the very singularity of that life) disjoined in the synthesis of a counter-effectualization, determined by the destituent power that such an impersonal and generative act imposes in itself.

For this reason, it is useful to highlight the continuous tension between the destituent and constituent force of power, in order to allow an instituting articulation to emerge with respect to the very concept of power. Which means understanding the latter as the disjunctive synthesis between the destituent and the constituent that remain active within its very meaning. In such a way that whoever speaks is always called upon to speak also in the name of his/her own singularity, and not to intervene in the name of rights alone, including when the rights of humans are at stake, but always in the name of life, of a particular life articulated in its own singularity. State and Law respond to the *molar* structure of what we may identify as a macrophysics of power, and in order to approach the exercise of power, its real and immanent dimension, it is necessary to recognize oneself within a *molecular* structure that is destituent in the process by which it constitutes itself within its own becoming. A philosophical act should therefore not orient the exercise of its own knowledge so as to formulate a general theory of state sovereignty, nor should it strive to define the form that the Law should acquire, or participate in the recognition of the global unity that claims to impose its domination. Rather, it should dwell essentially on the local and molecular exercise with which power articulates itself, and abstain from addressing statistical determinations. State sovereignty, the form of the Law or the global unity of domination, on the other hand, are exclusively oriented towards defining the ultimate forms of a transcendent principle of power. This does not mean there should be no State; nor does it mean the existence of Law is completely unnecessary. Rather, it means that the reflexive exercise of power, its force, is first and foremost a molecular movement that precedes all instances of statistical organization.[6]

The disjunctive synthesis of power, or of the plane of immanence

In *Marcel Proust et les signes*,[7] Deleuze highlights an essential difference between art and life that can be found in *À la recherche du temps perdu*.[8] In fact, art is referred to as that which does not rest on the becoming event of involuntary memory, but is rather grounded in the faculty of thinking exclusively aimed at grasping that which is essential. Essence, however, should not be understood in the Platonic sense, but as virtuality, as that which is real despite not being actual, as dematerialized entity that does not belong to the sensitive domain. It is a position, in other words, that views art as the only reflective mode capable of a real sublimation of the temporal experience that structures life, as opposed to the intrinsic limits that scientific knowledge, as well as philosophical knowledge, present with regard to this capacity. In this reading of Proust's work what emerges is a capacity of not putting forward a contrastive force with respect to the continuous tension exerted by the particle *not*, in such a way as to highlight how negation can act with respect to the tendency to concertation that characterizes philosophy: thought is, in other words, directed exclusively towards the determinations that force it to exercise itself. Thought is pushed to the edge of a coercive force that leads it towards an inevitable clash of forces. Time regained in lost time therefore exercises its own underlying motive thanks to the impressions that compel us to look, the encounters that compel us to interpret, and the expression that compel us to think.

It is not possible here to carry out an in-depth analysis of the extremely complex relationship between art and life. Although Deleuze highlights and carefully exposes the implications of the superiority that Proust attributes to art, we must nevertheless note that the book on Proust still presents the fundamental need for a counter-effectualization of this superiority through an immanent articulation of a life that is always embodied in its minority, in what is left out and is not subsumable. And so, despite the fact it is certainly not individuals who constitute worlds, but essences that determine individuals for the world they are, what still remains to be understood is the complex mechanism of reminiscence. That is, the mechanism by which what at first sight seems to respond to a direct associative pattern, does not in fact present a simple similarity between a present sensation and a past one, but rather an identical quality present in both. In going from an involuntary act to reminiscence, in fact, what is highlighted is how the present sensation is retrieved not so much in its original form, in continuity with the past sensation, but with a sense of splendour and authenticity that does not characterize experience itself, neither present nor past. Herein lies the fundamental importance of the concept of virtual in Deleuze. This concept is the outcome of a sort of shift: it is accentuated with respect to what we find in the work of Bergson, from whom it was borrowed (as can be seen clearly in the two fundamental books that Deleuze dedicated to cinema, *L'image-mouvement: cinéma 1*,[9] and *L'image-temps: cinéma 2*,[10] where his conception of film images is articulated together with an almost literal commentary on *Matière et mémoire*).[11]

Obviously, the concept of virtual would require a vast and detailed analysis too. The most important aspect is, however, that the virtual does not respond to the sole criteria of possibility, which means it cannot be equated with something purely imaginary that is articulated in all its determinations: if anything, it maintains the indetermination of the point in which this imaginary arises. It does not even coincide with the real, or rather, it constitutes its internal fault line. In such a way that the concept of virtual never posits the correspondence of something that is fully real, but rather the experience of something that is *not* experienced, which is not, however, to be understood as the imaginative force of what could have been and was not. Rather, this not-experienced is determined as the irruption of an inevitable destituent power, of a permanent action of revocation with respect to what being-in-progress does not in itself cease to constitute. This is a folding of being in action to be grasped in strictly temporal, not spatial, terms. Only in this way does virtual experience cease to respond to a mere identification of being with difference, preventing the articulation of being from being mere process of continuous differentiation. In this sense it is necessary to highlight the necessary shift with respect to Bergson's conceptualization, in which the virtual is viewed above all as a perpetually differential form, where the act of perception is continually subjected to a disintegration that forces, in a virtual way, to an always different actualization. The shift from this conception means that experience of the virtual no longer entails the belief that without the symbolic, without the tear that the negative exerts on experience, we would be crushed by the pressure of the real – which, moreover, is inevitably translated into the projection of something purely imaginary.

In this sense, it may be helpful to view the virtual through Lacan's three registers of the imaginary, the symbolic and the real. It is not a question of adding a fourth register to the first three, but rather of thinking of these three registers plus one. As far as the structure of the three registers is concerned, the real is presented as unbearable, as an event that cannot be experienced and whose irruption determines an inevitable traumatic response. Hence only *après-coup* is it possible to re-signify the event by retracing it with the symbolic, so that the impact is not projected onto the implications of the purely imaginary. With respect to this structure, we should think of the insertion of the virtual as a differential recording of the event. The virtual, in fact, does not coincide with the real, but corresponds to it only by temporally dilating its effects: we could say that the virtual is a differential experience in the time determined by the effects of the real.

A space opens up in the temporal experience of the event such that the real is no longer what leaves a hole. Only the symbolic is able to weave a possible pattern on the edges of this void. Therefore, the virtual reveals itself as a contrasting force with respect to the resignifying action of the symbolic, with respect to the unconditional trust placed in language; it allows to introduce a different spectrum though which to relate to the fundamental structure of the imaginary. What emerges, in other words, is the need for a paradigm shift, in part still to be explored in its implications, in which images play an essential role. Indeed, Roland Barthes himself (who was in many ways much more Proustian than Deleuze), when questioning the ontological nature of photography, and comparing it to the visual experience of Japanese haiku – to what characterizes its point of emergence, its instituting trait – dedicated his last university course to demonstrating how the brevity of the visual dimension contrasts the narrative proliferation of the symbolic.[12] Without investigating this point further, we can however say that his proposal for an iconological neo-structuralism represented a paradigm shift, whereby its field of reference required to radically rethink the very structure of the imaginary. The latter must be grasped in the point of incidence with virtual experience, which is disjointed from the determination of the real.

Hamlet, Bartleby or misconstruction

We might say that the stuntman of philosophical action in the political domain is Hamlet. Lacan clearly demonstrates that the Shakespearean hero is not at all incapable of acting[13] – when it comes to killing Polonius, Hamlet performs the deed swiftly, without the slightest sign of hesitation. Hamlet embodies the immanent experience of time, which is out of joint, and is the perfect expression of the need expressed by René Char, to be able to inherit without a testament. Hamlet is the product of a present in which time is no longer measured against movement, because movement is subordinate to time, it is articulated by what its condition dictates. Deleuze tells us that Hamlet is the first hero who actually needs time to act,[14] who senses the central void constituting the temporal structure and who draws the optics for his visionary ability precisely from this blind spot. His action, therefore, does not derive at all from the consequence of an original movement or from the implications of an aberrant action; he does not follow the testament that Greek tragedy artfully constructed to shed light on human life. Rather, he is aware that although things happen at different times, they are at the same time also simultaneous and do not cease to persist in any one time. The figure of Hamlet allows us to focus precisely on this 'any one': if time is out of joint, succession and simultaneity are nothing but ways of permanence of time. This is why Hamlet's character seemingly reflects a passive existence: like the actor or the sleeper, he no longer embodies skepticism or doubt, but orients himself exclusively toward the action of criticism. Hamlet is the subject who is barred at the origin. He has always been cut through by the form of time, in such a way that his permanence in that 'any one' is the formal event by which he is affected by himself. It is a form of interiority that never ceases to tear him, divide him, double him: it is a split that is however never complete. This event is shaped like vertigo, like the oscillation of a destituent power through which the process of its subjectification never ceases to institute itself.

If on the one hand Proust is the great creator of the symbolic capacity to sublimate life in art, on the other hand Hamlet is the virtual counter-realization of what has not been experienced that structures life itself. This non-lived experience is anything but what it could have been and was not, in that it is the experience of non-appropriability with respect to the action that the symbolic exerts between the imaginary and the real: a minor language being uninterruptedly carved into a major language. The language of mothers, of life, that we commonly call mother tongue, but that actually responds to the testamentary inheritance of the language of the father. This minority that belongs to a visionary language does not aim to the destitution of the symbolic force of language, but rather to its deposition, understood both in a theological sense, with reference to the immanent transcendence of the moment when the body of Christ yields to itself in all its weight, and in a juridical sense, as the counterpart of what Kafka described as the impossibility of testifying in the context of the constituent function of the Law. This minor language inside the major one is exemplified by Bartleby, Melville's scrivener.[15] 'I would prefer not to' is in fact a formula with a double temporality that never ceases to regenerate itself, to institute itself in the suspension determined by its fullness: it is the virtual emergence of an imaginary that evades utterance in a denotative form, as if the expression incorporated its punctuation, the colon, announcing the void of content that follows. This is why every time the lawyer, Bartleby's employer, hears the formula resonate in his office, he has the dizzying impression that everything must start again from scratch.

After all, the formula does not refer to something that still has to be said, which supposedly completes the sense of the statement. In fact, there is nothing more to be said or to be added. Here form is one with its own procedure, it overcomes the appearance of particularity without at the same time yielding to a universal. It discards the criterion of an alternative, creating a zone of indeterminacy in the very words composing it, a void in linguistic expression, which all the same remains active. It is Bartleby's own life that becomes waste (*déchet*), what Lacan calls *petit objet a*, in the sense that it does away with its function; he refuses to copy but this is expressed only as a preference, he never slips into the role of the rebel or the insurgent: he introduces a logic of preference within a logic of presuppositions. The dull timbre of his voice signals a disconnection between words and actions, so much so that Bartleby presents himself as the man without a reference, as he who is bound to always remain in his own position, in the a-grammatical correctness of his utterance.

Instituting power

Let us try, at this point, to reverse the terms of the discussion and follow the implications that arise when a radicalization of political theory prevails with respect to a position strictly anchored to philosophical reflection. A radicalization such as the one carried out by Claude Lefort with respect to the theoretical approach of his teacher, Merleau-Ponty.[16] In his work there is an effective reversal of roles: without rushing towards action, that is, remaining focused on an exquisitely theoretical position, political philosophers reveal the political inadequacy of an argumentation that is itself fundamentally philosophical. In fact, even though Merleau-Ponty's reflection opens to an a-subjective space, to a meta-political articulation of thought, his main focus remains the phenomenological project. According to Lefort, however, it is necessary to understand the whole of politics as an institution of the social, so that if the institution is, in itself, unequivocally political, on the other hand the sphere of the political cannot but manifest an inevitable instituting quality.[17] We witness a shift in the structure of the ontological argumentation that goes from the noun *institution* to the verb *institute*. The institution of the social should not be understood as a political institution located within society, but as the fact that society itself, as a whole, can only be instituted in its own form by the political.

This essential intensification of *institute* over *institution* cannot, however, leave out an essential reference to the force of what is maintained in action. In fact, in order to let its instituting nature emerge, the verbal form cannot but present a destituent articulation of its own normative quality. And it is precisely within this disjunctive synthesis between institution and destitution that we can think of democracy as the only political regime able to recognize the absence of a foundation as a constitutive part of its structure, in such a way that from a formal point of view power should be exercised through an intrinsic non-appropriability of divergent interests, the same way the process of socialization should always manifest itself as unoccupiable space. This means that the tendency inherent in the instituting process, while positing the need of a symbolic recomposition with regard to the void of the signifier, is at the same time counter-effectualized by the virtual medium of the image, by the iconological structure of its folds, whereby precisely in this contrast between vision and expression the temporal structure of its immediacy is revealed. It is a temporal dilation that is not so much achieved through the negative character of the law, but rather by means of a constant splitting operated by the diaphragm of imagination. In such a way that the instituting process, in its very essence, reveals itself as a living point of insurgence, as an immanence fault that destituent power determines in thought with respect to every precipitate that constituent power demands.

If thinking is first of all a relation between seeing and speaking, it is necessary to add that in this relation between these two simultaneous acts an essential disjunction arises. It is in this disjunction that the singular process of subjectification is established. In such a way that thinking does not take place only thanks to the relation between seeing and speaking, because its force always originates between the two: in the tear, in the fold that is between them; in the exact point in which seeing reaches the limit of its visibility (that is, it reaches what can only be enunciated). At this point of the disjunctive synthesis, seeing and speaking both reach the common border that connects them at the exact moment in which they are inevitably disjoined. It is therefore between seeing and speaking that thought sees and speaks, although it is also here that, at the same time, its potential virtuality arises: that is, it accesses the operative quality of a real imaginary. Here imaginary means the scenario of a power relation that is homogeneous both to seeing and to speaking, despite these two forms are different, that is, they are not homogeneous. This allows us to grasp the fact that the virtual is by no means that which is opposed to the real; rather, the virtual is the potential and immediate destitution of the real. The virtual is therefore inactual, but always real: what is indeed opposed to the real is not the virtual, but rather the possible. Only the eventual realization of the possible can, in fact, be deduced, following the criteria established by the relationship between seeing and enunciating. The virtual, on the contrary, can never be understood in terms of possibility because it is not implied by the logic of an eventual realization – in the instantaneous act of counter-effectualization the virtual is already a modality of the real. Virtuality never lacks reality, it lacks actuality: it is what rebounds on actuality ignoring its exclusive factuality, immediately counter-effectualizing every finality criterion, thus articulating the necessary incidence of the effects of singularity. This is why every actualization is in itself differentiation, a relationship of forces between surfaces and multiple singularities. The virtual, understood in this sense, reveals itself as too rich to be retraced back to unity, because it is articulated in division, without, however, this disjunction ever reaching a perfect dual form: it is the being in act of an instituting power whose political articulation presents itself in all its immanence.

Notes

1. Roberto Esposito, *Instituting Thought: Three Paradigms of Political Ontology* (New Jersey: Wiley, 2020).
2. Gilles Deleuze, *Différence et repetition* (Paris: PUF, 1968); Gilles Deleuze, *Logique dusens* (Paris: Minuit, 1969).
3. Giorgio Agamben, *The Use of Bodies* (Stanford, CA: Stanford University Press, 2016).
4. Hannah Arendt, *Between Past and Future: Six Exercises in Political Thought* (New York: The Viking Press, 1961).
5. Carl Schmitt, *Politische Romantik* (Berlin: Duncker & Humblot, 1919).
6. Gilles Deleuze, *Foucault* (Minnesota: University of Minnesota Press, 1988).
7. Gilles Deleuze, *Marcel Proust et les signes* (Paris: PUF, 1964).
8. Marcel Proust, *À la recherche du temps perdu* (Paris: Gallimard, 1999).
9. Gilles Deleuze, *L'image-mouvement: cinema 1* (Paris: Minuit, 1983).
10. Gilles Deleuze, *L'image-temps: cinéma 2* (Paris: Minuit, 1985).
11. Henri Bergson, *Matière et mémoire. Essai sur la relation du corps a l'esprit* (Paris: Flammarion, 2012).
12. Roland Barthes, *La preparation du roman. Cours au Collège de France 1978-79 et 1979-80* (Paris: Seuil, 2015).
13. Jacques Lacan, *Le Séminaire. Livre VII. L'èthique de la psychanalyse (1959-1960)* (Paris: Seuil, 1986).
14. Gilles Deleuze, *Sur quatre formulespoétiques qui pourraientrésumer la philosophiekantienne*, in Id., *Critique et Clinique* (Paris: Minuit, 1993).
15. Herman Melville, *Bartleby and The lightning-rod man* (London: Penguin, 1995).
16. Claude Lefort, *Le travail de l'œuvre Machiavel* (Paris: Gallimard, 1972).
17. Roberto Esposito, *Instituting Thought*.

Bibliography

Agamben, Giorgio. *The Use of Bodies*. Stanford, CA: Stanford University Press, 2016.
Arendt, Hannah. *Between Past and Future: Six Exercises in Political Thought*. New York: The Viking Press, 1961.

Barthes, Roland. *La preparation du roman. Cours au Collège de France 1978–79 et 1979–80*. Paris: Seuil, 2015.

Bergson, Henri. *Matière et mémoire. Essai sur la relation du corps a l'esprit*. Paris: Flammarion, 2012.

Deleuze, Gilles. *Marcel Proust et les signes*. Paris: PUF, 1964.

Deleuze, Gilles. *Différence et repetition*. Paris: PUF, 1968.

Deleuze, Gilles. *Logique dusens*. Paris: Minuit, 1969.

Deleuze, Gilles. *L'image-mouvement: cinema 1*. Paris: Minuit, 1983.

Deleuze, Gilles. *L'image-temps: cinéma 2*. Paris: Minuit, 1985.

Deleuze, Gilles. *Foucault*. Minnesota: University of Minnesota Press, 1988.

Deleuze, Gilles. *Sur quatre formules poétiques qui pourraient résumer la philosophie kantienne*, in *Critique et Clinique*. Paris: Minuit, 1993.

Esposito, Roberto. *Instituting Thought: Three Paradigms of Political Ontology*. New Jersey: Wiley, 2020.

Lacan, Jacques. *Le Séminaire. Livre VII. L'èthique de la psychanalyse (1959–1960)*. Paris: Seuil, 1986.

Lefort, Claude. *Le travail de l'œuvre Machiavel*. Paris: Gallimard, 1972.

Melville, Herman. *Bartleby, and, The lightning-rod man*. London: Penguin, 1995.

Proust, Marcel. *À la recherche du temps perdu*. Paris: Gallimard, 1999.

Schmitt, Carl. *Politische Romantik*. Berlin: Duncker & Humblot, 1919.

4

Vox Populi, Vox Dei: On the Vocal Substance of the Present

Federico Leoni

The myth of the word

It is not possible to question the state of contemporary democracies without questioning a kind of colossal shift that has occurred over the last century, a shift in what we could call the conditions of possibility of democracy, which concern the public sphere as a sphere of democratic discussion and deliberation. There is no democracy without a certain set of discussion and deliberation procedures centred on what we could call 'the word'. There is no democracy without the advent of a humanity educated in a certain use of the word, which provokes the appearance of common objects of discussion and deliberation, as well as subjects who share the vision, the evaluation and the organization of a conflict around those objects.

A beautiful and famous page from Hannah Arendt's *Vita activa* portrays this dimension of the word as a powerful tool of democracy and the public sphere, just as the Greek city would have articulated it for the first time:

> In the experience of the polis, which not without justification has been called the most talkative of all bodies politic, and even more in the political philosophy which sprang from it, action and speech separated and became more and more independent activities. The emphasis shifted from action to speech, and to speech as a means of persuasion rather than the specifically human way of answering, talking back and measuring up to whatever happened or was done. To be political, to live in a polis, meant that everything was decided through words and persuasion and not through force and violence. In Greek self-understanding, to force people by violence, to command rather than persuade, were prepolitical ways to deal with people characteristic of life outside the polls, of home and family life, where the household head ruled with uncontested,

despotic powers, or of life in the barbarian empires of Asia, whose despotism was frequently likened to the organization of the household.¹

We can find almost the same order of considerations in Jürgen Habermas, whose *History and Critique of Public Opinion* was published only four years later than Hannah Arendt's *Vita activa*:

> In the fully developed Greek city-state the sphere of the *polis*, which was common (*koiné*) to the free citizens, was strictly separated from the sphere of the *oikos*; in the sphere of the oikos, each individuali s in his own realm (*idia*). The public life (*bios politikos*) went on in the market place (*agora*), but of course this did not mean that it occurred necessarily only in this specific location. The public sphere was constituted in discussion (*lexis*), which could also assume the forms of consultation and of sitting in the court of law. [...] The realm of necessity and transitoriness remained immersed in the obscurity of the private sphere. In contrast to it stood, in Greek self-interpretation, the public sphere as a realm of freedom and permanence. Only in the light of the public sphere did that which existed become revealed, did everything become visible to all. In the discussion among citizens issues were made topical and took shape. In the competition among equals the best excelled and gained their essence, the immortality of fame.²

The Lutheran reader

We could say that the above is an idealized image, and that Greek democracy was anything but democratic, as Arendt and Habermas know well and show in those same pages. We could add that even today we are very far from that ideal image, and that democracy is still to come, because the kind of word that constitutes the condition of possibility of democracy is itself still to come. But many signs seem to suggest that this is not the case.

Perhaps democracy has already come, as far as it was possible for it to come. Perhaps the kind of word that constitutes the condition of possibility for democracy has also already come, as far as it was possible for it to come. Perhaps it is that word's decline that has made it so perceptible, so visible to the gaze of twentieth-century political theory. Perhaps it is because we now look at it from the outside (from elsewhere, from afterwards) that it lends itself so well to our investigations. The owl of Minerva begins its flight at sunset, when the day has ended, and events are easily offered to her belated apprehension. As anticipated, a gigantic shift seems to have reconfigured the conditions of possibility of the public sphere and its forms of subjectivation and objectivation. Something like another word – or something other than what we have so far called word – has taken hold. And with it, a new kind of subjects and objects, and a new kind of bond, have been put into play.

In his *History and Critique of Public Opinion*, Habermas drops, almost in passing, an observation that reveals a glimpse of this landscape of 'the word after the word'. Habermas writes:

> Throughout the Middle Ages, the categories of public and private were handed down in the definitions of Roman law. One could think of the public sphere, defined as *res publica*. Undoubtedly, it is only with the formation of the modern state and this distinct sphere of bourgeois civil society, that these categories find an effective application from a legal and technical point of view. They serve both the political notion of self and the legal institutionalisation of a bourgeois public sphere in its specific sense. In the meantime, namely in the last century, its social foundations have in fact been disintegrating. The trend towards the disintegration of the public dimension is unmistakable. While its sphere is expanding more and more visibly, its function is becoming more and more impoverished.[3]

In the course of his work, Habermas illustrates the long and complicated genealogy that brings the public sphere to that maximum of effectiveness in the eighteenth and nineteenth centuries. He meticulously investigates the spread of the first gazettes. They had, in the seventeenth century, been linked to the internal needs of certain commercial professions. Those information sheets gradually devoted themselves to broader discussions, no longer limited to the themes and problems of this or that professional category. In part they do this to attract new sections of the public. In part they sought to create the wider audience they seem to presuppose. The newspapers of the nineteenth century, which had already added to their repertoire a range of political, economic and military discussions, began to further broaden their interests into literary, artistic and cultural themes. They no doubt tried to attract a wider and less specialized audience. Increasing sales was a way of making the production of an increasingly complex and expensive object more sustainable. And in doing so, they built up, piece by piece, the public they seem to presuppose, a public that is increasingly united by a set of shared objects and methods of discussion.

Habermas shows how all this intersects with a similar movement within the administrative arrangements put in place by the largest European states. These are initially rather fragmented devices. Each is intended to regulate or monitor a certain area of social life: the education of the population, the productive activities, the collection of revenues, and so on. But under the pressure of state centralization, these devices flow into more and more complex, coherent and binding systems. They end up constructing a set of observation coordinates that are increasingly homogeneous, or a field of survey objects that is also increasingly homogeneous, and a set of subjects that are also increasingly accustomed to think of themselves as homogeneous elements of a whole. Without this overall movement, which on several levels mobilises what we might call a set of new media, which are highly specific in their tasks and effects, there would be no public sphere of discussion and deliberation, no democracy in the modern sense. The public sphere, the space of democracy, is neither an idea nor a functioning, but an *artefact*, a product of these new media.

It is on this point that we must take leave from Hannah Arendt and certain pages by Habermas himself. These new media, in all evidence, are centred not on the word but on writing. Or, if you prefer, on the transcribed word. Think of the testimony of the merchant who informs his shipping company, the note of the administrative official who reports on the tax situation in a distant province, the minister's speech that the reader can read in the gazette of the capital, the journalist's reflection on the events of the week or the month. All this is certainly something we can attribute to the order of the word, as Hannah Arendt suggests. But it is a word that lies motionless on the page of a document, as Habermas shows. The subject who belongs to the modern public sphere is essentially a reader, not an orator. Similarly, the object of discussion and deliberation that involves him or her is essentially a written object. An object that is not only encountered, but first and foremost evoked, aroused and shaped through the written page. The common amniotic fluid of these objects is the proliferating but converging variety of textual documents that the state demands and multiplies in every direction. And that it will not cease to demand and multiply in an ever more pervasive manner, right up to our present.

Habermas shows us this set of transformations, but does not seem to give them specific importance. Nor does he seem to give them a function that we might go so far as to define as transcendental – to borrow an old metaphysical word. It is rather his Canadian contemporary Marshall McLuhan who puts the transcendental function of the medium at the centre of his reflection on contemporaneity. Curiously enough, it was in Germany, where Gutenberg invented the printing press, that McLuhan isolates the decisive shift.[4] Whoever reads a printed page reads with a cool mind and understands what he or she is reading at a distance. They evaluate these words and objects with the relative freedom that this distance allows them. They suspend that more passionate and immediate reaction that the spoken and heard word often brings. They ask themselves what to think and what to do. McLuhan shows that Luther taught to use that distance first of all in the presence of the highest and most powerful word, the word of the Scriptures. And he shows that it is precisely because the word of the Scriptures was no longer the spoken word, or the word annotated on difficult and irregular manuscripts in need of slow and painstaking decipherment, that the praying subject became a reading subject and a doubting subject.

Thus, it is not the word as such that constructs that sphere of discussion and public deliberation which Arendt and Habermas see as the basis of Western democracy. It is the written word and therefore the read word, the word which has been transcribed and therefore removed from the vocal sphere, from the affection of hearing, from the transport of musicality, from the power of enunciation, from the hypnosis of listening. If Hegel could say that reading the gazette is the daily prayer of the bourgeoisie, it is because the prayer of the man who held Gutenberg's Bible in his hands had also become an entirely bourgeois prayer, an entirely intellectual operation, an entirely critical rite. Now, at every level, from the smallest town council to the highest chamber of parliament, from the primary schools in the most remote countryside to the most prestigious university in the capital, the same device is in action. We are faced with a sphere made up of written words. We are faced with a sphere of solitudes summoned in front of these immobile words. We are faced with a sphere of common objects, on which those innumerable solitudes reflect and deliberate. Those solitudes share words that can no longer be believed, but around which it is inevitable to reflect, discuss and decide. We are faced with a sphere of solitudes united by their very solitude, and thus in a certain sense by this freedom they have with regard to the enigmatic objects of their questioning – a sphere of free subjects, we could say; provided that we ask ourselves what freedom means, for instance by folllowing McLuhan's analysis. Ultimately, it means the end of an old type of subjection and the beginning of a new one: the end of subjection to the spoken word and the seduction of its music, and the beginning of subjection to the written word and the seduction of its silent distance.

Vox populi, vox dei

Let us read this story backwards. If the public sphere was born as the product of those media, and today it is disintegrating with increasing acceleration, it must be because those media that had designed the conditions of possibility and constructed the playing field of democracy are disintegrating. This is the point at which we find ourselves today. A point at which the public word, the word that not only circulates in the public sphere but most crucially *establishes* the public sphere, is being overwhelmed by something we might call a 'return of voice'.

This strange phenomenon should be understood in its most common sense. It is what happens in certain public situations when a speaker picks up a microphone that captures the voice at the moment it is emitted by the speaker. But at the same time the microphone captures that voice after it has been amplified. That voice now comes from elsewhere, it is now a stranger to the speaker. The voice that came from here, and resounded over there, now returns from over there. It invests the speaker as something that is of their own, but also not of their own. The speaker is now both themselves and also something other than themself. Something other than the subject they were, perhaps even something other than a subject.

In a sense, this presence of the voice, or voices, within the field of public speaking is nothing new. It could say something about the people and its social substance, long before that the people became the people of democracy, the people inscribed in those procedures of discussion and deliberation that Arendt or Habermas seem to attribute immediately to the magical virtues of a mediologically unspecified word. Much sooner than as a people of Lutheran solitudes, which takes the floor within certain procedures formalized by certain media, it is as a people that listens to and emits voices, as a vociferous people traversed by vociferations, that 'the people' announces itself in the history of Europe.

The Latin syntagma *vox populi* is already attested in Roman times, as historians show.[5] Its later variant, *vox populi, vox dei*, is obviously from the Christian era. In particular, it inherits in discontinuous but evident ways one of the major traits of Christianity. The one, we could say briefly, expressed for example in the Sermon on the Mount and in the preaching of Christianity as the religion of the least. This trait is valuable and yet disregarded by the history of Christian institutions, which perhaps, precisely because it is a history of institutions, has had to come to terms with this vocal dimension, finally evacuating and removing it. The syntagm *vox populi, vox dei* must have circulated widely in the early Middle Ages, but it is only documented for the first time towards the end of the eighth century. We find it, as George Boas explains,[6] in a letter from Alcuin of York to Emperor Charlemagne, of whose court Alcuin is an influential organic intellectual. Alcuin's letter, from around 798 CE, is a particularly instructive text. First of all, the simple fact that a personage like

Alcuin feels the need to deal with this expression, naturally to refute it, shows that this expression must have been sufficiently widespread to create some concern for the emperor and his circle. No one dares to refute a rumour, except when it is riskier to let it circulate without contesting it than to contest it, thus giving it further opportunity to circulate. The refutation of our syntagm occurs *en passant*, of course. Alcuin is talking about something else. He is talking about the problem of inheritance. Does he mean the general question of inheritance? Does he mean a particular inheritance, the legacy of a specific personage? Does he even mean the legacy of Charlemagne, who was now elderly and probably worried about the fate of the Empire after his death? This would be all the more significant, but historians invite us to leave the question open.

It is enough, for us, to note that Alcuin wonders about who should be listened to, which opinion should prevail over others, in resolving such important and controversial issues. And it is at this point that he observes that the voice of the people should certainly not be listened to. The word of those, whom Alcuin calls 'the men who have a position,' is much more reliable. Deciding on an inheritance, be it large or small, requires listening to an authoritative word, and not to a voice circulating among the plebs. But in carrying out this obviously traditional argumentative manoeuvre, a whole theory of voice is conjured up. Alcuin's argument is constructed around two blocks. The first one reflects on the status of the body. A body without a head, we read, is a body whose individual limbs are destined to languish. It is from the head that the strength of the organism, the solidity of its parts, the very fact that they form a whole, descend. This is not a new thesis, of course. The second block moves on to the terrain that interests us. 'The people,' writes Alcuin, 'according to the law of God, must be led, and not followed.'[7] He observes that 'when witnesses are needed, it is men who have a position, who must be heard.' No credit, he argues, and here comes our motto, 'to those who are wont to say that the voice of the people is the voice of God'. For, he concludes, 'the clamour of the *vulgus* is close to madness'.[8]

Here too, we might say, nothing is particularly new and unexpected. But between these two rather predictable theses there is more than one implicit link, and this link is, by contrast, extremely original. It is worth dwelling on it. It is a link between body and speech, or rather a parallel between the good constitution of the organism and the good constitution of speech. We have a body without a head and a people that speaks, a people that vociferates, a people close to madness. And we have a body endowed with a head, the strength of which invigorates the limbs, making them a whole, the counterpart of which is that of a discourse endowed with a head, a word endowed with a subject, we might say.

Aluin says that to the senseless clamour of the people we must prefer that significant clamour, the voice 'endowed with a head', the word endowed with meaning, which is the word uttered by 'men with a position'. We are entitled to suspect that the man with the highest position is the man who guarantees in the surest way that the mad vociferation of the *vulgus* is translated into a fully meaningful word. And it can be deduced that the fragmented and delirious body of the vulgar takes on the features of a people only when it is guided by the word of a man 'endowed with position.' But a final remark quickly brings us back to our problem. While it is not possible for us admirers of democracy to discard this word that Alcuin defends as an authoritarian word, this word which lies in the salvific hands of the emperor is structurally homologous to the democratic word admired by Arendt and Habermas. Did we not say that the Lutheran word was the premise to the democratic word precisely because it was a word looked at from the outside? A word contemplated by a subject who is foreign to it, and is therefore pondered from a vantage point, removed from the mad immanence of the voice? A word which is inscribed in the transcendence of a subject whose property or faculty it constitutes, rather than as a power that passes through them as an impersonal event?

True and false hallucinations

A century of psychoanalysis seems to have moved on a similar path. Indeed, a similar double path or double track. The first body a child comes into the world with, psychoanalysis explains, is a chaotic, fragmented, disorganised body. The expression 'body in fragments' comes from Jacques Lacan.[9] Only when those scattered limbs are knotted together into a unity thanks to the vantage point of an external gaze, namely a mirror image, does that body avoid the risk of psychosis by assuming a certain compactness, a properly organized structure. On the other hand, a body which has not known this transcendent knotting remains an unstable body, and is thus open to psychosis.

It is quite interesting that, in Lacan's teaching, the same logic applies to the experience of voice. Here the voice too is a sort of chaotic reverse of the word, a signifying and unorganized materiality capable of corroding the well-organized word and the perfect transparency of the meanings it conveys. A sort of reversal of oneiric prehistory when not actually mad, of a predecessor somehow removed but always on the point of returning to the scene. The word, in Lacanian terms, never happens without a return of voice, just as the body knotted around the 'caput' of the specular image is never without jolts, without a certain edge which remains unaware of specular capture.

Let us refer to two passages in Lacan's text that allow us to define this general landscape. On the one hand Lacan says that the voice is the reverse of the word. More precisely, that 'the voice' is 'the otherness of what is said'.[10] The voice is the other of saying or wanting to say. It is in some way the antagonist of the intention to say or wanting to say something. It is the signifier – if we assume that the signifier is the antagonist of the signified – which is not taken for granted and may be not entirely correct. It is the signifier insofar as the signifier makes itself heard when the word that wants to say something fails, namely when the word that belongs to that subject who intends to say something (the word which is inscribed in the field of a subject who has made himself or herself its master) fades away. Seen from the point of view of the subject who has taken possession of his voice as a means to an end, the voice is an anti-subject. It is a matter that turns a deaf ear to the intentions of subjectivity; an instrument that displays something monstrous in its rebellion against the intentionality of the discourse – no different, after all, from every instrument that takes on an autonomous life and returns within the human field, with human features, while being radically inhuman underneath. It is a classic scene from a horror film or novel – think for instance of Stephen King's novel *Christine*.

We could define the above as an 'imperial' conception of the voice, in the double sense retained by the term 'imperial': that which brings water to the emperor's mill; and that which presupposes an anthropology where the voice is the vulgar element, that which must be lost (together with the insanely dispersive body of the perverse polymorphic child) so that a word can become body and a body can become word – a word that is one, univocal, endowed with a single voice, a single meaning, and a body that is compact, a well-coordinated tool subordinated to the subject's intentions. To the Christian priest Alcuin – for it seems that this extraordinary early medieval intellectual became a priest towards the end of his life – this imperial conception of the voice must have posed at least one problem. That is to say: is God, then, also crazy? If God's people are the lowest people, and if the lowest people madly vociferate instead of speaking reasonably, is the Christian God also a mad and vulgar God, nothing more than a vast, fragmented and vociferating body? If God is infinite, how can we exclude the fact that his voice resounds everywhere, not only at the head of the empire but also in the margins? And perhaps in the lowest possible parts of the body, in the very genitals of the empire, where the so-called 'proletarians' live and make love?

On the other hand, Lacan reflects on the ways in which the voice returns. He knows, as a psychoanalyst, that the removed voice does nothing but return. Even though it has fallen under the bar of the Saussurian algorithm, which places the signified at the top and the low materiality of the signifier below underneath the bar. The voice does nothing but return as a more or less hallucinatory experience, whether it occurs in a neurotic subject as a slip of the tongue, as a momentary lapse of mastery; or in a psychotic subject as a siege, a civil war in which an almost powerless sovereign is periodically visited by a rigorously acephalous, a-subjective power. Lacan recalls in his Seminar III, *The psychosis*,[11] how already classical psychiatry observed that the patient suffering from verbal hallucinations performs, more or less mutely, a series of phonation moves in which a sufficiently attentive observation recognizes the articulation of those same voices he claims to hear: 'There were people having verbal hallucinations who could be observed, by quite obvious signs in some cases and by looking slightly more closely in others, to be uttering the words they accused their voices of having spoken to them, whether or not they were aware of it.'[12] Lacan adds that verbal hallucination is a speech that the subject is unable to recognize as his or her own. The subject speaks and hears his or her speech, but without managing to recognize himself or herself as the one who is speaking. That is, without arriving at the point where the circle of hearing oneself speak is welded together, and without appearing as the very welding point of the circuit. This is a more or less illusory appearance, or rather an illusion that sometimes is more effective, sometimes less.

It would be difficult to evoke in an adequate manner in what way Lacan explains this failed constitution, or this fragile illusion of the welding point. We would have to summon up his entire analysis of the so-called *other* and of its function of recognition. The scene Lacan has in mind is quite ordinary. The other gives back to the child who cries that same cry as a meaningful word, by the very fact of responding and answering in a certain way. The other's response, we might say, 'will have been' the meaning of a signifier; or more precisely the meaning of that thing which, after receiving a meaning, will become a signifier. But Lacan notes – and this is for us the most interesting point – that sometimes 'the other doesn't agree'.[13] Sometimes the other does not keep to this game of question and answer, sometimes the other shirks its Hegelian task. Then the place of the voice remains an uncertain terrain, where no answer installs the *après coup* effect of a meaning.

Is this always the case, to some extent? Is the answer of the other always to some extent vague, erratic, elusive, enigmatic? Would not a certain madness of the voice, a certain hallucinatory return of the voice in the word (even the most coherent word) be a structural datum to be used, rather than an unfortunate case to be lamented, or a psychopathological situation to be healed? One detail seems to be able to make a difference and deserves more attention. It is only *après coup*, Lacan shows, that the cry will appear as the negative of that positive which is meaning, as the chaotic and potentially hallucinatory signifier of that meaning which presents itself instead as transparent, ordered, meaningful. We might observe that in itself the *terrain vague* of the voice is neither a signified nor a signifier, neither a meaningful word nor a simply chaotic voice and inarticulate cry. That the voice as such seems chaotic, this is an *après coup* effect of a certain established order. That the signifier is the place of chaotic materiality and senseless fragmentation is what the emperor tells us, what his advisor Alcuin fears, and what his official psychoanalyst sometimes repeats. But Lacan, who sometimes seems to be the official psychoanalyst of the empire, is also an unofficial psychoanalyst. He seems to leave us the possibility of going in another direction. Is there something like a good hallucination, or a good use of hallucination? Is there a voice that is not just the formless matter of the word that belongs to 'men with a position'? Could Lacan go so far as to affirm that *vox populi, vox dei*?

Phenomenology of rumours

We could devote ourselves to a kind of transcendental deduction of the structure of the current public sphere from the structure of this Lacanian voice thought *juxta propria principia*. The first way in which this return of voice to the field of democratic speech announces itself is precisely as a voice claiming to be, as a matter of fact, the voice of the people. This claim must be thought of, not taken for granted or disqualified as such. What does this voice look like? First of all, it looks like a voice that murmurs contrary to the word that speaks from above, and the language that frequents the ethereal regions of written meaning. It is a voice that rises from below and rumbles against the presumptuous word of the literate citizen, dedicated to free and solitary meditations. A voice that shatters the illusion of those common objects and discussions and decisions that, tautologically, unite only subjects and only objects formed within that field. Outside that field, completely different kinds of subjects and objects see the light. Vocal subjects and vocal objects, we could say. But to say so, we would need to rely on an assumption, namely that in that field there are no subjects nor objects, since there is no Lutheran distance, no disconnectedness of silent readers in front of silent books, no transparency capable of differentiating myself from the object I am dealing with. Subject and object fall together with the fall of the word, and overflow into each other when voices return to that field investing it with their a-subjective power. There are voices without subjects; voices that it is not even sufficient to ascribe to the register of the voice to understand them properly. That thing we call voice is, in the final analysis, always already measured on the basis of its function as a support of the word; it is always looked at from the point of view of its 'becoming a word'. What would a voice-in-and-for-itself be? And a people corresponding to that voice?

The second way in which the voice of the people manifests itself is as noise; the rumour that passes from mouth to ear; the whisper that never makes it possible to identify a sender or a receiver, as the semiologists say. Here the subject is essentially a place of transit. The voice that the subject emits is simply a voice that someone else has emitted before him or her. That voice passes through the subject to reach another subject, who will in turn be passed through and forgotten. The movement of rumour has, in other words, the structure of contagion. If the written word lies motionless before the reader's eyes, as the object of their reflection and the matter of their decision, the voice of the people runs from subject to subject, remaining immune to subjective elaboration. It is the voice of the people, and fundamentally this has to do with an object moving from subject to subject without belonging to any subject or being modified by contact with any subject. If rumours change, from day to day or from hour to hour, this happens according to the logic of rumours themselves, and not according to their subjective elaboration.

But a voice or a rumour without a subject is also without an object. This is why the third way in which this strange word without subject or object manifests itself is the allusion, the essentially enigmatic hint, the ultimately unverifiable conjecture. A voice cannot be attributed to someone who is responsible for it, and does not designate any object for which it can be called to account. If the word is relative, relational, correlated to a subject and an object, the voice, when it returns, it returns as an absolute. A rumour fully encloses, in its own place devoid of otherness and exteriority, what remains of the subject and of the object. It segregates in its perfectly self-sufficient space those who seem to be the emitters, the receivers, the referents. All the categories of semiotics must be rethought and redistributed, so to speak. They are no longer arranged in exteriority with respect to one another, but in interiority, within the absolute sphere of rumour. Perhaps the rumour emanates from someone, perhaps it seems to address someone, perhaps it seems to speak of something. But we must not deceive ourselves: its structure is in no way intentional. Like any absolute, a rumour essentially speaks of itself and to itself.

Therefore, the fourth way in which rumour imposes itself is as a disturbing power, a force that the subject feels as foreign even when its content seems positive, or simply amusing, or indifferent. A rumour is by definition threatening for the subjects of the word, or what remains of them. For in no way does rumour fit with the subject's reflexive habit, with their illusion of being able to establish the truth or falsity of a certain statement by moving within the framework of a common discussion; or with the subject's inclination to decide on those objects of discourse after having tested their truth or falsity. A rumour draws on an undecidable field, and for that person who is entirely identified with their own presumed power of decision, the undecidable is by definition a hostile terrain, a field destined to denounce a fundamental impotence, an unmanageable swamp in which every discussion and deliberation is destined to wander indefinitely. A rumour, after all, is never really true or verifiable. There is no subject that can take on this task. There is no object around which to promote any verification.

For this reason, the fifth way in which a rumour presents itself is the way of truth, but absolute truth, a truth that is beyond true and false, a truth defined by something eternal and indestructible. The rumour's truth is the truth of the absolute space within which disputes may be opened – essentially, precarious discussions or confrontations that must necessarily take the form of bickering, quarrels that explode between positions that are in fact incommensurable and incommunicable. A rumour, being an absolute, always wins, even when it looks as though it will lose. Those who speak in favour and against a certain kind of rumour actually draw a path that they are never tired to travel, perhaps in different directions, as they could travel a kind of large concave surface, like the endless internal curvature of a bubble.

The sixth way in which this noise is presented beyond subjectivity and beyond objectivity is then the way of reassurance and faith. In the field of rumour, the a-subjective and the unobjective are finally at home. But this home is still to be thought of. More precisely, what remains to be thought of is whether it is a home or a landscape of ruins.

On the use of the vocal substance of the contemporary

At this stage in the discussion, we could attempt a definition of populism entirely based on an exploration of that unprecedented battlefield which is the battlefield of the voice. If democracy takes shape when the voice of the people becomes the democratic word, populism takes shape when the democratic word is visited by the voice of the people or by the people as pure vocality.

What we call 'the people' is nothing other than that unassignable voice, or the asymptote of that unassignable voice. An asymptote, that is to say a line that is never really touched, but sometimes carefully cultivated. Thus, democracy is nothing but the voice of the people once it is assigned to the regime of the word, inscribed within the communicative circuit of writing. It is also an asymptote, evidently presupposed by both the theory and the practice of democracy, but never actually realized and perhaps now definitively unrealizable.

We could take the *Leitfrage* of vocality to attempt not only a definition of populism and democracy and their strange topological relations, but also a historiographic periodization. Like any periodization, this one too is politically significant. The whole of the last century, from 1922 to 2022 – i.e. from the March on Rome, which gave rise to the Fascist dictatorship in Italy and the season of European totalitarianism, up to today – unfolds like strange comings and goings, a back-and-forth movement made up of shifts and bounces, more or less violent, between two extremes that we could define in purely mediological or psychoanalytical terms. One extreme is that of the removal of the voice, the other is that of the return of the voice. One extreme is that of the media of the written word, the other is that of contemporary vocal media, and more generally of media that take as their chosen terrain the impersonal matter of experience, the impersonal quota of experience that always embodies our subjectivity. This is not the place to inventory the vast array of these new media, which we could include in a single genre stretching from the radio and the phonograph – which Mussolini's or Hitler's speeches have frequented and exploited so effectively – to apps such as Facebook, Youtube, TikTok and so on. This is also not the place to show that although the image has become more and more overbearingly mixed with these vocal media, the image itself has very often taken on what we might call a vocal function, mixing with, rather than replacing, what remains today of that fetish of twentieth-century thought that is language as the ultimate transcendental form. The images in TikTok videos are more similar to what we might call voice-images than representation-images, that is, the iconologically organized and ultimately linguistically designed images that had hitherto governed the Western use of the image, and in particular the use of the image in the political field.

Voice, thus, is the terrain not of populism, but of the dissolution of democracy as a product of a certain technology of the word. This is a terrain that populism colonizes in its own way, taking over that vocal element that is radically foreign to democratic treatment, and which in any case escapes the grasp of its writing devices. It is interesting, moreover, that populism takes charge of the voice not as such, *juxta propria principia*, but as democracy itself imagines it. It is instructive, in other words, that populism values the voice in the same (basically, purely negative) terms in which the democratic public sphere is forced, by its media structure, to encounter the voice itself. That is to say, as a misfortune, a rumour which is mere noise, chaos. It is also significant that democracy's response to this populist takeover of the vocal dimension is, in its own way, a regressive and restorative response, since it simply aims to reinscribe it within the technologies of the word which constitute the condition of possibility of democracy. Thus, caught between two false opponents who quietly agree in seeing the voice as a chaotic element (which one would have to liberate) and the other regiment, that vocal element which is the very substance of the contemporary political field, will continue to remain inaccessible. In turn, the political field will continue to oscillate indefinitely between the false alternatives of populist pseudo-revolution and pseudo-democratic restoration. This is as much as to say that the challenge that the contemporary scene presents us with has nothing to do with the populist liberation of the vocal instance, nor with the re-democratization of the voice as word. Instead, it has to do with intercepting the energies belonging specifically to this unprecedented vociferous humanity. It has to do with the alliance that can be established with the vocal element and the vocal devices of the present.

Notes

1   Hannah Arendt, *The Human Condition* (Chicago: University of Chicago Press, 1998), 26–27.
2   Jurgen Habermas, *The Structural Transformation of the Public Sphere. An Inquiry into a Category of Bourgeois Society*, transl. T. Burger (Cambridge: MIT Press, 1991), 3–4.
3   Ibid.
4   Marshall McLuhan, *The Gutenberg Galaxy. The Making of Typographic Man* (Toronto: University of Toronto Press, 1962).
5   George Boas, *Vox Populi. Essays in the History of an Idea* (Baltimore: The Johns Hopkins Press, 1969).
6   Ibid., 9.
7   Ibid.

8   Ibid.
9   Jacques Lacan, 'The Mirror Stage as Formative of the *I* Function as Revealed in Psychoanalytic Experience,' in *Écrits*, transl. B. Fink (New York: Norton & Company, 2002), 75–81.
10 Jacques Lacan, *Anxiety. The Seminar. Book X*, transl. A. R. Price (Cambridge: Polity Press, 2014), 275.
11 Jacques Lacan, *The Psychosis. The Seminar. Book III*, transl. R. Grigg (New York: Norton & Company, 1993), 16–28.
12 Ibid., 24.
13 Ibid., 40.

Bibliography

Arendt, Hannah. *The Human Condition*. Chicago: University of Chicago Press, 1998.

Boas, George. *Vox Populi. Essays in the History of an Idea*. Baltimore: The Johns Hopkins Press, 1969.

Habermas, Jurgen. *The Structural Transformation of the Public Sphere. An Inquiry into a Category of Bourgeois Society*. Cambridge: MIT Press, 1991.

Lacan, Jacques. *The Psychosis. The Seminar. Book III*. New York: Norton & Company, 1993.

Lacan, Jacques. 'The Mirror Stage as Formative of the *I* Function as Revealed in Psychoanalytic Experience,' in *Écrits*. New York: Norton & Company, 2002, 75–81.

Lacan, Jacques. *Anxiety. The Seminar. Book X*. Cambridge: Polity Press, 2014.

McLuhan, Marshall. *The Gutenberg Galaxy. The Making of Typographic Man*. Toronto: University of Toronto Press, 1962.

Part Two

Ideology

5

Neo-plebs and Elites in the Global World

Matteo Vegetti

In our globalized world, we are witnessing the progressive dissolution of social groups that are linked to the idea of class. It is not that classes in the Marxist sense are vanishing, but rather that the radical transformation of modes of production, the liquefaction of the state as a biopolitical agent, disruptive technological innovations, the transformation of the price system and of the relationship between income and salaries, and the dismantling of what is left of Fordism, are progressively eroding the effectiveness of a social interpretation based on traditional economic models.

The bourgeois universe, with its various stratifications, seems to be crumbling under the weight of a strong internal polarization, which has affected above all the middle class. Correspondingly, the face of poverty has changed. It is no longer identified with the proletariat or the remains of the by now 'classical' working class; it does not produce any progeny nor is it capable of developing an antagonistic social project.

At the same time, however, since the 1990s economic disparities have grown enormously, and along with wealth, power too has been concentrated into the hands of a narrow social group that no longer responds to the guidelines of industrial capitalism. Manuel Castells (1996) was perhaps the first thinker to warn that a declining national bourgeois class was being replaced by a cosmopolitan elite intrinsically linked to the rise of the 'network society' and the global space of flows. From the moment capitalism learned to create forms of wealth that are uncoupled from material production and the resources producing it, the classic triad of the modern age, namely the relationship between labour, capital and nature, began to crumble. This epochal shift has been most costly for the lowest strata of the population and the middle classes.

In *Harvest of Rage* (1998), the American writer Joe Dyer predicted the birth of a new generation of 'rural right' on the back of the devastating effects of the decade's political-economic transition, mass impoverishment, collapse of welfare, drastic cuts to healthcare and the impossibility of reacting in any meaningful political way, given the absence or weakness of any organs of collective representation. The result was the decay of an entire social class and the birth of a diffuse, sometimes virulent, resentment against the system, the *res publica*, immigrants, ethnic minorities, the law, the cultured metropolitan class, public information, and science.

Three years earlier, in *The Revolt of the Elites and the Betrayal of Democracy* (1994) – a prophetic book if one thinks, for example, of the assault on Capitol Hill on 6 January 2021 and what made it possible – Christopher Lasch described the dramatic economic erosion and cultural decline of the American middle class:

> In the United States, 'Middle America' – a term that has both geographical and social implications – has come to symbolize everything that stands in the way of progress: 'family values', mindless patriotism, religious fundamentalism, racism, homophobia, retrograde views of women. Middle Americans, as they appear to the makers of educated opinion, are hopelessly shabby, unfashionable, and provincial, ill-informed about changes in taste or intellectual trends, addicted to trashy novels of romance and adventure, and stupefied by prolonged exposure to television. They are at once absurd and vaguely menacing – not because they wish to overthrow the old order but precisely because their defense of it appears so deeply irrational that it expresses itself, at the higher reaches of its intensity, in fanatical religiosity, in a repressive sexuality that occasionally erupts into violence against women and gays, and in a patriotism that supports imperialist wars and a national ethic of aggressive masculinity.[1]

Insofar as they are typically American, the analyses of Dyer and Lasch seem to me to capture a general trend, or rather a crisis so deep that it brings forth unprecedented social groupings lacking in internal cohesion and for which we lack adequate categories. As a preliminary step, in anticipation of further theoretical reflection, I propose to call these groups neo-plebs, referring to those segments of the population on both sides of the Atlantic who have been struck by the combined effect of the economic and social devaluation of work, the withdrawal of welfare and the precarization of life.

The neo-plebs can be thought of as corresponding to the same process that led to the formation of the global 'elites'. While being polar opposites, both are the result of the new economic and social structure, that is to say, of today's deterritorialization of the economy; and both are expressions of a certain individualistic anarchism. It should be said right away that the neo-plebs do not have any relationship with the Roman plebs other than a metaphorical one, and the term does not allude to the rebirth of the idea of Empire. Rather than ancient tradition, I will refer to the modern one, in which the idea of the plebs, adapted to a social universe transformed by capitalism, can be measured with legal and political concepts like the people, citizenship and classes.

Phenomenology of the plebs

In his *Anthropology from a Pragmatic Point of View*, Kant distinguishes between the concepts of the people, nation and plebs, thus inaugurating a long and fertile critical tradition:

> By the word people (*populus*) is meant a multitude of human beings united in a region in so far as they constitute a whole. This multitude, or even the part of it that recognizes itself as united into a civil whole through common ancestry, is called a nation (*gens*). The part that exempts itself from these laws (the unruly crowd within this people) is called a plebs (*vulgus*),[2] whose legal association is the mob (*agere per turbas*) – conduct that excludes them from the quality of the citizen.[3]

With these words, the plebs enter modern philosophical thought as the product of exclusion: they are part of the people, and yet do not belong to the nation (*gens*). But the most interesting aspect is that the reason for this resides not in some discrimination that they are subjected to, but rather in the fact that *the plebs do not recognize themselves* as connected to the civil unity that founds the national community of which they are a part. Kant insists twice on the fact that the plebs enact their own exclusion: they self-exclude because they do not feel part of society, and because they refuse the norms of civil life through a movement of sedition that places them outside of citizenship and the people. From this, two deductions can be made: the first is that the plebs carry out an act of social repudiation that brings about terrible consequences not so much through the effect of their actions (at worst, unrest without any political valence), but because they contest from within the ideal contours of the nation, the people and citizenship – their necessity and thus their desirability. While Kant does not move far beyond this intuition, which is otherwise extremely valuable, Hegel takes it up again in his *Elements of the Philosophy of Right* (1821) and brings it to a higher level of critical elaboration. The plebs [*Pöbel*] represents for him that part of civil society that refuses to integrate itself into its rules, that does not want to be subjectivized through the dynamics of the universal mediation of work, and thus refuses to play a role in national economic life.

Paradoxically, the Hegelian concepts of the plebs and the seigniory hold a distinctive trait in common that defies bourgeois reason insofar as it is completely foreign to the ethics of capital: the refusal of work as a lever of citizenship and economic condition upon which all members of society depend. But the most scandalous aspect of the plebs is their irreducible character: they refuse the logic of poverty, of admitting to a condition of lack that needs to be negated in order to become something other than itself, thus evading any process of redemption or social liberation. The plebs, says Hegel, are 'dependent on contingency',[4] that is to say on chance, and on the search for immediate pleasures which excludes any desire for change.

However, in the unexpected paragraph 244 of *Elements of the Philosophy of Right*, Hegel also notes an unintentional social function of this phenomenon:

> When a large mass of people sinks below the level of a certain standard of living – which automatically regulates itself at the level necessary for a member of the society in question – that feeling of right, integrity, and honor which comes from supporting oneself by one's own activity and work is lost. This leads to the creation of a plebs [Pöbel],[5] which in turn makes it much easier for disproportionate wealth to be concentrated in a few hands.[6]

In the first part of the quote, adopting a measure of valuation typical of bourgeois culture, Hegel rebukes the plebs for that form of immorality that derives from the renunciation of earning one's freedom through work, which is the only source from which the subject can obtain dignity, consciousness of his own rights, and righteousness. As Kant had already suggested, the plebs want to be as they are: they desire the exclusion of which they are victim; with their own existence they negate the rationality of progress and civilization; and deny the necessary link between work and enjoyment. But at the end of the passage Hegel adds that despite all this, the plebs are not entirely unproductive. Paradoxically, they produce the conditions that cause social disparities to increase enormously, allowing a small number of individuals to accumulate an unheard-of concentration of capital. We will return to this important issue below.

For now, it should be noted that the Hegelian analysis shows in each step a typical approach that begins with the intention to delineate the plebs as a social object but slides continually towards moral condemnation, guilt, and reproach. Aesthetic and moral degradation, vulgarity coupled with arrogance, seem to be integral parts of the concept of plebs. Thus, every judgement on the plebs also refers back to the one who is speaking about the plebs. Because the plebs are politically mute, we find in the discourses that concern them the same categories used to analyse, evaluate and denigrate them, or in some cases revalorize, justify or idealize them.

More frequently, however, those who speak about the plebs use words like 'rabble' [Plebs,], 'thugs' [*Lumprenproletariat, Lumpenpack*], 'lowlives' *[canaille du peuple]*, '*voyou*' (Flaubert),[7] or '*racaille*' (to use the expression with which Sarkozy stigmatized the revolts in the Parisian banlieues in 2015). From this standpoint, the plebs have always horrified the bourgeoisie and alarmed the proletariat. The former, however, has an option that the latter lacks, namely avoidance, suppression, rejection or circumvention. The proletariat, on the other hand, sees in the plebs an image of an anthropological decline that is viewed from close. This is also the reason why Marx constantly took pains to distinguish between the plebs and the proletariat: to keep them separate from one another, to reinforce a border that is in fact very fragile, given its irreducibility to economic criteria. Here one inevitably recalls the Marxian figure of the *Lumpenproletariat*, which appears for the first time in *The German Ideology* (1845–46) precisely as a synonym for the Roman plebs, but is then adapted to the modern context in several justifiably famous passages from *The Class Struggle in France 1848–1850* (1850) and *The Eighteenth Brumaire of Louis Napoleon* (1852).

It should be noted that critics have often mistakenly conflated the prefix *Lump-* with the substantive *Lumpen* (rags), failing to note that the actual root refers to 'Lump' (brigand, lowlife, boor; social scum, dangerous classes, ragamuffin or ragged-proletariat). The difference is significant, because even if it is the case that the *Lumpenproletariat* largely corresponds to that social layer beneath the proletariat, what qualifies them (or better, *disqualifies*) is not income, but moral conduct.

For this reason, Marx always uses the term in a politically discriminatory way that designates a social subject that is as close to as it is different from, even opposed to, the proletariat. It is a class that is paradoxically characterized by being devoid of any class consciousness, yet opportunistic and always willing to betray the workers' cause:

> The 'dangerous class', [lumpenproletariat] the social scum, that passively rotting mass thrown off by the lowest layers of the old society may, here and there, be swept into the movement by a proletarian revolution; its conditions of life, however, prepare it far more for the part of a bribed tool of reactionary intrigue.[8]

The clearest example of this phenomenon is the revolts of 1848, when the *Lumpenproletariat*, in accordance with political impulses mysteriously connected to its 'way of life', was easily instrumentalized by reactionary and counterrevolutionary forces to combat the proletariat. Once again, the elites and the plebs found themselves on the same side, to the extent that Marx sees an affinity between the two on the level of desire: 'In the way it acquires wealth and enjoys it the financial aristocracy is nothing but the lumpenproletariat reborn at the pinnacle of bourgeois society.'[9]

In the ways in which the financial aristocracy, the true elite, enjoy their accumulated wealth, Marx thus recognizes the characteristic traits of the *Lumpenproletariat*: wastefulness, contempt for work, and the absence of limits. Only in *The Eighteenth Brumaire*, however, do we find a kind of phenomenology of the members of this class that remains unconscious of itself, of this 'disintegrated mass' known as the *Lumpenproletariat*. Here, we learn that it is comprised of outsiders without shared interests, yet united in their refusal to politicize their own condition:

> Decayed roués with dubious means of subsistence and of dubious origin, degenerate and adventurous offshoots of the bourgeoisie, rubbed shoulder with vagabonds, discharged soldiers, discharged jailbirds, escaped galley slaves, swindlers, mountebanks, lazzaroni, pickpockets, tricksters, gamblers, maquereaux, brothel-keepers, porters, literati, organ-grinders, ragpickers, knife-grinders, tinkers, beggars: in short, the whole of the nebulous, disintegrated mass, scattered hither and thither, which the French call *la bohème*; from this kindred element Bonaparte formed the core of the December 10 Society. A 'benevolent society' – in so far as, like Bonaparte, all its members felt the need to benefit themselves at the expense of the laboring nation. This Bonaparte who constitutes himself chief of the lumpenproletariat, who here alone rediscovers in mass form the interests which her personally pursues, who recognizes in the scum, offal, and refuse of all the classes the only class upon which he can base himself unconditionally.

Through the long catalogue of socially marginal subjects that opens the passage, Marx points towards a polymorphous and disconnected mass, a docile and corruptible social material always ready to side with those in power, here represented by Napoleon III.

Returning to Hegel, we could say that the plebs elude dialectical understanding not only because they do not produce developments in a teleological sense (since they fail to recognize the lack that qualifies their existence), but also undermine the certainty that there is a social unity mediated by work, that dynamic and evolutionary reality identified with the market by Adam Smith. In this sense, the plebs are the only social components that the market cannot bend to its needs. And because the market directs the spontaneous convergence of individual interests towards collective interests, the plebs are necessarily destined to remain foreign to these interests themselves, as well as to that natural convergence between economic and moral order in which Smith always believed.

In the *Addition* to the paragraph 244 of the *Philosophy of Right*, Hegel – profoundly influenced by Smith's theories – turns again to the moral valence of the concept of the plebs, but this time adds something that changes the picture significantly. While the plebs had previously depended on a certain threshold of material subsistence, now this criterion does not seem to be enough: poverty relates to the plebs, but only partially and not by necessity:

> The lowest level of subsistence [*Subsitenz*], that of the plebs, defines itself automatically, but this minimum varies greatly between different peoples. In England, even the poorest man believes he has rights; this differs from what the poor are content with in other countries. Poverty in itself does not reduce people to a plebs; a plebs is created only by the disposition associated with poverty, by inward rebellion against the rich, against society, the government, etc. It also follows that those who are dependent on contingency become frivolous and lazy, like the lazzaroni of Naples, for example. This in turn gives rise to the evil that the rabble do not have sufficient honor to gain their livelihood through their own work, yet claim that they have a right to receive their livelihood. No one can assert a right against nature, but within the conditions of society hardship at once assumes the form of a wrong inflicted on this or that class.[10]

Hegel then traces the condition of the plebs to three different origins: the renunciation of fighting for the recognition of one's own rights, the claim to be able to live without taking active part in society, and indignation against the powerful, government, and the very society to which one does not belong, but from which a symbolic reward is expected. In this sense, the plebs are the precise opposite of Rousseau's *volonté générale*, and in a certain sense are completely inscribed within this political/moral antinomy.

Furthermore, in a more objective sense, the plebs are such by virtue of not being part of any association. Because they lack public representation, they lack the essential condition that allows workers to obtain the dignity of social beings, fully participating in civil society (*bürgerliche Gesellschaft*). The bitter conclusion that Hegel draws from this fact (§ 245) is that the plebs cannot be eliminated in the capitalist world. Only two paths would seem to be available. The first would imply taxing the richest members of society to subsidize the plebs and thus make it possible for them to live on the fringes of the world of labour, outside the market, in a condition that today we would call 'being on welfare'. While this solution may seem possible, in truth it is impracticable not merely due to costs, but for a much more essential reason: if this were to occur, the founding principle of liberal civil society would be discredited, namely the one according to which only work confers on human beings the right to citizenship, i.e., rights *and* citizenship. This ethical-political principle cannot therefore be undermined without delegitimizing the values established by the bourgeois revolution, which is based on the replacement of social rank and rent with work and profit. One might note here, incidentally, that from this point of view the much-debated Universal Basic Income would be a contradiction in terms for Hegel.

The second solution to the problem would be to include the plebs in the world of labour. For civil society, according to Hegel, this would in fact be an imperative ethical duty (today we would speak of the right to work and the duty to exercise this right). However, this road too proves to be impracticable. To employ the plebs would mean producing an excess of manpower, and consequently a degree of overproduction that could make capitalism collapse. Hegel is perfectly aware that in its modern phase of development, the economy has much greater need for consumers than for producers. However, we also need to look at this matter from the opposite perspective. While it is true that civil society has for Hegel the obligation to provide everyone with adequate public education (§ 239) and above all to include every individual in the market so that they can support themselves (Addition § 240 and § 238), it is evident that all this collides with the interests of capital, which, as we have just seen, always requires a social remainder that cannot be integrated in the world of production.

Civil society and capitalism are therefore two partially incompatible universals. The latter establishes the former but at the same time delegitimizes it, preventing it from fulfilling its obligations and responsibilities. Ultimately, what prevents civil society from fulfilling itself, from living up to its own concept and truth, is precisely that shameful and irrepressible social residue that takes the name of plebs. Yet, as long as the mechanization of production causes a surplus of labour force and a reduction in wages, for Hegel the plebs are destined to grow, and the spiral of social injustice along with it.

In terms of our present time, it is difficult to compare the contemporary plebs with those described by Hegel. Despite the historical distance, however, it is also difficult to deny certain similarities. We might for example add that in the post-

Fordist era the dismantling of trade unions and welfare accompanies the automation of production, and that all of this, combined with the economic crises that cyclically recur in the global world, inexorably feeds the exodus of the neo-plebs from civil society, as well as that multiplication of socioeconomic inequalities that Hegel connected precisely to the growth of the plebs.

The plebs do not exist

In an interview with Jacques Rancière, Michel Foucault speaks of the plebs as an insubstantial category, devoid of sociological reality, and yet *not* non-existent. On the contrary, as the 'permanent and ever silent target for the apparatuses of power', the plebs are presented as a fluid element that permeates the whole of society in different ways:

> The plebs certainly have no sociological reality. However, there is always something in the body of society, in the classes, the groups, and in the individuals themselves, which evades power relations in a certain sense; something that is not more or less malleable or recalcitrant raw material, but rather a centrifugal movement, a contrary, liberated energy. The plebs undoubtedly do not exist, but there is 'something' plebeian (*il a 'de la' plèbe*). There is something plebeian in the bodies and soul, it is in individuals, in the proletariat, in the bourgeoisie, but with various expansions, forms, energies and origins.[11]

Foucault thus indirectly elucidates another decisive element of the discourse surrounding the plebs: they are certainly a product of the contradictions of the systems, but precisely because, as Hegel had already understood, they cannot be reduced to the economy alone, 'there is something' of them in the bourgeois universe. Although Foucault does not delve deeply into the issue, he invites further analysis through categories that are not strictly related to the economy. In my opinion, it is here that the notions of 'social capital' and 'cultural capital' developed by Bourdieu could make a very valuable contribution.

Bourdieu writes that social capital is 'the ensemble of existing or potential resources that are related to the possession of a sustainable network of more or less institutionalized relations of knowledge and mutual knowledge; or, in other words, to belonging to a group, as a set of agents who are not only endowed with common properties [...] but are also united by permanent and useful links.'[12]

Social capital is a value shared by members of groups of various kinds (cultural, political, associative) that can be mobilized for the benefit of individuals to elevate their positions.[13] The value of the social capital accumulated and incorporated into groups thus allows for the possibility of forming relatively closed social circles joined together by 'habits' of aesthetic, cultural or other nature. In turn, cultural capital, which has its roots in class, but which also develops through educational institutions and their own social objects (titles, certificates, diplomas etc.), legitimizes privilege in a way that is more objective, but intimately connected to the logic of social capital.

From this point of view, the neo-plebs, ousted from the circuits of production and reproduction of social capital, constitute a kind of immaterial poverty to which material poverty is sometimes (but not always) added. Deprived of social recognition and public respectability (to use Bourdieu's terms) they develop, in response to exclusion, that understandable form of resentment towards civil society for which the whole modern tradition reproaches them. What is crucial here is the perception (not necessarily conscious) of being excluded from the mechanisms that regulate social mobility.

Thus, in its way – or rather, from an opposite perspective to that of liberal individualism – the plebs also contest the existence of a supposed organic and all-encompassing totality called 'society' (and it is here that one finds the origin of that anarchic character with which, for better or worse, they are constantly associated). But by denying that something like 'society' exists, the plebs at the same time deny the social significance of their own exclusion, and thus fall victim to what Bourdieu would call 'symbolic violence', one that is not perceived as such by the one who suffers it, and thus is carried out with their unwitting complicity.

Going back to Foucault, we need to consider another issue. Once it has been established that the plebs as such do not exist but are a social gradient variously distributed through the population, his approach can be linked to Kant's, although adding a different, perhaps even opposite, dimension. Foucault writes:

> The part of the plebs forms less of an outside in relation to the power relations, but rather perhaps their boundaries, their flip-side, their echo; this plebeian reacts to every advance of power with an evading movement; this motivates every new development of the constellation of power.[14]

Foucault argues that the control of the plebs can be implemented in three ways: through subjugation, through their use as plebs (the reference is to the example of delinquency in the nineteenth century) or through a strategy of resistance and containment. The idea of subjugation of course does not refer to simple repressive practices, but to the use of biopolitical tools aimed at normalizing those parts of social life that exceed the order and goals of a given social organization. Modernity moves in this direction, creating governmental institutions and devices aimed at making school education compulsory, managing abandoned children, improving housing conditions, and inculcating the discipline required for modern work. Making the plebs part of the people means retracing the path described by Kant in the opposite direction, while mobilizing modern pastoral techniques for this purpose. The second method seems to me to refer to the idea that, on the one hand, crime can be tolerated by power as a parallel economy, a source of livelihood for that part of the population that is not part of the production system, and on the other hand it can be exploited as a justification to implement, if necessary, forms of police control over territory, repression, and stricture of liberal freedoms.

The last modality, although only briefly sketched out, probably alludes to strategies of isolation, confinement and spatial separation. It is worthwhile to reconsider these three possibilities of government in the light of the technologies of contemporary power. But to return to the initial theme, I would now like to focus on the conclusion of Foucault's text: 'I do not think that this can be confused in any way with a neo-populism that would substantiate the plebs or with a neo-liberalism that would exalt their primitive rights.'

Since the terms 'neo-populism' and 'neo-liberalism' have become partially juxtaposed today, we can measure the historical distance that separates us from Foucault. At the end of the Fordist age, the socialist (or at least 'labour') parties often proved to be the object of the indignation of the neo-plebs (as they were excluded from the privileges of traditional employee jobs, trade union corporations, and from the processes of production and reproduction of social capital) while the forces of neo-liberalism, the elites of the economy and of power, whose policies have marginalized an enormous mass of people in the last thirty years, paradoxically often enjoy their consensus.

It therefore seems that Hegel was not wrong to stress a certain reciprocity between the plebs and the production of unreasonable socioeconomic differences. Our world offers proof of this, as neoliberalism moved precisely in a direction that favoured the social reproduction of the plebs.[15] The dismantling of welfare, the privatization of education and healthcare, the war on any form of political mediation, the exaltation of individualism and its 'fundamental rights' (not least, in America, the right to bear arms), the culture of competition as the sole form of social bond, the deregulations of markets and competition, and a contempt for the common: all of this contributed to the growth and cultural legitimization of social differences, while the global financial crisis of 2008 dramatically worsened things. The new plebs are thus at once a cultural by-product of neoliberalism and of contemporary modes of production: they are something that the processes of delocalization and automation have rendered redundant to production in an apparently irreversible manner. On the other hand, they still provide a large reservoir of consensus for those forms of neopopulism that give voice to their 'indignation'. Their dominant trait, unsurprisingly, is their being 'anti-system', which means disowning, first internally and then publicly, the civil unity to which they belong (to use Kant's words).

In following a well-recognized psychological defence mechanism, the exclusion that one has suffered can be transformed into self-exclusion, because turning frustration into an active feeling, or aggressive movement, makes it more bearable. Kant (and then Hegel, Stirner and Dávila) clearly saw this phenomenon – the voluntary detachment of the plebs from the social body – even though they then gave it a heavy moral connotation.

And yet one cannot avoid suspecting that such explanations reassure those who make them, neutralizing the more scandalous character carried by the plebs: something that consists not so much in their voluntary secession from civil society (Kant), nor in their refusal to integrate themselves through labour and the market (Hegel), nor, finally, in their lack of class identity (Marx), but in the fact that, in the final instance, the plebs, with their conduct and their 'form of life', could signify that civil society and the bourgeois world as a whole are undesirable.

The governance of the neo-plebs

The neo-plebs are a mobile and fluid social galaxy that today takes many and often incompatible forms. There are (or rather: there may be) plebs in irregular immigration, chronic unemployment, criminal labour, youth gangs, white trash, contemporary *Lumpenproletariat* and even in a certain 'Lumpenbourgeoisie' (as Andre Gunther Frank called it); in the men and women cut off from the networks in which social and cultural capital is reproduced, in the marginalization that has made the margin itself a guarantee of its social invisibility, in those who Geiger called proletaroids,[16] and in whom today we recognize the profile of self-exploiting self-employed workers; precarious, deprived of any union protection and group membership, and systematically exposed to global economic crises.

Of course, since no statistical parameter in principle captures its existence, a phenomenology of the plebs does not exist. The idea of the plebs is conceivable only as a residue of a triple exclusion: material (restructuring of productive forms), social (foreclosure of the status of citizenship, exclusion from public recognition and from collective representative bodies), and epistemological (inability to grasp its essence and needs with the help of traditional analytical tools).

Although the plebs do not exist 'objectively', they have always been the cause of a significant problem for government, which can be summed up in the simple question of 'what to do with them'. In my opinion, the answer to this question can be found in five different technologies of government that rework solutions as old as the plebs themselves.

The first one is the army conscription of the plebs, an almost exclusively American prerogative that is nevertheless difficult not to mention, not least because of the long tradition behind it. I will limit myself to noting that it is such an ancient strategy that it was already mentioned by Titus Livius, in *Ad urbe condita libri*, in respect to the reform of 407, which for the first time paid a salary to the soldiers of the Roman army.

The second technology consists in what Guy Debord called the 'society of the spectacle', which can be understood as the industrialized and technological update of the ancient uses of the public spectacle. Debord himself speaks of 'the empire of the spectacle', connecting this expression to modern 'lonely crowds': a new widespread proletariat, educated by the propaganda of commodities, which the spectacle brings together only as separate. In this sense, it is useful to remember that the verb 'entertain' comes from *intra-tenere*: to hold inside, to hold off, to retain within oneself. Entertainment is therefore a postmodern figure of internment, and in this sense it lends itself to being thought of as a form of control of the neo-plebs. The entertainment industry, meanwhile, has a desperate need for consumers of images and goods, and the neo-plebs function exactly like a 'reserve army' for consumption, since the universe of commodities directs their desire towards the immediate possession of goods, logos, styles, which make up for the lack of social recognition and belonging to the civil life of the dominant groups.[17]

As it happened throughout the history of capitalist accumulation, political economy saw in the proletarian only a worker, or the one who had to receive the minimum amount of money in exchange for his wage labour; in the post-Fordist age, however, it sees in the neo-plebs only the consumer. This is generally made possible by the instrument of private debt, which in turn is an effective government lever in the hands of various agencies.[18] But this is not the crucial point. What matters is that the universe of goods plays a fundamental role in controlling the plebs because, by intervening between their desire and their subjectivity, it prevents them from encountering their own lack. In short: it allows them not to feel poor like the poor part of the people, who are objectively captured and sometimes tormented by what they lack (in general: income or work). The neo-plebs do not want to be the poorest part of the proletariat, the one that yearns to improve, or more often to fight for its social status tooth and nail. From this point of view, the discourse of social democracy is doomed to fail in both of its two fundamental variants. The more typical and never exhausted version is the one that followed the Marxist approach of the German SPD, according to which the *Lumpenproletariat* had to be excluded from any consideration and political strategy, marginalized by trade union interests, and discredited on a moral level. Faced with the dramatic dissolution of the mediating social bodies and the industrial organization of work, the expanding universe of the neo-plebs would thus have remained completely extraneous (or even hostile) to the social project of the left parties (like the proletaroids, ignored or even despised for being entrepreneurs and proletarians at the same time). But the other, more inclusive version of the relationship between social democracy and the neo-plebs, characterized by a fundamental misunderstanding, was doomed to fail too. As we have just seen, the will to abolish the plebs by including them in the world of work, and therefore in 'the people' (or the working class) risks running into an theoretical misunderstanding the moment it presumes the desirability of such an assimilation.

For better or for worse, the very facticity of the plebs creates resistance: they do not allow themselves to be disciplined or assimilated. And on this note it seems to me there is a certain convergence between the bourgeois moralism of Kant and Hegel, which sees in the plebeian exception a repulsive socio-anthropological deviance, and the anti-bourgeois and anarchic one of Bakunin, Foucault or Pasolini, which in several ways re-evaluate this same exception as a form of resistance, albeit unconscious, to the capitalist *ratio*. What is essential in this critical convergence is not the type (positive or negative) of judgment, but the recognition that people and plebs are different concepts in a qualitative sense. The plebs, by definition, escape the political categories of the Enlightenment due to their internal lack of homogeneity, their fluid and metamorphic character, their hybrid status (inextricably bringing together economic, social, moral, aesthetic and psychological characteristics), and their intimate resistance to both liberal utilitarianism and the anthropological assumptions of social democracy.

I would also like to add one further comment. Hegel's anthropological portrait of the plebs may have seemed to veer towards the picturesque, particularly when lingering on their passion for games, gambling, and chance (as opposed to work and its intrinsic social virtues). However, if one thinks of the social significance that the liberalization (and institutionalization) of gambling, lotteries, video-poker, sports and other types of betting have taken on today, I think one should realize that Hegel grasped an aspect that is only apparently marginal. Does not today's success of these forms of entertainment lie in a sort of 'magical' compensation for the gap that stops the plebs from upward social mobility? Does it not feed into the conviction that fate is more powerful than will and history, and does it not perhaps profit from that same superstition that sees fortune and misfortune as caused by personal destinies?

There are, however, other and more dramatic elements connecting Hegel's and Marx's plebs to their current form. For example, what we refer to today as 'addictions' (to alcohol, drugs, and so on) – a social problem of ever-increasing proportions across all classes – is in fact one of the most characteristic prerogatives ascribed to the plebs.

This brings us to the third strategy of control of the neo-plebs which, as Foucault suggested, relates to the submerged galaxy of illegality. If instead of immediately thinking of criminal organizations, drug dealing, or theft, one thinks of the economic continent of 'undeclared work', it is easier to understand how this strategy consists of tolerating the existence of a parallel and 'informal' economy with its own rules, often radically different from the competitive and rational ones of 'formal' capitalism. But since this is not generalizable, the State must give itself other means to control the neo-plebs and guarantee them the minimum threshold for subsistence. The most common are precisely the welfare benefits deprecated by Hegel, such as the citizen's income, which today are on the verge of becoming a government tool.

The fourth technique is based on the action of the new *tribuni plebis*, i.e. the populist leaders capable of creating a direct and personal relationship with the sections of the population that are cut off from traditional mechanisms of representation, promising them protection from the threats of global capitalism and cosmopolitanism (or immigration) and at the same time amplifying the indignation towards the state, the 'system', and the enlightened bourgeoisie (the elite understood as a class), and social democracy.

Populist propaganda focuses on the recovery of imaginary forms of power by carefully choosing a vocabulary based on autarchy, resentment, the selfish primacy of the interests of the nation and the individual, the liberating power of secession, the threat of turmoil and insurrection, the de-legitimization of public information channels and third-party institutions.

And yet the word 'populism' is inadequate to describe the government of the neo-plebs, who as we have seen do not even align with the concept of the people. In this case too, Hegel provides theoretical assistance. Following his suggestion, we should call 'ochlocracy' (government of the multitude) that type of government which arises from the degeneration of democracy: 'Its degeneration is the ochlocracy or domination of the plebs, when that part of the people that has no property and it is animated by iniquitous sentiments diverts honest citizens from the affairs of the state.'[19]

It is therefore clear that, while plebs and citizenship are irreconcilable concepts, ochlocracy remains a possibility that pertains to democracy, and is indeed inherent to it: just as the people can fall into the plebs, so democracy can lapse into the ochlocratic regime. To gain further direction about this concept, however, it is necessary to turn to Polybius, who first coined the term in book VI (chapter 9) of the *Histories*. According to the Greek historian,

> As long as some of these survive who have experienced the evils of oligarchical dominion, they [...] set a high value on equality and freedom of speech. But when a new generation arises and democracy falls into the hands of the grandchildren of its founders, they have become so accustomed to freedom and equality that they no longer vlue them, and begin to aim at pre-eminence; and it is chiefly those of ample fortune who fall into this error. So when they begin to lust for power and cannot attain it through themselves or their own good qualities, they ruin their estates, tempting and corrupting the people in every possible way. And hence when by their foolish thirst for reputation they have created among the masses an appetite for gifts and the habit of receiving them, democracy in its turn is abolished and changes into a rule of force and violence.[20]

In a certain sense, the theses of Hegel and Polybius complement each other: the first attributes the origin of the ochlocracy to the crisis of citizenship and to the ethical-social involution of the people, while the second finds it instead in the decline of the economic elite, which having now forgotten the value of democracy, and more particularly the value of the extraordinary political achievements of legal equality and freedom of expression, aim for power by flattering and corrupting the people; that is, by transforming them into *óclos*, a disordered, atomized, headless multitude, prey to demagogic agitations and exploited in a subversive sense by the wealthiest classes.

The fifth and final technology of governance of the neo-plebs is that of physical separation, that is, their ghettoization, or the self-ghettoization of the affluent classes (for example, through the urban model of gated communities).

Mike Davis has illustrated this strategy in his *City of Quartz*, which traces back to the 1990s the testing of this and other governmental technologies (interdiction, video surveillance, concealment, law enforcement) connected to control over public space through both legal and extra-legal means. After all, whether it is a question of marginalizing the plebs through the soft methods of gentrification or through walls and gates, it concerns making the most of the natural potential of space to separate, hide, and remove. The marginalization that affects physical mobility does not replace the marginalization that affects social mobility; rather, it completes it, even assigning to it a certain degree of public visibility.

Remnants and waste

I previously defined the neo-plebs as a 'remnant', a 'residue', or an 'excess'. At this point, however, this idea is no longer entirely adequate. The 'remnant' is whatever is left after a division or subtraction. The social remnant continues to refer to the totality, to the whole from which it derives. The plebs do not seem to respond to this logic, but rather to what (with Lacan) I would connect to the notion of 'waste'. By its very nature, waste is in fact unavoidable: it is what *resists* the 'nothing-ization' processes that produce it. Something is left over, but it is not representable, economizable, subjectivizable and therefore governable. Waste is what detaches itself from the social body that produces it. And the plebs, as mentioned above, are always in the process of detaching themselves from the people, of falling out of civil society. From this point of view, the problem posed by waste – that is, what to do with it – turns out to be a decisive question for the order of the present and future global world.

On the other hand, the concept of waste designates an anti-economical dynamic, linked to wastefulness, excess, and transgression, in which Bataille recognized the most archaic and irrepressible trace of sovereignty, of anthropological resistance to the bourgeois logic of accumulation.[21] In waste there is always something that takes precedence over the logics governing work and its ethics. Its typical manifestations are laughter, tears, the comic, the tragic, intoxication, music, celebration, the horror of death, the sense of the sacred, vice, crime and violence, extreme misery or extreme wealth, luxury, and profligacy: in short, everything that goes beyond the world dominated by the primacy of the useful, in both economic and social sense. Once again, the discourse of the plebs seems inseparable from their 'form of life', as Marx called it in passing. Or rather, from a form of thinking complementary to the tradition we have considered up to now, which accepts its excessive character rather than discarding it on principle. This way of thinking of the plebs as a potentially revolutionary ethico-political excess is inscribed in the tradition that goes from the 'vulgar common people' of Machiavelli to Spinoza and Deleuze and finally Negri's 'multitude', in which all the elements of mediation from the Hegelo-Marxian tradition are overturned, while its fluid, desubjectivized, shapeless, immediate, instinctual and revolting (in both senses of the word) nature is celebrated. It is not a matter of pitting one tradition against the other, as if they were opposite and complementary or incompatible. It is perhaps more interesting to note how in both approaches the very question of the plebs takes on a political-existential meaning that cannot be reduced to the juridical-political categories of the modern, and perhaps for this reason continues to be so 'scandalously' relevant.

Notes

1 Christopher Lasch, *The Revolt of the Elites and the Betrayal of Democracy* (New York: Norton & Company 1994), 28–9.
2 I have replaced the word 'rabble' in the English translation with 'plebs' as it adheres more closely to the German word 'Pöbel.' As we shall see later, in the English version of the Hegelian texts, translating the terms 'Pöbel' or 'Plebs' with 'rabble' does not seem correct as it severs the word's link to its ancient tradition (and also its modern one, for instance Machiavelli's). In a small note on the plebs, Kant also adds an anthropological connotation by referring to Plautus, which will become central in Hegel: 'The insulting name of *canaille* (*la canaille du peuple*) probably derives from *canalicola*, idle people who loitered along a canal in ancient Rome, mocking people at work (cavillator et ridicularius, cf. Plautus, Curcul.).'
3 Immanuel Kant, *Anthropology from a Pragmatic Point of View*. Translated and edited by Robert B. Louden (Cambridge: Cambridge University Press, 2006), 213.
4 Georg Wilhelm Friedrich Hegel, *Elements of the Philosophy of Right*, trans. H.B. Nisbet (Cambridge: Cambridge University Press, 1991), § 244, 266–7.
5 I have changed the word 'rabble' to 'plebs'. See note 1.
6 Hegel, *Elements of the Philosophy of Right*, 267.
7 Flaubert used the word *voyoucratie* ('thugocracy') to express the ghastly, transgressive, violent nature that plebian counter-sovereignty can assume. Derrida (2003), meanwhile, reminds us that 'the word *voyou* has an essential relation with the *voie*, the way, with the urban roadways [*voirie*], the roadways of the city or the

polis, and thus with the street [*rue*], the waywardness [*dévoiement*] of the *voyou* consisting in making ill use of the street, in corrupting the street or loitering in the streets, in "roaming the streets" [...] In the wake of Baudelaire, Benjamin, or Aragon, all this would be part of another portrait of "modern life," of the modern city in the urban and capitalistic landscape of industrial civilization from the nineteenth century to the present' (Jacques Derrida, *Voyous*, Paris, Galilée, 2003, 65).

8   Karl Marx, Friedrich Engels. *The Communist Manifesto*, trans. Samuel Morse (London: Pluto Press, 2008), 49.
9   Karl Marx, 'The class struggles in France: 1848 to 1858', in Karl Marx, *Surveys from Exile*, trans P. Jackson (Harmondsworth: Penguin 1973), 39.
10   Hegel, *Elements of the Philosophy of Right*, 266–7.
11   Michel Foucault, 'Powers and Strategies' (1977), in Michel Foucault *Power/Knowledge: Selected Interviews and Other Writings 1972–1977*, edited by Colin Gordon (New York: Pantheon Books, 1980), 137–8.
12   Pierre Bourdieu, 'Le capital social', *Actes de la Recherche en Sciences Sociales*, 31 (1980): 2.
13   Pierre Bourdieu, 'The forms of capital', in *Handbook of Theory and Research for the Sociology of Education*, edited by John G. Richardson (New York: Greenwood Press, 1986), 241–58 (249).
14   Foucault, 'Powers and Strategies', 137–8.
15   See Marco D'Eramo, *Dominio* (Milano: Feltrinelli, 2020).
16   In Weimar Germany, Theodor Geiger (1932) identified, alongside the proletariat, an elusive social subjectivity, the result of the great crisis of 1929, which he baptized *Proletaroid*. The name refers to the figure of a day worker, not bound by a boss (and in this different from the wage worker); a constitutively precarious worker, with no professional identity, class or group culture, which brings together the functions of the employer and the employee. Geiger's proletaroids are that part of the old middle class or traditionally self-employed that, faced with their progressive economic marginalization, have now resigned themselves to their condition, but feel forsaken by both the state and socialism, whose policies are reserved for employees, former workers, or unemployed employees, or for the productive middle classes (technicians, specialists, figures of the new professions). For this reason, among other things, the autonomous proletaroids would have been more susceptible to the appeal of the Nazi agitators.
17   If, at the same time, the neo-plebs are the breeding ground for fake news and so-called 'post-truth', this can be at least partly explained precisely through the spectacularization of life: 'The spectacle, which obliterates the boundaries between self and world [...] also obliterates the boundaries between truth and false by repressing all directly lived truth beneath the real presence of falsehood maintained

by the organization of appearances' (Guy Debord, *Society of Spectacle* (London: Rebel Press & London, 1992, §219), 116–17).
18 See Paolo Perulli, *Il debito sovrano* (Milano: La nave di Teseo, 2020).
19 G. W. F. Hegel, *Nürnberger und Heidelberger Schriften, 1808–1817* (Berlin: Suhrkamp Verlag), 248. My translation.
20 Polybius, *The Histories* (Cambridge, MA: Harvard University Press, 1922), 287–8.
21 See Georges Bataille. *La souveraineté* (in Georges Bataille, *Ouvres complètes*, VIII, Paris: Gallimard, 1976).

Bibliography

Bataille, Georges. *La souveraineté*. In *Oeuvres complètes*, VIII, Paris: Gallimard, 1976.
Bourdieu, Pierre. 'Le capital social'. *Actes de la Recherche en Sciences Sociales*, no. 31 (1980): 2–3.
Bourdieu, Pierre. 'The forms of capital'. In *Handbook of Theory and Research for the Sociology of Education*, edited by John G. Richardson, 241–58. New York: Greenwood Press, 1986.
Bussard, Robert. 'The "dangerous class" of Marx and Engels: The rise of the idea of the Lumpenproletariat'. *History of European Ideas* 8, no.6 (1987): 675–92.
Castells, Manuel. *The Rise of the Network Society* (*The Information Age: Economy, Society and Culture* Vol. I.) Oxford: Blackwell, 1996.
Debord, Guy. *Society of the Spectacle*. London: Rebel Press, 1992.
D'Eramo Marco. *Dominio*. Milano: Feltrinelli, 2020.
Derrida Jacques. *Voyous*. Paris: Galilée, 2003.
Foucault, Michel. 'Powers and Strategies' (1977), in Michel Foucault *Power/Knowledge: Selected Interviews and Other Writings 1972–1977*. New York: Pantheon Books, 1980, 134–145.
Frank, Andre Gunther. *Lumpenbourgeoisie and Lumpendevelopment: Dependency, Class and Politics in Latin America*. New York: Monthly Review Press, 1972.
Hegel, Wilhelm Friedrich. *Elements of the Philosophy of Right*. Cambridge: Cambridge University Press, 1991.
Hegel, Wilhelm Friedrich. *Nürnberger und Heidelberger Schriften, 1808–1817*. Berlin: Suhrkamp Verlag, 1986.
Kant, Immanuel. *Anthropology from a Pragmatic Point of View*, translated and edited by Robert B. Louden. Cambridge: Cambridge University Press, 2006.
Lasch, Christopher, *The Revolt of the Elites and the Betrayal of Democracy*. New York: Norton & Company, 1994.
Marx, Karl. 'The class struggles in France: 1848 to 1858'. In Marx, Karl. *Surveys from Exile*. Harmondsworth: Penguin, 1973.

Marx, Karl. *The Eighteenth Brumaire of Louis Bonaparte*, Beijing: Foreign Languages Press, 1978.
Marx, Karl, and Friedrich Engels. *The Communist Manifesto*. London: Pluto Press, 2008.
Perulli, Paolo. *Il debito sovrano. La fase estrema del capitalismo*. Milano: La Nave di Teseo, 2020.
Polybius. *The Histories*. Cambridge, MA: Harvard University Press, 1922.

6

On the Theatricality and Historicity of the Political[1]

Gregor Moder

In his own contribution to *Žižek and Performance*, Slavoj Žižek analyses what he calls 'the most elementary *theatricality* of the human condition'.[2] But contrary to what an unsuspecting reader may expect, what Žižek has in mind is not the way in which we usually discuss social and political practices as performances, as roles that we have to play within a given set of social rules. He argues that when we face a profound challenge to our normal understanding of the world and our place in it (such as in moments of deep trauma), we may of course doubt the meaning and the purpose of those usual practices, but at the same time our 'bare existence' appears at these points theatrical – in a very different sense from everyday performances. Commenting on the 1977 western *The White Buffalo* (dir. J. Lee Thompson), Žižek writes:

> What we encounter here is a surprising reversal: common sense tells us that we 'perform' and obey complex rules in our polite everyday interactions and exchanges, while the moments of encountering a Real are the moments when, under its traumatic impact, the symbolic protective network disintegrates and we are exposed to the raw impact of the Real. *The White Buffalo* turns the relationship around: it is precisely the traumatic encounter of the Real Thing that has to be constructed, its stage organised like the scene of a performance.[3]

The aim of this chapter is to explore the distinction between the theatricality of 'polite everyday interactions and exchanges' on the one hand and the theatricality of 'a staged Real' on the other hand as a way to introduce a distinction also in two concepts of performance in Žižek's political theory. Žižek himself inscribes this problematic in the political theory when he discusses the reenactment of the Storming of the Winter Palace in Petrograd on the third anniversary of the October revolution. What fascinates him is the enormousness of the project which ended up involving many of the protagonists of the original storming who were thus performing their own role in the revolution. Žižek suggests that this staging of one of the central events of the revolution is far from what Walter Benjamin criticized as the aesthetization of the political; instead, he understands it as an example of what the 'staging of the Real' may look like in the political domain.[4]

My claim is that in addition to the atemporal analysis of the two types of the political performative discussed by Žižek, we should also introduce a dimension of historicity which we can find in Hegel's political philosophy. To an extent, philosophy has always relied on theatrical metaphors and privileged the sense of sight when describing cognitive processes and the truth itself, the truth beyond any process of knowledge. Just think of Plato's notion of the 'idea' and his notorious allegory of the cave, with puppet masters on the one side of the wall and passive observers of the shadowy spectacle on the other. Even the common etymology of words 'theatre' and 'theory' indicates that they are both related to the practice of observation, to the function of sight. This chapter, however, aims beyond such general parallels and explores the double claim that (1) Žižek's political thought not only relies to a great extent on an explicit theory of performance but also that (2) his concept of performance allows us to better understand the phenomena in our contemporary political regime of power as well as to articulate the conditions of the possibility of thinking beyond it.

Žižek's concept of performance

Let us begin by exploring the extent to which Žižek's conceptual arsenal employs the metaphor of theatre. The first thing to note on this count is that the two major sources for Žižek's theory – Jacques Lacan and especially his linguistic intervention into psychoanalysis and G. W. F. Hegel and his radicalization of the project of the philosophy of German idealism – themselves rely massively on theatre or performance as the privileged metaphor. For our purposes here, the first important concept to examine is Lacan's idea of the 'master signifier', especially because Žižek puts it in close proximity to Hegelian conceptual apparatus.

Lacan's notion of the master signifier was developed in his seminar on *The Other Side of Psychoanalysis* in 1969–70, where he explicitly referred to the master–slave dialectic in (Alexandre Kojève's interpretation of) Hegel's *Phenomenology of Spirit*. Nevertheless, the groundwork for this concept in

Žižek's use was laid out much earlier, already in *Ecrits*, where Lacan draws on the developments in the structural linguistics from Ferdinand de Saussure to Émile Benveniste.⁵ Recall how Saussure, discussing the nature of the sign, distinguished between the signifier and the signified in terms of the 'sound image' of the sign and its 'concept', insisting on the contingent, unmotivated way the one is coupled with the other.⁶ However, this distinction is perhaps only provisional, or even misleading. As Benveniste argued, the signifier and the signified are 'consubstantial', and their connection is not arbitrary or contingent, but 'has to be recognized as *necessary*'.⁷ Lacan took the idea of the consubstantiality of the signifier and the signified to its ultimate consequence. Anything that we may construe as the signified in terms of the concept is ultimately still just another signifier (or a series of signifiers). Thus, the signified as an independent entity evades us; all we have is an apparently endless stream or flow of signifiers.

The more we speak and utter words, or write down sentences, the more it becomes clear that we are immersed in signifiers. For Lacan, this means that we must account for the emergence of meaning differently. His innovation can be summed up as the claim that apart from the signifiers pointing to other signifiers in the signifying chain, there is also such a thing as the master signifier, a signifier with the capacity and the function to stitch the signifying chain to the subject, effectively ending the chain and making it legible for the subject. The crucial point to be made in this process is that for Lacan, the meaning thus emerges *only in retrospect*; that strictly speaking, the chain of signifiers was 'meaningless' until the advent of the master signifier.

On this specific point, Lacan's account of the process of understanding or interpretation of a given text must be sharply distinguished from (Heideggerian) hermeneutics, where the subject of understanding is always already working with an *anticipation* of meaning; in a sense, hermeneutics argues that one always already 'knows', albeit incompletely or inexplicitly. For Lacan, any anticipation of the future meaning must strictly be explained as the *retroactive effect* of the master signifier, as the consequence of its work: only once the master signifier has rendered the signifying chain legible and we have grasped the meaning, it becomes evident to us that, looking back, we have *always* known what was coming.

There is another, equally important distinction between Lacan's theory and phenomenological hermeneutics. Hermeneutics assumes that the conscious subject of understanding is already given, irreducible from the process of reading and interpreting. In this regard, even Heidegger's account of human subjectivity as being-there (*Dasein*) remains within the confines of the Cartesian project. For

Lacan, the situation is more complex, because Lacanian psychoanalysis presupposes that our subjectivity is split between what we could call the unconscious and the conscious subject (and Lacan himself would distinguish as the subject of the unconscious and the ego) and argues that the latter only emerges in the process of understanding, with the advent of the master signifier. The very supposition that I am, in fact, the subject of my own thoughts, is precisely what constitutes me as the conscious subject in the Cartesian sense. In other words, it is not only the signifying chain that gets its definitive form with the advent of the master signifier, producing the retroactive effect of meaning – it is the subject of knowledge itself that is constituted in this process. The master signifier does not only stitch the chain of signifiers to the subject, making it legible to the subject, but in the very same movement also stitches the subject to the signifying chain, constituting it in its conscious identity. The subject itself becomes 'legible', disponible to the signifier. In grasping the meaning of a text, the subject also grasps itself – understands itself – as its addressee.

Žižek's early rendering of the concept of the master signifier, and of what its intervention means for the subject, is found in the second lecture he held at the occasion of the establishment of the Society for Theoretical Psychoanalysis in Ljubljana, Yugoslavia, back in 1982. The lecture is dedicated to the 'point of suture', which is basically Lacan's concept of the anchoring point (or quilting point, *point de capiton*) interpreted through Jacques-Alain Miller's phrasing it as the 'suture'. Žižek introduces the concept by recalling Lacan's own example, the encounter between the high priest Jehoiada and the military officer Abner in Jean Racine's 1691 play *Athalie*. The background for the meeting of Jehoida and Abner is the biblical tyrant Athaliah who turned away from the true Jewish faith and began worshipping Baal. The officer Abner is haunted by suspicions and fears, and wants to offer an alliance to the high priest against the queen. In terms of mitigating Abner's many worries, however, the priest does not offer any concrete assurances; instead, when Abner points out that dire fate awaits the priests under the tyrant's rule, Jehoiada simply says that he fears only God. Surprisingly perhaps, this works: Abner's worries, as Žižek writes, 'miraculously' dissipate. In Žižek's rendering of Lacan, the claim is that there is no counterbalance of hope to conciliate the fears of the military officer; instead, the entire series of fears is replaced with a much greater one – with the absolute fear of God. It is this absolute fear, evoked in Jehoiada's reply, that has the calming effect on Abner; it works on Abner as the master signifier, transforming him into a devout supporter of the cause.[8]

Žižek offers several further examples of the miraculous functioning of the 'point of suture', including one that is of central interest to us – the concept of monarch in Hegel's *Philosophy of Right*.

> Hegel says here exactly the same thing as Lacan does in the seminar *The Other Side* ...: the displacement between the state bureaucracy and the monarch corresponds precisely to the displacement between the battery of 'knowledge' (S2) and the 'point of suture', the 'unary' master signifier (S1); the bureaucratic 'knowledge' requires an external, 'non-bureaucratic' unary point to 'suture' its discourse, to 'totalize' its discourse from the outside and to confer upon it a performative dimension by giving it an empty, self-referential 'signature', a purely formal 'dotting of the i'. What Hegel is trying to do is to completely isolate the 'point of suture', to consider it as an empty point of formal 'decision', the subjective 'I will it' without any concrete 'content'.[9]

Based on Žižek's reading, we could argue that Hegel already gives us not only an *example* of a performative utterance – the ceremonial declaration of a new law – but also an early *concept* of such utterance. Following Žižek, we could sketch the Hegelian performative, first of all, in Lacanian terms as the intervention of the master signifier, and secondly, as a decision which is purely formal and ultimately groundless, since there is no final number of reasons or grounds that could amount to and outweigh what Hegel describes as the 'ultimate decision of the will'.[10] Žižek characterizes this with the tautological formula where 'one is subjected to the king because he is the king'.[11] Hegel himself, however, described the self-referential, groundless nature of the monarch's decision as belonging to the same logic as the notorious ontological proof of God's existence. As far as Hegel is concerned, what is at stake in both is the 'transformation of the absolute concept into being', and both rely on what is simply the nature of truth as the 'unity of the concept and existence'.[12]

Unity of the concept and existence does indeed constitute the basis of the ontotheological tradition, yet we may be wary of accepting such unity as 'simply the truth', as Hegel put it. This notion of truth becomes much more reasonable when we consider the truth in the symbolic realm, for instance with regard to legal entities such as the state – which is precisely what is at stake in Hegel's *Philosophy of Right*. Legal entities such as states or companies indeed exist solely by virtue of being declared as existing by the appropriate authority, by the sovereign (the monarch or the people, depending on the form of government), but this ultimate authority of the law is always self-declared and self-evident (in monarchy, the legal authority is usually derived from God or other divine beings, but this only defers the self-referentiality of the law to the 'higher' level: the authority of God is self-declared and self-evident).

Theatricality of fascism

Žižek's concept of the performative, whether based on Lacan's master signifier or on Hegel's purely formal decision of the monarch, is inextricably bound to the questions of political power and the source of legal authority. What I find especially interesting and relevant for contemporary political theory is the question of the relationship of the concept of such political performance to what has often been described as political theatre. The obvious example here is the theatricality of fascism, an often-discussed propensity of fascism to perform and act in the public domain as if on a stage. Bertolt Brecht spoke of 'kleine Dramatisierungen (...) die für den Nationalsozialismus so charakteristisch sind', naming *Reichstagsbrand* as a good example.[13] Of course, all politicians and political parties tend to deploy rhetorical and theatrical tricks in order to pursue their political goals – in democratic processes just as well as in any other. Nevertheless, many have made the point that in the case of fascism, theatre is not simply one of its tools in the political arsenal or its preferred method of appearance; fascism is theatrical by its very nature. Even Walter Benjamin's famous formula of fascism as '*aestheticization of politics*' could be read as supporting this point:[14] fascism is not simply an introduction of some cultic or aesthetic elements into the already established political domain, it is a genuine grasp and articulation of the political domain as such. More generally, fascism is not simply an introduction of certain radical content – racism, unity of the nation, cult of the leader, rapid industrialization etc. – within what is otherwise a perfectly neutral political domain. Instead, fascism is an arrangement of the political according to a set of very specific aesthetic principles, where the vanishing remnants of the 'aura' – of that which binds the work of art to its specific temporality and to its original location, to its *native ground* – make a claim to modernity by re-appropriating the means of technological reproduction (photography, film).

And indeed, as soon as Žižek introduces the idea of the decision of Hegel's monarch as necessarily groundless, he goes on to separate the functioning of the monarch from the functioning of totalitarianism. For Žižek, what characterizes the totalitarian system is ultimately the very absence of the 'point of suture':

> When does the state bureaucracy become 'totalitarian'? Certainly not when the S1, the point of the 'irrational' authority, puts too much pressure on it, but, to the contrary, when such point is completely *absent*, when *there is no* unary 'point of suture' to totalize the discourse of bureaucracy from its outside, when the S2, the field of the 'bureaucratic knowledge', 'runs amok' and begins functioning 'all by itself', without any reference to an external point, which would confer the performative dimension to it...[15]

Hegel claimed that 'Das Wahre ist das Ganze', and so it is perhaps no coincidence that Žižek sharply distinguishes between totalitarianism from what he calls totalization – far from being a path to totalitarianism, totalization is precisely what is necessary for meaning to emerge beyond the endless chain of reasons or grounds. For our discussion here, I think it is especially important to emphasize the 'performative dimension' supplied to the political domain with what is ultimately a groundless decision. While Žižek also discusses the performativity of fascism and even a kind of 'Stalinist performative', it seems that the proper concept of performative in the Žižekian sense is what he observed with regard to the master signifier and the ceremonial monarch. In fact, when discussing the performative function in fascism, he explicitly designates it as a kind of false theatre: 'The fascist discourse therefore truly puts the ideological dimension on display (...), but it does this by literally "staging" or "acting" it: it theatrically "imitates," "feigns" the (pre-bourgeois, mediaeval) "discourse of the master".[16]

The falsity of fascist theatre does not mean, for Žižek, that fascist performances are only an external veil that covers some other discourse, some other interest – personal gain, for instance. It means that the distance of the subject to the fascist rituals he or she takes part in is ultimately irreducible; there is no point of suture, no true performative function in the sense described above. Totalitarianism is the very absence of the point of suture.

Let me add an historical remark. From our contemporary point of view, Hegel's political idea of the constitutional monarchy, which took shape well before the advent of fascism, can only seem utterly naïve. The idea that the modern political commonwealth can be stitched together, or totalized, through a purely ceremonial act of signing bills into laws; or, in other words, the idea that the conflicts and contradictions (to use a more Marxist term) of the bourgeois society can be adequately addressed and perhaps even resolved with the separation between the institution where the political discussion takes place (the parliament) and the institution of ultimate sovereignty (the monarch), this idea has been amply rebuked by the history of the nineteenth and twentieth centuries.

What concerns Žižek's article, the central point is that fascism is not what results from Hegel's idea of the monarch as the point of the final decision of the will, because Hegel's monarch is not the supreme leader who knows better than anyone else what is to be done. Quite to the contrary, Hegel's monarch is someone who needs not to know anything. This is why, for Žižek, fascism, or totalitarianism in general, is precisely what you get when the decisions of the Leader do not appear merely as 'dotting of the i's' but rather as the incessant, unstoppable, endless functioning of the realm of reasoning.

Coupling Žižek's argument with Benjamin's historical one, I claim that we can make a step further and distinguish between two concepts of the performative dimension in politics. The first concept would designate an event within the political field which completely rearticulates it, such as a political revolution in the sense of an emergence of a new legal-political order, one that, strictly speaking, cannot be reduced back simply to an element within the former regime of power and should therefore be perceived as radically groundless. The second concept of the performative would designate performance in the sense of 'business as usual', politics as the realm of means to an end, as the realm of reasons or grounds, where fascism (or totalitarianism) is never a necessary result, but always a potential threat. In a sense, this is how I understand that other notable remark by Walter Benjamin, that 'behind every fascism is a failed revolution'. One could say that fascism is what you get when an *historical* 'point of suture' (a revolution, dictated by the immense conflicts within a given society, opening a possibility of a new world) is replaced with a *regressive* 'point of suture', one which recognizes social contradictions but neutralizes them by translating them into already known terms (yes, the conflicts and the suffering are real, and we all know who's behind it: the Jew).

The ceremonial monarch and the world-historical individual

In the extant literature, the difference between theatricality and performativity is often spelled out in the sense of separating between 'bad' theatricality and 'good' performativity, between merely acting out or merely playing something on the one hand and genuinely, authentically doing it (performing it) on the other. I want to carefully separate the distinction sketched above, between the two concepts of performativity in the political, from such attempts. The simple distinction between good and bad performance seems to reproduce, at least to an extent, the old Platonic distinction between genuine truth and 'mere' appearances. For Plato – and similarly for Rousseau and many others – the problem of theatre is not only epistemological (firstly, by focusing on imitations it hinders cognition; secondly, the poets only know how to imitate/represent, they possess no true knowledge of what they write about) but also political (by watching tragedies and comedies we may become tragedians and comedians ourselves, that is to say, bad role models we see in theatre will make us become bad citizens). Plato's solution is seemingly quite intuitive: just as we have to separate between true science (well, true philosophy) and sophistry, we also have to separate between true politics and politics as theatre. Does the separation between the two kinds of performance in politics such as I presented above, along the lines of Žižek and Benjamin, not reproduce this 'ancient quarrel between philosophers and poets', as Plato puts it?

In response to this objection, one is perhaps tempted to claim that the terms performance and theatre already suggest that they are reflexive categories, whereas the terms truth and mere appearance (to which Plato oftentimes reduces theatre in *Republic*) are unmediated, direct. However, this is not entirely true, at least not when Plato applies these categories to political theory. In *Laws*, Plato even goes as far as to declare that the only proper response to tragedians asking for admittance to the state is this:

> Most honored guests, we're tragedians ourselves, and our tragedy is the finest and best we can create. At any rate, our entire state has been constructed so as to be a 'representation' of the finest and noblest life—the very thing we maintain is most genuinely a tragedy. So we are poets like yourselves, composing in the same genre, and your competitors as artists and actors in the finest drama, which true law alone has the natural powers to 'produce' to perfection.[17]

The claims that the state is a *representation* of the finest and noblest life, and that that true law is the finest *drama*, are strikingly Hegelian. The quote specifically refers to representation – to mimesis – and it is clear that it cannot be interpreted as 'mere imitation', or 'mere theatre'. Especially the idea that the true law is a kind of drama – indeed, the finest kind – seems to suggest that laws are not to be construed as some external restrictions to human capacities, but as the very condition for those capacities to truly come to fruition in the first place. In Hegelian terms, it is only within the state governed by (good) laws that human capacities – indeed, human freedom – are something not merely abstract, but something *actual*. If we were to use contemporary terminology of anthropology or sociology, we would probably say that Plato understands the state as a (perlocutionary) performance of its laws.[18]

The core of the objection is this: if the distinction between the two concepts of the performance in politics reproduces the distinction between true being and mere representation/imitation, then it is fair to assume that it also reproduces the problems of that distinction. And what is the main problem of the clear-cut distinction between being and appearance? Well, precisely the fact that it disregards the performative character of social practices! If the state is its own live performance, the finest drama, just as Plato seems to claim, then its true being is not hidden behind the veil of external appearances, because it dwells in those very appearances themselves: they constitute the actuality of the state. This objection thus puts pressure on the clear-cut distinction between two kinds of performances, between a genuine performance and the 'merely' theatrical politics: by adopting it, have we not lost the very concept of the performative?

As for Žižek, the semantic problem of the terminological nest of 'performance' is not really pertinent, because he is not committed to the distinction between performativity and theatricality of social practices – as indicated above, he often uses these terms synonymously. But this objection is still pertinent to our discussion about Žižek's concept of the performative in politics, because it forces us to distinguish between the Žižek's performative as a *historical* 'point of suture', as an event that rearranges and rearticulates all political reality on the one hand – a revolution – and what we could call the general theory of performativity of all social practices on the other hand – the normal, 'polite' everyday flow of political life, where the 'point of suture' merely denotes the beat, the rhythm of everyday exchange. I suppose one could argue that the difference between the former and the latter is in their temporality, or to be more precise, in their historicity. While societies clearly change and transform over time, and new social and political facts are produced within social practices continuously and incessantly, the sum of all those new facts, which may be a result of so many incessant and continuous social performances, never truly amounts to what we could call an historical event. An historical point of suture is still required in order to arrange all of those facts and performances according to a meaning that would retroactively make them a prehistory of the historical event they were all leading to.

Perhaps we could use the old structuralist distinction and say that the point of suture is a concept that can be addressed either in a synchronic or in the diachronic way. The synchronic way to think about the point of suture is to look at the social and political practices and performances – marriages, contests, legislative procedures – insofar as they can be said to appear on a formal plane, as if the sequence they imply is of the mathematical rather than of the temporal order. If we consider the point of suture in the diachronic way, however, we are interested precisely in the *historicity* of political practices, which means that we are interested precisely in the conditions of how one political plane is transformed into another. In other words, while the synchronic approach analyses how new social facts are produced through the performative practices within a given social or political formation, the diachronic approach is interested in the very conditions of possibility of the formation of a (new) political order as such. In short, there is a difference between the performativity of practices within the domain of the existing lawful order and the performativity of the very constitution of a new lawful order.

This point becomes even clearer when we compare two of Hegel's political concepts – the world-historical individual from his *Philosophy of History* and the ceremonial monarch from his *Philosophy of Right*. The first thing to note about these two concepts is that the ceremonial monarch is certainly not a world-historical individual – a personality like Caesar, Napoleon or Alexander, someone who stood in the very centre of world events and whose name has become synonymous with great historical upheaval and long-lasting political change. It is absolutely crucial to note, however, that the world-historical individuals are not simply great leaders of men, endowed with qualities like iron will, strategic thinking, great military leadership etc. that make their rule an historically important one. In fact, as it becomes especially apparent in Hegel's comments on Caesar, they are not even important so much, historically, for what they did as living individuals – which was no small feat, to be sure – but rather for what they did as *signifiers*.

What I refer to here is Hegel's idea of 'historical repetition', a fascinating concept which attributes the historical agency, even historical subjectivity, not to any particular individual or class of individuals, but to history itself. Discussing the death of Caesar at the hands of 'the noblest men of Rome' – Brutus, Cicero and others who wanted to protect the republic – Hegel remarks that the senators considered the rule of one individual (clearly an allusion to monarchy) as only contingent, and that all that is required to defend the republic is to get rid of that particular, contingent individual. Hegel argues that this is precisely why Augustus had to 'repeat' Caesar – in order for the rule of one to become something 'actual' and 'confirmed'.

> Spite of this we see the noblest men of Rome supposing Caesar's rule to be a merely adventitious thing (*etwas Zufälliges*), and the entire position of affairs to be dependent on his individuality. So thought Cicero, so Brutus and Cassius. They believed that if this one individual were out of the way, the Republic would be *ipso facto* restored. (...) But it became immediately manifest that only a *single* will could guide the Roman State, and now the Romans were compelled to adopt that opinion; since in all periods of the world a political revolution is sanctioned in men's opinions, when it repeats itself. (...) By repetition that which at first appeared merely a matter of chance and contingency (*zufällig und möglich*) becomes a real and ratified existence.[19]

My claim here is that we should consider the instance of historical repetition – and not the personality of a world-historical individual – as the conceptual correlate of the ceremonial monarch from the *Philosophy of Right*: it is the instance of historical repetition that has the performative task of confirmation, of producing actuality from something only contingent and possible. In short, on the stage of world history, the only true 'monarch' is the history itself, precisely inasmuch as it produces 'repetitions'. If I argue that Caesar is important for Hegel's concept of history not so much as an individual with a certain set of positive qualities (which only pertain to him as a contingent individual), but rather as a *signifier*, I wish to underscore precisely the repetition that he is inexorably bound to: the series of emperors who followed and repeated him in keeping his *name*, thus even giving the name, in many European languages, to the form of government they embodied (*Kaisertum, cesarstvo*, etc.).

To make one further point, I want to argue that the idea of historical repetition is a much better example for the Žižekian performative (as the *political* point of suture) than the idea of the ceremonial monarch. True, with the ceremonial monarch making laws actual by declaring them, it is much more obvious that it fits J. L. Austin's definition of 'performative utterances'. However, the functioning of a ceremonial monarch is only conceivable 'in the long periods of peace',[20] when the state is operating like a well-oiled machine and the political spectacle is going on without interruptions. In other words, the concept of the ceremonial monarch is ahistorical almost by definition and thus blind to what I described above as the diachronic aspect of the performativity in politics. In this sense, the example of the monarch is also somewhat misleading: Žižek's interest in Hegel's political philosophy lies, primarily, beyond its normative, timeless aspect, beyond the orderly, ideal functioning of the state.

From Althusser's theoretical theatre back to the point of suture

Another frequent example (early) Žižek uses to illustrate the concept of the point of suture is Louis Althusser's notion of ideological interpellation. In the text of the 'Three Lectures', Žižek quite directly claims that what Althusser calls ideological interpellation is precisely something like the miraculous transformation of the anxious military officer in a devout supporter of the cause in the first act of Racine's *Athalie*.[21] Moreover, there is no doubt for Žižek that the ideological operation in Althusser's theory is performative – the ideological subject is produced in the very recognition that he or she is, indeed, the addressee of the ideological Call, that he or she is, indeed, the ideological subject. And finally, the tautological affirmation of the king that he is the king, which Žižek touts as the formula of the groundlessness of the (monarchic) law, does indeed remind us of what Althusser denotes as the 'obviousness' of the ideological recognition that I am, in fact, precisely me.[22]

The most famous example Althusser gave us of the ideological interpellation is something he calls 'my little theoretical theatre': a man is walking down the street; behind him, he hears the police shout 'Hey, you there!'; he turns around, and in this turn – in the recognition that he is the addressee of call – he is transformed into an ideological subject.[23] But for the purposes of this chapter, it is especially interesting that Althusser immediately adds that the reality of the interpellation transpires on a completely different plane, and *not* on the street: it was only 'for the convenience and clarity' that he has 'had to present things in the form of a sequence, with a before and an after, and thus in the form of a temporal succession'.[24]

Žižek has always been suspicious of this move by Althusser, throughout his oeuvre, but the reason is complex. In *Absolute Recoil*, Žižek argues that 'what the "timeless" character of interpellation renders invisible is a kind of atemporal sequentiality that is far more complex than the "theoretical theatre" staged by Althusser invoking the suspicious alibi of "convenience and clarity"'.[25] In other words, Žižek finds Althusser's concept of interpellation unsatisfactory, and he points the finger at Althusser's concept of the 'timelessness.' For Žižek, the problem is not atemporality itself, rather, the problem lies in the fact that with the timeless character of the process of human subjectivation, Althusser has effectively obscured the locus of the *proper* atemporality that pertains to human subjectivity. For Žižek, as mentioned in the first part of this chapter, human subjectivity is split into the ego (the Cartesian conscious subject) on the one hand and the subject of the unconscious on the other hand – and it is this *other* subject, the subject of the unconscious, that is 'timeless' in the proper sense. In Žižek's own words:

> What remains 'unthought' in Althusser's theory of interpellation is thus the fact that, prior to ideological recognition, we have an intermediate moment of obscene, impenetrable interpellation without identification, a kind of vanishing mediator that has to become invisible if the subject is to achieve symbolic identity, to accomplish the gesture of subjectivization. In short, the 'unthought' of Althusser is that there is already an uncanny subject that precedes the gesture of subjectivization.[26]

The 'subject prior to subjectivization' is where the proper timelessness resides for Žižek, the one described by Freud as the timelessness of the unconscious. What Althusser describes as timeless, on the contrary, is the functioning of human subjects in a well-oiled mechanism of the state apparatuses. It is in this sense that Althusser declares that ideology is eternal. Many criticized Althusser precisely for proposing a theory of ideology which is only capable of explaining its success, but not its failure.

Hence, we must conclude that there is timelessness and then there is timelessness. If we follow the distinction I sketched above, between the historical and the 'timeless' performativity in Hegel – the historicity of the 'repetition' of the *individual* Caesar in the *name* and the *concept* of Caesar versus the 'timelessness' of the ceremonial monarch in the endless life of the state – one may be inclined to think that this is contrary to Žižek's theoretical endeavours, which clearly demand a concept of timelessness. However, I argue that the ceremonial monarch is timeless in the 'bad' meaning of the term – simply explaining the well-oiled functioning of the state in perpetuity. And I argue that there is a completely different idea of timelessness involved in the concept of historical repetition, which I take to be the concept of the performativity of history itself (its 'repetition,' as Hegel put it). I do not argue that Hegel's concept of the historical repetition is something that we may be able to compare to the psychoanalytic concept of the timelessness of the unconscious. But I do claim that Hegel's concept of historical repetition is atemporal in the sense that one cannot place it *within* the flow of history itself; 'repetition' does not appear on the stage of history, it is the idea of history itself taking on the role of the 'monarch'. While the monarch, ceremonial or not, is always an actor perfectly visible on the historical stage, the historical repetition is a deeper mechanism which drives history itself, it is simply another formulation of what Hegel also described as the 'cunning of reason'.

We can now return to the question raised earlier in this chapter, which was the attempt to distinguish between two concepts of performance in politics. If we do insist on distinguishing between them, we should not assume that the distinction runs along the dividing line between authentic performance and mere representation or imitation, such as is sometimes used in the ordinary language (e. g., 'the president's speech was mere rhetoric and theatrics, mere performance'). As is the case perhaps even in Plato's *Laws*, the functioning of the state in its practices and rites is never *mere* mimesis, *mere* drama; it does not function as a veil to cover other interests. In Althusser's theory of ideology as imaginary reality this is explicitly stated as the claim that practical ideology means the practical organization of human daily life, and not a conspiracy by 'a small number of cynical men' to rule the uninformed masses.[27] And for Hegel in the *Philosophy of Right*, the actuality of the state is never *mere* appearance to be judged against some ideal; it is the fundamental tenant of Hegel's philosophy that the actuality of the ideal lies precisely in its appearance (in concrete practices).

In other words, if we consider the political domain as theatrical in its very nature, this is not to question its authenticity or truthfulness, defending true human freedom outside of the political and social existence; it is simply to recognize the fact that political life (and in fact, all social life) is organized as a complex web of performances within a given set of rules. However, as I tried to demonstrate in this chapter, Žižek allows us to articulate a very different concept of the political by borrowing from Lacan, one where the given set of rules is transformed, in a historical development, into a different set of rules – so that one political regime is replaced with another – but without assuming that such replacement is even dreamed of, much less deliberately intended, by any players or actors recognized in the existing political field. If we take the concept of the point of suture seriously, it implies that the new political stage is, strictly speaking, impossible to articulate in the terms and in the 'costumes' of the old regime. There can be no anticipation of meaning: it is only *retroactively* that we can recognize the events before the inauguration of the new regime as necessary and logical steps leading to it. Strictly speaking, caught in the world events themselves, we are always profoundly blind as to what future conditions they are leading us to. In this sense, albeit in a different context, Žižek even speaks about the 'elementary *theatricality* of the human condition'.[28] This is what Hegel means when he discusses the 'cunning of reason': we could say that this other theatre, the stage of the historical political events, is a place where we can never assume the role of the spectator, and much less that of the director, for we are bound to perform the roles of individuals striving for their particular goals, perishing, and thus sacrificing their passions on the altar of the idea – just like Caesar had to die as an individual in order to be 'reborn', to be 'repeated' as a concept.

Notes

1   This contribution is a result of the work conducted within the research project 'Theatricality of Power' (J6-1812), financed by ARRS, the Slovenian Research Agency. A version of this chapter will appear in German in Erik Vogt (ed.), *Slavoj Žižek und die Künste* (Vienna and Berlin: Turia+Kant).
2   Slavoj Žižek, 'Notes on Performing, Its Frame, and Its Gaze' in Broderick Chow and Alex Mangold (eds), *Žižek and Performance* (London: Palgrave, 2014b), 236–52 (247).
3   Ibid., 237.
4   Ibid., 250–1.
5   See also Geoff Boucher, 'The Lacanian Performative. Austin After Žižek', in Broderick Chow and Alex Mangold (eds), *Žižek and Performance* (London: Palgrave, 2014), 13–32 (15).
6   Ferdinand de Saussure, *Course in General Linguistics*, trans. Wade Baskin (New York: McGraw-Hill Book Company, 1966), 12.
7   Émil Benveniste, *Problems in General Linguistics*, trans. Mary Elizabeth Meek (Coral Gables, FL: University of Miami Press, 1971), 48.
8   See especially Slavoj Žižek, 'Tri predavanja [Three Lectures]', *Problemi* XXI: 4/5, 1983, 11–13 (author's translation).
9   Ibid., 21.
10 G. W. F. Hegel, *Elements of the Philosophy of Right*, trans. H. B. Nisbet (Cambridge: Cambridge University Press, 1991), 308.
11 Žižek, 'Tri predavanja', 21.
12 Hegel, *Elements of the Philosophy of Right*, 322.
13 Bertolt Brecht, 'Über die Theatralik des Fascismus', in *Werke*, vol. 22 (Berlin: Aufbau and Frankfurt am Main: Suhrkamp, 1993), 563.
14 Walter Benjamin, *Das Kunstwerk im Zeitalter seiner technischen Reproduzierbarkeit* (Frankfurt am Main: Suhrkamp, 2003), 44.
15 Žižek, 'Tri predavanja', 21–2.
16 Ibid., 10.
17 Plato, 'Laws', trans. by Trevor J. Saunders, in *Complete Works* (Indianapolis: Hackett, 1997), 817b-c.

18 It has even been argued that this goes for theatrical performances as well, which is why tragedies are competing with laws in the same genre. In his detailed analysis and interpretation of Plato's *Laws*, Marcus Folch argues that Plato 'develops an early theory of the performative properties of poetry, music, song, and dance', and argues that for 'Plato, what is being performed on the Athenian stage and in the theatrical audience – reflectively and reflexively – is the city itself' (Marcus Folch, *The City and the Stage. Performance, Genre, and Gender in Plato's Laws*. Oxford: Oxford University Press, 2015, 61).
19 G. W. F. Hegel, *The Philosophy of History*, trans. J. Sibree (Kitchener, Ontario: Batoche Books, 2001), 332.
20 Jure Simoniti, 'Hegel and the Opaque Core of History', *Problemi* LVII: 11/12, 2020: 222.
21 Žižek, 'Tri predavanja', 17.
22 Althusser writes: 'It is indeed a peculiarity of ideology that it imposes (without appearing to do so, since these are "obviousnesses") obviousnesses as obviousnesses, which we cannot *fail to recognize* and before which we have the inevitable and natural reaction of crying out (aloud or in the "still, small voice of conscience"): "That's obvious! That's right! That's true!"' (Louis Althusser, *Lenin and Philosophy and Other Essays*, trans. Ben Brewster. London: NLB, 1971, 172).
23 Ibid., 174.
24 Ibid.
25 Slavoj Žižek, *Absolute Recoil. Towards a New Foundation of Dialectical Materialism* (London: Verso, 2014), 63.
26 Ibid., 64.
27 Althusser, *Lenin and Philosophy and Other Essays*, 163.
28 Žižek, 'Notes on Performing', 247.

Bibliography

Althusser, Louis. *Lenin and Philosophy and Other Essays*, trans. Ben Brewster. London: NLB, 1971.

Benjamin, Walter. *Das Kunstwerk im Zeitalter seiner technischen Reproduzierbarkeit*. Frankfurt am Main: Suhrkamp, 2003.

Benveniste, Émil. *Problems in General Linguistics*, trans. Mary Elizabeth Meek. Coral Gables, Florida: University of Miami Press, 1971.

Boucher, Geoff. 'The Lacanian Performative. Austin After Žižek', in Broderick Chow and Alex Mangold (eds), *Žižek and Performance*. London: Palgrave Macmillan, 2014, 13–32.

Brecht, Bertolt. 'Über die Theatralik des Fascismus', *Werke*. Vol. 22. Berlin: Aufbau and Frankfurt am Main: Suhrkamp, 1993.

Folch, Marcus. *The City and the Stage. Performance, Genre, and Gender in Plato's Laws*. Oxford: Oxford University Press, 2015.

Hegel, G. W. F., *The Philosophy of History*, trans. J. Sibree. Kitchener, Ontario: Batoche Books, 2001.

Hegel, G. W. F. *Elements of the Philosophy of Right*, trans. H. B. Nisbet. Cambridge: Cambridge University Press, 1991.

Plato. 'Laws', trans. by Trevor J. Saunders, *Complete Works*. Indianapolis: Hackett, 1997.

Saussure, Ferdinand de. *Course in General Linguistics*, trans. Wade Baskin. New York: McGraw-Hill Book Company, 1966.

Simoniti, Jure. 'Hegel and the Opaque Core of History', *Problemi* LVII: 11/12, 2020, 201–29.

Žižek, Slavoj. 'Tri predavanja', *Problemi* XXI: 4/5, 1983, 1–38.

Žižek, Slavoj. *Absolute Recoil. Towards a New Foundation of Dialectical Materialism*. London: Verso, 2014.

Žižek, Slavoj. 'Notes on Performing, Its Frame, and Its Gaze' in Broderick Chow and Alex Mangold (eds.), *Žižek and Performance*. London: Palgrave Macmillan, 2014, 236–52.

7

A Critique of Biopolitics

Maurizio Lazzarato

After Foucault's death, the concept of biopolitics enjoyed great success but it also generated a number of misunderstandings about capitalism, Marxism, and the reality of class struggle – all of which have turned out to be politically damaging. The abandonment of the analysis of general or institutional forms of domination – that is to say, the repudiation of the analysis of struggles between classes in favour of the analysis of 'techniques and procedures by which one sets about conducting the conduct of others',[1] as enunciated by Foucault in 1983 – appears to me as a capitulation to the spirit of the time, and to its governance.

Governmentality claims to provide the means to organize a decentralised, flexible, mobile power, capable of adapting to the heterogeneity of the struggles which flared up at the end of the 1960s and at the beginning of the 1970s. In the face of a conflict that can arise from anywhere, governmentality opposes a continuous state of emergence, a permanent crisis, a politics of bio-security. It thus seeks to dissolve classes by disaggregating them into a new partition between population and individuals, thereby inverting Marx, who had imagined the theory of class struggle precisely against the theory of populations formulated by bourgeois economists.

I argue that we must remain faithful to Marx, thereby extracting classes – understood in the plural, i.e., class of sex, race and workers – from populations. The apparatuses of regulation and integration, aimed at avoiding political rupture, are used not against the populations as such, but against the struggle between the capitalist class and the working classes (men and women, whites and non-whites). Foucault completely closes off this political space by replacing it with a double model, which is both legal-political (aimed at 'subjects') and biopolitical (aimed at 'populations'), where the former refers to the state and the latter to the economy. The goal of the Foucauldian operation, whether conscious or unconscious, is to suture the Marxian breakthrough which, by introducing classes and their struggles, had opened up the space made inaccessible by the people/population and state/economy couples. In this respect, Foucault's suture intervenes with perfect timing, since it coincides with the exhaustion of the working class's revolutionary struggle and its historical defeat. Today, sovereignty and biopolitics (state and extra-state governmental techniques) have won: there is only political space left for counter-action, struggles against 'too much power', subjectivations that aim directly at 'freedom' within the system, without going through the process of 'liberation' (revolution).

The Foucauldian reconstruction of the closure of political space is not a simple repetition of what the economists did. Rather, it innovated the ideology of the capital/state machine by turning the economy into bio-economy, something concerning 'life' and 'the people'. The Foucauldian novelty, which posits that 'biological existence is now reflected in political existence',[2] is therefore deeply problematic, because living human beings are *always qualified politically*. The machine of power always concerns workers, women, slaves and the colonized. Biopolitical policies are not about birth, death, disease or health, but about the relation between workers, women, slaves and the colonized with the oppressors. In other words, biopolitics must produce differentials between human lives that are thus qualified.

The dual legal-political and biopolitical model ignores capital and its classes, which nevertheless gradually reconfigure the legal-political system and give meaning and direction to biopolitics. Biopolitics, then, seems to ignore this power over life and bodies which preceded it by a few centuries, and of which it is the belated and mutilated conceptualization. The seizure of power over *living bodies* is first achieved through the violent appropriation and the normative formation of the classes of women, workers, slaves and the colonized, who are forced into 'production' through their exclusion from the political domain (or even from humanity as such).

Since its origins, the capital/state power machine has never had as its objective the taking care of the population and its lives, but, on the contrary, to exploit and dominate it by dividing lives and bodies, by valuing certain lives and bodies and devaluing others. The lives of slaves, natives, women and, in the West, of workers, are reduced and classified as close to natural phenomena. They are therefore, like all products of nature, appropriable and exploitable. Thus, biopolitics is always and necessarily racist, sexist, classist, in the sense that it must produce and reproduce not the population and its individuals, but the divisions of men and women, of whites and racialized people, of capitalists and workers.

If we follow Foucault, the great reversal of the historical-political order into the biological one took place from the second half of the eighteenth century. In truth, it was already at work throughout the long sixteenth century, when classes were formed (including workers, slaves, natives and women of the inferior races) and humans reduced to their organic dimension. Foucault's Eurocentrism traces racism back to the biopolitical measures deployed in the old continent from the eighteenth century. However, the 'Code noir' ('Ordinance on the slaves of the islands of America'), which was promulgated by the king of France Louis XIV, already marks, in March 1685, the end of a first stage of the state's control of the biological. This transformation, then, started with the conquest of the Americas, which can also be defined as the time of the biological invention of race.

In this respect, Foucauldian concepts work, as it were, on one leg: the European leg. The Foucauldian version of governance is an unrecognized consequence of the strategic division between the proletariat of the South and the proletariat of the North. As capitalism developed, it gave rise to a differentiation in the way power was exercised: relative integration of workers in Europe vs maintenance of slavery and serfdom elsewhere (and domination of women everywhere); constitution and law in the metropolises vs state of emergency in the colonies; *relative* valorisation of the labour force by welfare policies in developed countries vs violent devaluation of bodies and lives in the Third World.

In this regard, Giorgio Agamben further exasperates the limits of Foucauldian biopolitics. His repeated references to antiquity and the theologico-political realm obscure, even more than Foucault himself did, the specific difference that is constitutive of capitalism. The inescapable role that capital plays in political organization since the 'long sixteenth century' emerges clearly if we compare the functions of slaves and women (and artisans) in Greek society, with slaves, women and workers in capitalist societies. In the Greek polis, the work of slaves and the work of women aimed at the reproduction of the *bios politikos* (making it possible for free men to live 'without working'), while in capitalism the living bodies of slaves, workers and women operate within an entirely different *oikonomy*, in which the goal of production is production itself.

Chrematistics ('production for the sake of production' as Marx calls it) was known and much feared in Greek society. Its development was opposed in several ways (political, social, religious, ethical etc.), while in our societies it constitutes the rule of rules (*Grundnorm*). In capitalism, all the barriers that hinder the expanded repetition of the same (money that produces money) must be broken down (this is the correct definition of liberal praxis) so that the economy can separate itself from society and constitute an autonomous and hegemonic domain.

The inclusion of the oppressed in production by their exclusion from the political space is not the same in antiquity and capitalism. The first is static, the second dynamic. Production, having its own goal, must continually expand (this is the enlarged reproduction of capital), which means that it must continually increase the number of workers, slaves, women and their exploitation. Under certain conditions, it must even transform them very rapidly into consumers, because surplus-value must be realized (the rich and their lavish spending are not enough for this task). The political danger that biopolitics must avert is the intensification of conflicts and ruptures that the production and reproduction of classes inevitably generate.

The thinking that informed 1968 considered this functioning of capital as specific to the time of Marx, and therefore largely outdated. This great misunderstanding resulted in a collective blindness to the strategy of the capital/state machine, to which Foucault's work at the end of the 1970s testifies in an exemplary manner. At the end of the governmental phase of his work, power in Foucault assumed autonomy and independence from capitalism, which today we should be able to see as being clearly misplaced. In 1978, Foucault made a gross error of judgement: he claimed that, if the nineteenth century was haunted by the rise in wealth production and by 'the impoverishment of those who produce it'[3] – that is to say, by capitalism proper – at the end of the twentieth century this problem no longer occurred with the same urgency. For Foucault, contemporary societies are traversed by a completely different type of anxiety than the production of profit: 'the overproduction of power'. He adds: 'So that, just as the nineteenth century needed an economy which had as its specific object the production and distribution of wealth, one could say that we need an economy which is not about the production and distribution of wealth, but an economy that would focus on power relations.'[4] Here, 'overproduction of power' is obviously another name for *biopower*. What matters, 'even more than the economic stake, is the very modality in which power is exerted'.[5] Therefore, struggles should be 'primarily aimed at the effects of power themselves, much more than at something like economic exploitation, or inequality'.[6]

According to Foucault, medicine played a fundamental role in the biopolitical narrative. Through its growing body of knowledge, it has developed techniques for managing epidemics, madness and abnormal behaviour, thus constituting a new exercise of power. These 'control and regulation' strategies, set up in collaboration with the policing of populations, allow medicine and its techniques to solicit, induce and bring about behaviours capable of ensuring order and the health of society. The great reversal concerns not only the passage from 'the historical to the biological', but also that 'from the political to the medical'.

Foucault's misunderstanding concerning biopolitics and capitalism – which has deceived, both politically and theoretically, generations of activists and researchers – appears as particularly striking in a text from 1982, which can be read in connection with the 2020 pandemic. Foucault equates the political problem with the effects of power as such. Thus, according to him, the criticism levelled by political movements of the 1970s against the medical profession had nothing to do with their being 'a profit-making sector', but concerned their exercising 'uncontrolled power over the body, the health of individuals, their life and their death'.[7]

I argue that the Covid-19 health catastrophe invalidates the above hypothesis of the subordination of capitalism to the 'overproduction of power' (biopower). In fact, it shows the exact opposite. The strategy chosen by the capitalist machine (including the role of the state) from the 1970s onwards involves a return to profiting from the health systems. It puts the production of wealth and poverty at the centre of economic exploitation and the widening of class differences; and it does so by applying its profit/rent-making tools precisely to bodies, health, life and death.

For years, medical staff have criticized the way in which public health is managed – even more under the pressure of the pandemic – precisely for being enslaved to profit-making, thus aiming at productivity and competition between hospitals and services, which imposes the 'fee-for-service' logic, thus measuring the economic value of each medical procedure. Why was the health system in Western countries so ill-prepared to treat the population during the pandemic? Because the executives of hospitals, research, pharmaceutical companies and the state have never been concerned with biopolitical goals, namely a power intended to produce forces and to make them grow. The health system has a completely different objective, common to all capitalist production, insofar as the growth of the forces of production is subordinated to the goals of accumulation, that is to say to the generation of profits, to making any act of care profitable, to transforming research itself into a profitable business, amenable to the financial rent machine. The state and biopolitics must encourage, solicit and make possible the imposition of a New Public Management – modelled on industrial management – on all public services from hospitals to the police.

The management of vaccines by multinational pharmaceutical companies has revealed – in case it was missed by proponents of biopolitics – the exact meaning of the industrialization/financialization of public health (in other words, for fifty years now we have witnessed the industrialization/financialization of what we know as biopolitics).[8] Richly subsidized by vaccine research funds, pharmaceutical companies are paid handsomely a second time after they make their vaccines available. With the complicity of the state, these companies have imposed shameful contracts for their exclusive benefit and taking no risk in relation to adverse effects.

Also, they unilaterally decide where, how and when to deliver vaccine doses, thus speculating on profit opportunities, just like with any commodity. They can also hijack the delivery of the vaccines if they discover that they can earn more by distributing them elsewhere. They categorically refuse – always with the consent of the state – the provision of patents (intellectual property requires limiting the places of production as much as possible, thus generating artificial scarcity), which alone can ensure that the contagion is stopped. The defence of profit, intellectual property and monopoly is incompatible with the health of the population. We know as much at least since the AIDS epidemic.

While the financialization of hospitals has made much progress, it is with the production of drugs that the whole process is pushed to the end. While the strategy of capitalist appropriation of health is centred on the construction and management of hyper-technological hospitals treating the most profitable diseases, it is the pharmaceutical multinationals which, through their monopolies, impose the complete subjugation of life to the logic of profit. The greed of these multinationals stops at nothing, including putting billions of people in danger of death.[9] Big pharma – the result of an unprecedented concentration and centralization of production and power – promoted and encouraged by the state, are virtually a monopoly, thus fixing the prices of drugs which, having no relation to the costs of production, constitute, quite simply, rents. 'More than industrial groups, they are first and foremost financial groups, juggling billions, assets and patents. Rather than carrying out research on their own, they find it preferable to buy start-ups, take back their patents and develop them. The dream is to get a blockbuster: the drug that exceeds one billion dollars in sales.'[10] Their only real problem here is certainly not the 'life' of populations, but how to be able to increase their stock price on the market. Shareholder value becomes the cardinal point of their entire strategy. The pharmaceutical monopolies are only accountable to their shareholders.

The 'advanced' Western countries were unable to cope with the pandemic because they have completely abandoned prevention and the promotion of the health of the population in the territory, since it is difficult to centralize and financialize health. The Italian region which suffered the highest number of deaths during the pandemic (one-third of the total), Lombardy, is the one where the industrialization/financialization strategy is the most advanced.

During the pandemic, the 'power of life and death' was a prerogative of companies (pharmaceutical and medical) which, with vaccines, distribute death and life according to profit opportunities; or of the state which, with vaccines, distributes death and life according to the opportunities of geopolitical power. In both cases, according to principles that have nothing to do with biopolitics – or (even less) with necropolitics, which is a lazy concept because it avoids the analysis of the connection between the production of profit and power. The concept of biopolitics in its different versions (immunity/community, bare life, state control of the biological) is unable to provide the slightest explanation for the reorganization of the institutions which 'govern' the health of the population, a process that could be correctly defined as financialized biomedical capitalism built on the individualization of disease.

If 'society does not exist' and if there are only individuals, public health is a false problem. A disease is understood within the strict limits of the 'biomedical', and the biological is completely naturalized while it continues to exist in symbiosis with the social, the economic and the political, so that 'the biological is reflected in the political' in a more radical way than in Foucault's theory, since it is reflected in class difference.[11] This is a double truth that the pandemic has brutally made explicit.

The individualization of disease reduces the human body to just a compound of the cells, tissues, organs that the pharmaceutical industries and medical technology turn into highly profitable markets. For structural and ideological reasons, neoliberalism was not prepared to fight the pandemic, or its socio-political and ecological dimension.

Marx here is much more useful, despite his 'socialist' vocabulary, because he focusses on what biopolitics believes to be outdated: capital and its thirst for profit. When something – health in this case – is produced according to the principle of accumulation, 'capital and its self-expansion appear as the starting and the closing point, the motive and the purpose of production; that production is only production for capital and not vice versa, the means of production are not mere means for a constant expansion of the living process of the society of producers'.[12] The thanato-political (or necro-political) explanation is largely insufficient because it avoids the specific analysis of the murderous logic of capitalist production. In fact, to add insult to injury, the concept of biopolitics has become familiar with the 'sharks' who run pharmaceutical multinationals, the personification of capital in the field of health.

The health system in the US, the cradle of neoliberalism, perfectly represents today's biopolitical logic. It is designed and organized to enrich insurance companies – the prototype of any biopolitical device – much more than to treat populations. This process is taken to the point of caricature because 'to "make" live and to "let" die'[13] is strictly dependent on the condition of the patient's bank account.

For years, health policies have been at the heart of a hard-fought class struggle. The poor fight for universal insurance, which aims to reduce inequalities in the face of disease, while the rich fight so that private insurances reproduce their privileges even in terms of medical care. The pandemic has shown that health policies do not serve the population, but the dominant classes, since the virus perfectly matches inequalities in income, race and heritage.[14]

Paradoxically, the population is produced not by biopolitics, but by class struggles, in the sense that, when the latter are deployed, universal insurance and welfare for all become possible (the right to health, to housing, to personal development for all, and so on), and therefore an increase in the power of life is achieved. When the revolution is defeated, biopolitics only redistributes health, income and personal development, according to the hierarchies of class, race and sex, in other words by diminishing the power of life of the oppressed people.

The Covid-19 disaster is not exogenous to capitalism. It is rooted in all kinds of inequalities, in the plundering of nature and in the demolition of public health operated by finance. The pandemic (in Foucault's terms, an exemplary manifestation of the 'pressure of the biological on history') made it possible to accelerate and reinforce the policies of centralization and concentration of power carried out by the monopolies (big pharma, digital platforms, banks etc.), with the complicity of the state which, in turn, accomplishes the centralization and concentration of political power. The two processes are parallel and convergent. The catastrophe was not anticipated, but rather prepared by its biopolitical character, for none of the biopolitical devices aim at 'increasing the power of life' or curing it in general, but rather at creating conditions so that each life, at each of its stages, depends on income and wealth.

Michel Foucault thought of biopolitics as a device of autonomous power animated by universal principles which are specific to it – essentially, to make people live and to let them die. However, it is easy to ascertain that biopolitics always remains subordinate to forces that go beyond it and bend it according to their needs and desires, producing imbalances, neutralizing all compensation, widening inequalities, contributing to the affirmation of one class over other classes.

Public welfare policies are part of the arsenal of the ongoing social war. In the nineteenth century, workers (men, women, children) left their lives and health in factories. What we call biopolitics took charge of them when they organized and became dangerous, likely to threaten the established order. During the whole of the nineteenth century, the insurance systems were the backbone of the bosses, aiming to strengthen their power while pacifying industrial relations. In the twentieth century, welfare (the result of the balance of power determined by the Soviet revolution, the struggles of the workers at the end of the First World War, the crisis of 1929, the seizures of power by the Nazi and fascist parties etc.), became more favourable to workers *solely for political reasons*. This is why proletarian life is still split between the valorisation of the male worker's life and the devaluation of the life of unproductive workers, first and foremost women.

In this regard, Sylvia Walby shows that welfare organizes the passage from private patriarchy to public patriarchy by reproducing and reconfiguring the relations between the class of men and women. Welfare is not only sexist, but also racist. Jill Quadagno reminds us that welfare, like all public policies, is not only marked by sex, but also by colour.[15]

A radical alternative to biopolitics (in its double version, i.e. Foucault's and Agamben's) was presented by French materialist feminism in 1977, in the editorial of the first number of the journal *Questions féministes*. Here the key questions (in what way is the biological political? What political function does the biological have?) are not posed from the point of view of the state, as in Foucault's case, but from the point of view of class (in what ways and why do the social classes of sex correspond to the biological classes of sex?), thus breaking with an ideology (the biological as an ideology that rationalizes the political) which has poisoned even so-called critical thinking. Biopolitics has as its object not *the life* of the human species, but the lives of the classes of women, the colonized and the workers.[16]

Biopolitics quietly *let blacks die* and *helped whites live* in the United States, as long as the collective political organization of blacks remained powerless, unable to impose other power struggles. In his book on the Welfare State, François Ewald, a student of Michel Foucault, not only ignores the way in which biopolitics governs populations according to a logic rooted in class struggles, race and sex; but he also, by defining welfare through 'risk' and 'insurance techniques', anticipates and legitimizes the Third Way in politics (Tony Blair) and in theory (Anthony Giddens, Ulrich Beck), which is an integral part of one-dimensional thinking (*la pensée unique*).

At present, the welfare state is not the continuation of untraceable biopolitical principles. Rather, it is strictly subordinated to a double capitalist strategy: on the one hand, it is the object of a process of privatization which must generate profits/rents and drastically reduce so-called social public spending – that is to say, it must enhance the life of capital and devalue the life of workers, women and racialized people. On the other hand, the restructuring of public policies aims to intensify class dualisms, which, far from dissolving in the double form of populations and individuals, deepen their divisions.

Biopolitics is therefore caught in a double bind: undoing classes by reducing them to the population/individual pair; and categorically reproducing the dualisms of sex, race and class, without which capitalism would collapse. We do not live in a biopolitical regime, but in a society still, as always, dominated by capital.

To account for our condition, it is imperative to exit the biopolitical framework (governmentality, populations, individuals) in order to rediscover the existence of classes. Biopolitics represents the point of view of the capital/state machine, from which, as such, we will never be able to escape. If we are to pass to the other side of the power relation, as Foucault wanted to do, either we have to be there from the start (Marx), or we will never be there at all. After 1975, with his new categories of biopolitics, population and governmentality, Foucault operated a radical depoliticization of his thought, whose dissemination was taken care of by his followers. His articles on the Iranian revolution were the ultimate testimony of this transformation: by seeing Khomeini as the one who finally emerges *outside politics*,[17] Foucault expelled the revolution from his discourse.

Notes

1 Michel Foucault, *The Government of Self and Others: Lectures at the Collège de France 1982–1983*. Trans. Graham Burchell (London: Palgrave Macmillan, 2010), 4.
2 Michel Foucault, *The History of Sexuality, Volume 1: An introduction*. Trans. Robert Hurley (New York: Pantheon Books, 1998), 142.
3 Michel Foucault, 'La philosophie analytique de la politique', in *Dits et écrits II, 1976–1988*, ed. D. Defert and F. Ewald (Paris: Gallimard, 2001), 534–51 (536). All translations from French by the author.
4 Ibid., 536.
5 Ibid., 546.
6 Ibid., 545.

7   Ibid.
8   'The world of health is systemically linked to industrial interests, from research, the training of healthcare professionals, regulatory expertise, to the practices of physicians, and public information. This set of links of interest influences care, and this influence presents a risk for public health as well as for the balance of social accounts. It constitutes a loss of opportunity for patients.' ('Some lessons from the crisis', Association for independent medical information and training, *Formindep*, 3 July 2020. See https://formindep.fr/quelques-lecons-de-la-crise/).
9   In an interview given at the release of his 2001 novel *The Constant Gardener*, John Le Carré explained that, to account for the looting and exploitation of the Third World, he could not find anything more relevant than the pharmaceutical sector. The book itself comments on the global pharmaceutical trade 'testing dangerous drugs on the world's poor, corrupting governments and doctors alike and ruthlessly silencing critics in the pursuit of super-profits'. Le Carré said that the novel stems from events he witnessed 'on the ground' in Africa as well as his discussions with non-governmental organizations, doctors and dying patients. Le Carré rejected the claim that his depiction of drug companies is 'wicked and unreasonable', adding that their actions are 'far more awful than anything [he has] written about. [...] And if we don't stop it, then we're guilty of genocide by neglect, that's what it amounts to' (Ray Moynihan *Australian Financial Review*, 3/1). Biopolitics – if that is what we want to continue to call the industrialization/financialization of 'life' – is a neo-colonial strategy.
10 Martine Orange, 'What Sanofi says about French industrial policy', *Médiapart*, 3 February 2021. https://www.mediapart.fr/journal/economie/030221/ce-que-sanofi-dit-de-la- french-industrial-policy.
11 According to the latest advances in science, biological life (*zoe*) and qualified life (*bios*) are inseparable since their functioning is symbiotic. Biologist Carlo Alberto Redi demonstrated that 'the genome (DNA) of each cell of the millions of billions of cells that make up a *con-dividuo* [defined by a multiplicity of organs, elements, internal and external relations, as opposed to *in-dividuo*], in the different phases of development, is exposed to a variety of chemical and physical agents as well as to social environments of different nature (family, education, religion, work, income etc.): these material and immaterial factors are able to epigenetically mark the functioning of the genome in such a way that the degree of exposure and the social structure convey advantages or disadvantages of the good or bad functioning of the genome' (Carlo Aberto Redi and Carlo Sino, *Lo specchio di Dionisio*, Milan: Jaca Book, 2018). Redi's research aims to clarify how the social enters the skin and becomes biological, how the social class enters molecules and cells. In other words, by being embedded in the body, social inequalities are translated into biological inequalities, and in health inequalities. Here, then, is a credible (class) biopolitics!

12 Karl Marx, *Capital: A Critique of Political Economy*, Vol 3 – Part 1 (New York: Cosimo Publications, 2007), 293.
13 Michel Foucault, *Society Must Be Defended: Lectures at the Collège de France, 1975–76* (London: Penguin, 2004), 241. For capitalism, of course, not all lives have the same price. Hundreds of millions of people continue to die from endemic diseases that affect the world's poor. The pharmaceutical industry has no interest in treating these insolvent populations. It prefers to concentrate its investments on the patients in the north.
14 The pandemic has brought to light all the class divisions that characterize our societies. The health issue throws into sharp relief the neo-colonial bias, that is to say it reproduces the policies of large multinational pharmaceutical companies whereby a small percentage of the world population (in the North) gets more than half of the vaccines against Covid-19.
15 'Although welfare reform is the political issue that most easily reflects the racial code, other social programs – urban renewal, vocational training, school choice – have similar connotations. Politicians say they are talking about social programs, but people understand that they are really talking about race. Americans have good reason to understand that coded social policy messages are substituted for discussions about race, because there is a real connection between race and social policy. Race first became inseparable from social policy during Franklin Delano Roosevelt's New Deal. The New Deal achieved a twofold objective: it established a floor of protection for the industrial working class and it reinforced racial segregation through social protection programs, labor policy and housing policy. These obstacles to racial equality remained intact until the 1960s, when civil rights movements made struggles for equal opportunity the predominant social issue of the decade' (Jill Quadagno, *The Color of Welfare: How Racism Undermined the War of Poverty*, New York, Oxford: Oxford University Press, 1996, v-vi). The victories of these movements created the political backlash that brought Trump to power.
16 The political class of men defines women as a biological class in order to find in nature the justification of its power and capacity for oppression. They only deploy sexual difference in one direction, because for them only women and blacks have a particular physical, biological constitution. Men do not show biological differences because they are universal beings. Others are always different, while men are the standard, the measure of everything. Again, it is crucial to emphasise that the reversal of the political in the biological finds its foundation and rationale in class division and not in 'naked life' or 'life in general'.
17 See Renzo Guolo, 'La spiritualità politica,' in Michel Foucault, *Taccuino persiano* (Milan: Guerini e Associati, 1998, 69–74). Guolo ruthlessly criticizes Foucault's positions on Iran. For Foucault, revolutionary Shiite Islam introduces a spiritual dimension into political life, a historical opportunity to fertilize politics through

spirituality. As such, politics would manage to oppose the categories of the 'political' and the 'revolutionary' as developed in Europe. Khomeini represents anti-politics because his refusal to mediate with the regime places him 'outside politics'. Guolo remarks that this perspective can only result in a deadlock: 'Foucault's hope in the political spirituality of revolutionary Islam will very quickly prove to be erroneous [...] The man who according to Foucault "does not do politics" immediately arises as a source of legitimation for revolutionary power [...] Politics, on the contrary, shows its soul of steel. On February 19, 1979, the Party of the Islamic Republic was born, the political arm of the Hezbollah movement and of the radical clergy. The Party plays a fundamental role and immediately aims for the elimination of all opposition [...]. On March 8, a demonstration of women was attacked by the Hezbollah militias [...]. In November, Khomeini, the anti-political, liquidates the liberals from the political scene and marginalizes the left [...]. Khomeini's political strategy is very lucid indeed.' Foucault's argument (that Khomeini attempted to 'to expel the revolution from its discourse') fails in the face of reality. The Iranian revolution is the latest translation of the Leninist revolution in the Global South.

Bibliography

Foucault, Michel. *The History of Sexuality, Volume 1: An introduction*. New York: Pantheon Books, 1998.

Foucault, Michel. 'La philosophie analytique de la politique', in *Dits et écrits II, 1976–1988*. Paris: Gallimard, 2001, 534–51.

Foucault, Michel. *Society Must Be Defended: Lectures at the Collège de France, 1975–76*. London: Penguin, 2004.

Foucault, Michel. *The Government of Self and Others: Lectures at the Collège de France 1982–1983*. London: Palgrave Macmillan, 2010.

Guolo, Renzo. 'La spiritualità politica', in Michel Foucault, *Taccuino persiano*. Milan: Guerini e Associati, 1998, 69–74.

Marx, Karl. *Capital: A Critique of Political Economy*, Vol 3 – Part 1. New York: Cosimo Publications, 2007.

Orange, Martine. 'What Sanofi says about French industrial policy', *Médiapart*, 3 February 2021.

Quadagno, Jill. *The Color of Welfare: How Racism Undermined the War of Poverty*, New York, Oxford: Oxford University Press, 1996.

Redi, Carlo Aberto and Carlo Sino. *Lo specchio di Dionisio*. Milan: Jaca Book, 2018.

8

Profit, Knowledge and *Jouissance*: Lacan and the Logic of Action

Matteo Bonazzi

Jacques Lacan claimed that 'The discourse of the Analyst is nothing other than the logic of action.'[1] Given that our time has been described as the era of the 'One-all-alone,'[2] and of the 'Other that does not exist,'[3] how might we rethink the ethical and political status of the act within the context of the contemporary social bond? Turning to the unconscious could again provide an answer, as long as we reconsider its status on a plane of immanence and therefore on the basis of a pragmatics and an economic theory oriented by what analytical experience has to teach us.

In so doing, we will refer to two thinkers, Pascal and Marx, and the use Lacan makes of them in his *Seminar XVI*. We will thus retrace via Pascal the ethics of the wager underlying every act, and via Marx the politics of profit that accompanies its economic use. This will introduce a shift with respect to our initial premise: at the point of the loss of knowledge, i.e. the loss of the guarantee that the Other seems to offer us, the One is simply the last step towards *another way* of positioning oneself with respect to knowledge. This other way does not fall under the framework of the unconscious structured as a language, which in the end is our master, and offers us the ethical and political possibility of a different economy of *jouissance*.

The political animal with the power of discourse and its subversion

There is another unconscious that concerns us here, to which Lacan began to give shape in the Seventies. This unconscious cannot be reduced to the formula according to which it is structured *like* a language, and yet it continues to be deeply linked to language, without which it would lose its Freudian orientation. Hence, there is no pre- or post-linguistic turn in Lacan's last work, to which we will refer here. We must rather ask which language, and based on which premises can we describe the relation between the unconscious and language.

If we remain close to what Lacan clarified in his first return to Freud, the language that structures the unconscious is precisely the field of the Other. The unconscious is that which speaks in me, above and beyond me, and therefore something (*ça*) by which I am spoken:[4] the parental discourse in which desires, hopes and worries become deposited, but also the mixture of drives and the economic strategies used by parents and all others within whose discourse I came into the world. Thus, *the unconscious is the discourse of the other*.

If this is the unconscious that Freud discovered, which – while bearing in mind the risk of lapsing into sociology – we could correctly equate with the social bond in which we are included,[5] its 'linguistic' side immediately takes on a very specific form.

Lacan's interest in language is strategic. It involves grasping exactly what, of that which speaks in me, above and beyond me, actually affects and decides upon my existence: the signifier. In this case however, we must understand precisely what is the signifier that Lacan isolates and uses when attempting to describe the unique features of analytical experience.

The signifier is marked by its twofold structural nature. On the one hand, it relays to other signifiers, creating a constellation of knowledge whose centre of gravity lies in the master signifier and which therefore leads us to equate knowledge with power. On the other, however, the signifier is first and foremost a trace. As such, it does not only relay 'forwards' towards other signifiers, it also stops when it is just about to be cancelled. 'These traces that are only effaced because they are there, an effaced embossing, these traces have a different support that is properly in the *in-form* of O in so far as it is necessitated by the fact that it makes an *o* that functions at the level of the subject'.[6] We can thus deduce that when traces are cancelled, on the one hand they lead the signifier to be born, in Lacan's words,[7] and on the other, precisely 'through *embossing*' (*en repoussoir*), borrowing an expression from painting, they unclose another support. This other side is the one we must investigate here, on the level of language and politics. This is the subversion of Aristotle's *political animal with the power of discourse*.

Let us begin with language. Linguistics does not fully grasp this twofold effect of the signifier, only approaching it thanks to its most spurious part, i.e. pragmatics, and still letting something go unnoticed. On the other hand, social determinism, in its structural Marxian sense as well, does isolate this aspect, but does not always see it through the lens of the subversion introduced by Freud's discovery of the unconscious. The individual is not determined by the relations of power and production under which it falls, but by the unconscious. And the unconscious, from this point of view, occupies at one and the same time the position of the master and the proletarian, as rightly noted by Samo Tomšič in his *The Capitalist Unconscious*.[8] This makes analysis an eminently political experience, because the conflict takes place on an intra-subjective level, and because only by going through this conflict analytically can one actually grasp what is at stake. The determination, therefore, is not linear but oblique. This helps us understand both the master's ambivalence with respect to the subject, whose functioning is explained by hysterics, and the contortion the proletarian must carry out to no longer remain suspended and go through the passage that awaits him, which has nothing to do with class consciousness.

Following May '68, Lacan began to put into question not only the usefulness of linguistics. Alongside this, and during those very same years, he reconsidered the exteriority of the unconscious which had marked his return to Freud. It is not that politics is unconscious, as we all too easily think. Rather, it is the unconscious that is politics,[9] in the sense mentioned by Lacan at the international Symposium *The Languages of Criticism and the Sciences of Man* held in 1966 at the Johns Hopkins Humanities Centre: 'The image that best summarises the unconscious is: Baltimore at dawn'.[10] This image is very beautiful and, ultimately, quite precise: it helps us grasp not only something about the unconscious and its political aspect, but also the position occupied by Lacan in listening to it, and thus the position of the analyst. We must attempt to draw the consequences from this position, politically speaking as well. The unconscious is the *polis*, the social bond, not at just any moment or in the midst of its activity, but just about to awake. As with the dream scene, 'the encounter, forever missed, has occurred between dream and awakening, between the person who is still asleep and whose dream we will not know and the person who has dreamt merely in order not to wake up'.[11] It is at the point of its onset that there is the unconscious and that one must go back to reading the surface of the social fabric, thus positioning oneself a bit after the dream and a bit before waking life. This state between sleep and wakefulness, as Plato said, is swarming with dreamt and unsaid, or said and forgotten, discourses that trace out the bond. That is where Lacan stands, at that precise distance and with that intensity of listening. That is where the analyst places himself in order to receive that which is continually erased from the fabric of political discourse: between the night-time and the daytime cities.

There is an awakening at stake with the unconscious, but this awakening, as with the prisoners in the famous sophism, can only take place if all are involved.[12] The act upon which the work of the unconscious is suspended is therefore political, and this act perforates the realm of truth that accompanies discourse – the daytime life of the *polis* – and exposes it to a passage that can only be undertaken by exposing oneself to the other and within a temporality that presupposes certainty in advance.

We can now better understand one of Lacan's earliest formulas that indicate, within a refined analysis, the political consequences of his experience. At first sight, this formula may seem to follow the outline of a Hegelian synthesis:

> The subject achieves his solitude [...] in the full assumption of his being-toward-death. But we can simultaneously see that the dialectic is not individual, and that the question of the termination of an analysis is that of the moment at which the subject's satisfaction is achievable in the satisfaction of all – that is, of all those it involves in a human undertaking.[13]

Rereading this in the light of what we have seen thus far, it no longer seems to convey an uplifting synthesis, but of a point of disjunction in which each individual finds the trait of their own singularity that allows them to achieve an act with which they take the act of the other by surprise. This is the logic of action towards which the experience of analysis ultimately tends. And this is the logic of action that makes the unconscious political: in order for the polis to awaken, it is necessary, above and beyond 'I' and 'we', for there to be an encounter with the inconsistency of the Other. The Other to which the unconscious politically reveals us, in Hegelian terms, through the *Aufhebung* of our particularity in the discourse in which we dwell, analytically reveals its own inconsistency, binding us to every other in a tension with no relation, out of which the act becomes possible for each, not however without the other.

But Freud did not only discover the unconscious. The analyst, 'an Eastern element that penetrated into the Western world',[14] according to Miller, marks a position that had never been occupied in this way before Freud. From a certain point of view, Lacan's entire work aims at clarifying something about the unconscious and this position or desire. These two issues are closely correlated. As Lacan wrote in *Position of the Unconscious*: 'psychoanalysts are part and parcel of the concept of the unconscious, as they constitute that to which the unconscious is addressed'.[15]

These structural elements allow us to establish one certain starting point: if the unconscious is politics and the unconscious also brings with itself the place of the analyst, within the political unconscious, or within the city that awakens at dawn, there must structurally be a place for what we might provisionally define as the analyst's position in the social bond. In what follows, we will work towards clarifying this position.

Losing in excess: Pascal

Lacan derives two elements from Pascal that help us greatly in understanding the logic of psychoanalytic action and its 'erotology' (*érotologie*),[16] which has nothing to do with psychology nor sociology, but rather with the unconscious, which is politics. On the one hand, its nature as an *automaton*, that orients its course; on the other hand, the *tuché* that signals what is at stake. It is a question, then, of writing down the way in which these two levels are knotted together, starting from a disjunctive point that does not lie along either of the two series but allows each to pass into the other. This point has to do with the object *a* and with the act suspended from it, in the knot between necessity and contingency.

Let us begin with the *automaton*, reading what Blaise Pascal writes about it:

> For we must not misunderstand ourselves; we are as much automatic as intellectual; and hence it comes that the instrument by which conviction is attained is not demonstration alone. How few things are demonstrated? Proofs only convince the mind. Custom is the source of our strongest and most believed proofs. It bends the automaton, which persuades the mind without its thinking about the matter. [...] It is not enough to believe only by force of conviction, when the automaton is inclined to believe the contrary.[17]

This reference helps us to grasp the automatism of analytic practice, which is one of its fundamental dimensions. From this point of view, we could speak of a real 'Lacanian behaviourism', as I have discussed elsewhere.[18] What interests us here, with respect to the politics of psychoanalysis, is not therefore intentional or accidental action, but the act that coincides with the subject itself. This act cannot be traced back to intentionality, which is always imaginary; rather, it must be grasped in the effect it produces and in the feedback that gives consistency to the existence of the subject. This is what we are ultimately responsible for: not for what we intend or do not intend to do/say, but for what, in the act, we make exist of the unconscious subject that speaks in us and beyond us. A political act is one that appears on the public stage with an effect of existential feedback towards the subject, who only in this way enters the scene, not at the level of conscious intentionality but of existential actuality. This is an effect of the automatism of practice and the incalculable nature of its consequences. Having established the tension within the automaton, between act and existence, we can move on to the second aspect: *tuché*.

What Lacan finds in Pascal's wager is this close link whereby there is no existence prior to the act that retroactively makes it occur. It is thus a question of grasping how the act can make the subject ex-ist in the field of the Other. Here, we should note an important passage within Lacan's work. In his 'classical' period, the question of subjectification revolves around the subject's tragic realization that the Other pre-exists him. The subject comes into the world in the Other's discourse, and does not possess any signifier able to represent him and thus give him a place. The ethics of psychoanalysis starts from the assumption of this constitutive impossibility to be represented by the Other, because the subject is precisely what 'one signifier represents for another signifier' and is therefore destined to the negative infinite of metonymic relay. In the late 1960s, Lacan reformulates the question. He reconsiders the priority of the Other not in the name of a naive priority of the subject but through a different topological writing. The existence of the subject depends not on the recognition of the Other or the (in)existence of a signifier capable of representing it in the field of the Other, but on its act. Analytic experience has revealed its secret: *the Other does not exist*. Therefore, the question is not whether or not there is a signifier in the Other that can represent me, but, far more radically, that there is really no Other there that can or cannot give me a place of existence. The subject now has no choice but to wager on what gives him consistency, the object *a*, in order to perform an act capable of making *his* Other exist. In this, Pascal once again helps Lacan: it is no longer a question of the God (Other) of philosophers, but the God (Other) to whom we turn in inner dialogue. It is in the use of discourse, as an act, that the object *a* that we ultimately are brings into existence that Other for whom there is retroactively a subject. Not because it is recognized or represented, but because it is produced in its 'particular foreignness', as though *included outside*, we might say. Pascal's God (Other) is thus unclosed only beginning with the consistency of that object, which precisely between the act and existence makes both possible. It then becomes a matter of grasping this *a* above and beyond any ideology. And this is where the reference to Marx appears, because the consistency of the object in question should be grasped not as a phantasmagoria of truth, but as a semblance that is realized starting from practice, what Lacan defines, speaking of the drive object, as a 'trace of the act'[19]. This is the 'erotological' practice that psychoanalysis politically gives us. We will have to better understand how to produce it on the level of the social bond. But let us remain for a moment with the idea of the wager.

What is wagered on the gambling table of the Other is always destined to be a pure loss, a loss that produces a gain not so much on another scale, but parallel to the former. What is wagered is always lost and precisely for this reason it reproduces the structure of the object: to grasp it means to lose it. The signifying 'mis-grasp'[20] makes it exist, because when it is grasped, the void that makes it possible is renewed. In this way, its edge is drawn, because the object is always 'the recess of a void'[21], and the 'the trace of the act' is then what makes it *ex-ist*.

The point is that *a* shatters any calculable framing of the Other. The object appears precisely where the Other shows its structural incompleteness. And it appears as a demonstration of the fact that, no matter how hard we try to turn the Other into a calculable universe, *a* is always in excess.[22] One must thus hold together this topologically intertwined series: the loss, the excess, and the gain between the two, according to a logic which, however, does not foresee any prediction or calculation and which, strictly speaking, operates with no guarantee.

We must therefore conceive a subtraction that is overturned into a production, which would mean, all things considered, rethinking castration without any transcendence that would turn the cut made by the Law into the generative propeller of the negativity inflicted in the flesh of *discourse-being*. Instead of desire and the Law as its condition of possibility, what emerges is the trace of this body that carves itself through the singular writing of its continuous division. There is no longer a repression that conditions our present from behind our back; repression becomes an extension of presence, with no *arché* nor *telos*.[23] This is the absolute immanence of an operation that, in the act, hollows out the void in the Other, so that *a* can trigger its productivity.

The premise underlying this operation is the observation that *the Other of the Other does not exist*. This is an ethically delicate passage. The ideological structure apparently attempts to account for the entire field, including the alternatives that seem to arise: on the one hand, 'Everyman', the knave, the right-wing *servant*, with his *rogue realism*, in search of his own herd; on the other, the fool, the left-wing victim, a *simple and retarded buffoon* who tells the truth: 'what is not sufficiently noted is that by a curious chiasma, the "foolery" which constitutes the individual style of the left-wing intellectual gives rise to a collective "knavery"'.[24]

Paradoxically, perversion underlies both positions. If, on the one hand, as common sense would also have it, a perverse person is precisely one who does not care about the existence of the Other, on the other, in a surprising but logically impeccable manner, Lacan emphasizes that a perverse person is precisely one who does everything possible to maintain the existence of the Other, 'one who devotes himself to filling this hole in the Other. [...] I would say that he is in favour of the Other existing, that he is a defender of the faith'.[25]

Analysis aims at going beyond this alternative, by radicalizing its most basic premise: if the Other does not exist, there is no Other to whom it can be demonstrated, or to whom one can demonstrate that, in spite of everything, the Other does exist. One must acknowledge this, to the point of letting the problem simply evaporate. In fact, it is one thing to take up the non-existence of the Other in order to use it as one pleases, as the "rogue" does, insisting on flaunting the empty truth in front of everyone else; it is quite another to take up this non-relationship through the experience, always singular, of 'a knowledge that is checkmated'.[26]

On the one hand, we see the elevation to a transcendental level of the cynical affirmation seemingly offered to us by *the truth about the true*; on the other, conversely, an implication in immanence, where *knowledge that is checkmated* becomes a specific way of experiencing its truth. This is because it is precisely where we encounter the *impasse*, the failure or the fall of the Other, provided we do not elevate it to *the truth about the true*, that the object *a* as a resource appears. Or again, to be precise, where *the more of this less* is produced.

Marx's profit

Marx's *Capital* not only offers a critique of political economy, but also tools for reading the economic structure underlying psychic functioning. If 'the collective is nothing but the subject of the individual',[27] within the logic of the capitalist system of production, exploitation and distribution, we can find something that helps us grasp the structure of psychic economy as well. More specifically, *Capital* allows us to see the logic of surplus value as revealing the functioning of the practice from which *discourse-being* is constituted. Surplus value will then have to be reconceived above and beyond the ideological framework that shapes capitalism through its phantasm. How are we to understand, at this point, the sacrifice to which we submit ourselves in order to produce surplus value, to be reinvested, without making reference to the phantasmal justification that the religion of the market creates as if by magic? How to understand the grammar of practice that Marx revealed to us in *Capital*, above and beyond the perverse faith in the existence of the Other of the market? This is the clinical use that can be made of this text: a logic of profit, and therefore of surplus value, freed from the illusion that there is an Other of the Other ready to enjoy it or to renew its theft in a deferred and future *jouissance*.

Let us begin, once again, with an initial quotation. In *Das Kapital*, we read that:

> Use value is, by no means, the thing '*qu'on aime pour lui-même*' in the production of commodities. Use values are only produced by capitalists, because, and in so far as, they are the material substratum, the depositories of exchange value. Our capitalist has two objects in view: in the first place, he wants to produce a use value that has a value in exchange, that is to say, an article destined to be sold, a commodity; and secondly, he desires to produce a commodity whose value shall be greater than the sum of the values of the commodities used in its production, that is, of the means of production and the labour power, that he purchased with his good money in the open market. His aim is to produce not only a use value, but a commodity also; not only use value, but value; not only value, but at the same time surplus value.[28]

Value is detached from use right from the outset: only in exchange does the object acquire the value that interests the subject. This initial transfiguration, going from use to exchange, rewrites the very status of the object, which loses its quality of simple immediate presence, becoming instead, once again in Marx's words, a true 'social hieroglyph'.[29] In order for this to happen, however, a primary renunciation must be operative: the subject loses the possibility of immediately enjoying the object in order to gain the possibility of making it an object of exchange, therefore, a phantasmagoria that fits into and sustains the social bond.

The object of exchange, then, is the object of the phantasm in which the social bond takes shape, covering up the scandal of the non-relation. What is thus veiled returns in the drive to produce a surplus: something favoured by the object itself precisely at the point where it shows its failure.[30] The subject, then, always wants more, precisely because this is what the object invites him to desire, based on the renunciation and failure it carries with itself.

The logic of action offered by analysis reveals here the twofold structure of its own way of proceeding: in turning every object into a commodity, something is lost, but something is also gained. In this transformation, goods become social hieroglyphs and bring into existence another *jouissance* which, so to speak, tends to go beyond good and evil. Here we have surplus-*jouissance*, an indirect effect of the non-relation that exchange tends to mask, as is well seen in Holbein's painting discussed by Lacan in his *Seminar XI*. What, however, does capitalism do with this other jouissance that practice produces, above and beyond itself? It reinserts it within the circuit of production/consumption, by converting it into surplus value. The object that makes the Other of the market exist thus appears: a profit that no capitalist enjoys in the first person without renouncing it, so that it can be enjoyed indefinitely in the full realization of the market as Other.

With respect to this logic, the psychoanalytic gaze introduces the fold produced by the encounter with its own secret, as we have seen: there is no Other of the Other. Two illusions thus disappear, involving future *jouissance* but also the solidity that the market, as a generalized Other, offers to presumed capitalist rationality. Emptied of its Other, the mechanism of surplus value tends to introduce an atrophy of the object, which may actually result in a certain depressive tone that always comes with economic crises: a loss of value, a fall of the phantasmagoria, a crisis in the social bond that commodities as hieroglyphs used to sustain. But here, at this point of crisis, we can also glimpse the possibility of recovering the precise point at which the object had not yet completely *sold* its effect of surplus-*jouissance* to its conversion into surplus value. Detaching the former from the latter clearly makes room for a different (economic) reading of depression.

The fall of the object, which with its phantasmagoria sustained the logic of surplus value understood as the use of profit in exchange, now becomes a chance for a different use of the object and of the surplus-*jouissance* it facilitates. The entropy of production leads to a surplus-*jouissance* that on the one hand is repeated, or on the other is recovered in profit by the capitalist's discourse.

This newly found object is certainly not the object whose use value was irretrievably lost, once and for all. It is also an object that exceeds the latter in exchange, fully displaying its own refusal: a stumbling block for the bond sustained by the illusion of the existence of the Other of the market. What is not exchanged in the exchange has first of all the effect of resisting, in its radicality, the logic of profit that tends to turn it into a surplus value. But resistance is simply a passing figure, because the object in question is not only that which interrupts and eludes the grasp of surplus value. This opens the phantasmatic creation of a possible newly found use, a realm of simple needs and regained immediacy, which is not a way out of capitalism, but its opposite. The object that resists use is nothing if not this very negativity that eludes it. And yet, it also conceals something affirmative.

'The real Punchinello'

'The more saints, the more laughter, that's my principle, to wit, the way out of capitalist discourse – which will not constitute progress, if it happens only for some.'[31] This laughter dismantles the justifying illusion that the Other of the market exists, revealing to us, using an expression Lacan borrowed from Nietzsche, the 'real Punchinello'[32] that underlies the mask of the capitalist.

Just as for Marx history repeats itself first as a tragedy and then as a farce, so it is for a life seen through the lens of psychoanalytic experience. Lacan testifies to this in his *The Youth* of *Gide, or the Letter and Desire*. Gide's tragedy comes to its conclusion precisely when he sees what was dearest to him vanish: those letters he had always written to his cousin Madeleine, who later became his wife, which she, with unwavering cruelty, decides to burn. A tragicomic fate, we might say, which concerns Gide's obsession with the destination, the destiny or the addressee of his writing. Faced with this extreme loss, what is the message that passes from Gide to his biographer Jean Delay and then reaches Lacan, who commented on the latter's *La jeunesse d'André Gide*,[33] and beyond, proceeding back and forth, towards Nietzsche and his 'real Punchinello'? *There is no secret other than the one written on the mask.*[34]

The Other falls, not only as a subject presumed to know, recipient and destination of writing in general, but also as the Other that guards what is most intimate and singular about the subject: the emptiness of which it is made – since, as Lacan says: 'There is no neighbour except for this emptiness that is in you, the void of yourself'.[35] Faced with this tragic fall, discourse-being is left with nothing but laughter. Laughter suddenly allows it to elude the logic that, in its own way and on a large scale, capitalism imposes: the logic of investment and secure protection of the loot, precisely so that it can be renounced when reinvested again.

In that laughter, all of a sudden, we discover that 'there is only the social bond' and that this, ultimately, is based not on presumed knowledge or identification, nor on love, the object that is most dear to us and that, like an *agalma*, we presume the Other guards just for us, but on *jouissance*. In this laughter, there is a *con-pleasure* that comes from participating in *in-common* enjoyment, always different and yet also capable of resonating among singularities. A *knowledge-jouissance*, a different knowing and a different jouissance that are produced upon the ruins of the Other and the now fallen object of love. This leads to another struggle, and another mourning awaits us: no longer in order to regain possession of the surplus labour that is taken away from us by the Other, but in order to produce, thanks to the Other, that which has no place in the Other – the element that is *most dear to us* (in Plato's words), the object that has always been lost and yet has always yet to be rewritten, above and beyond the imaginary trappings with which the inherited phantasm covered it. The excess – in loss – of this surplus-*jouissance* pierces the depressive frame that surrounds its fall, offering us the key with which to rethink, within the difference between the *jouissances* that are singular to each of us, the social bond in which we are.

Notes

1 Jacques Lacan, *Le Séminaire. Livre XVIII. D'un discours qui ne serait pas du semblant. 1971* (Paris: Seuil, 2006), 61.
2 Jacques-Alain Miller and Antonio Di Ciaccia, *L'uno-tutto-solo. L'orientamento lacaniano,* (Rome: Astrolabio, 2018).
3 Jacques-Alain Miller, Eric Laurent, *L'Autre qui n'existe pas et ses Comités d'ethique*, Course held at the Department of Psychoanalysis at the University of Paris VIII in 1996–97, unpublished.
4 Jacques Lacan, *Le Séminaire. Livre XXIII. Le sinthome. 1975–76* (Paris: Seuil, 2005), 95.
5 'In the final analysis, there's nothing but that, the social link', Jacques Lacan, *The Seminar. Book XX. Encore 1972–73* (New York, London: W.W. Norton & Company, 1998), 54.
6 Jacques Lacan, *Le Séminaire. Livre XVI. D'un Autre à l'autre. 1968–69* (Paris: Seuil, 2006), 315.
7 Ibid.
8 Samo Tomšič, *The Capitalist Unconscious: Marx and Lacan* (London: Verso, 2015).
9 'The unconscious is politics', Jacques Lacan, *Le Séminaire, Livre XIV. The logic of the phantasm. 1966–67,* unpublished, 10 May 1967.
10 Jacques Lacan, 'Della struttura come immistione di un'alterità preliminare', *La Psicoanalisi* (Rome: Astrolabio, 2016), 14.
11 Jacques Lacan, *The Seminar. Book XI. The four fundamental concepts of psychoanalysis* (New York, London: W. W. Norton & Company, 1981), 59.
12 Jacques Lacan, 'Télévision', in *Autres écrits* (Paris: Seuil, 2001), 520.
13 Jacques Lacan, *Écrits* (New York, London: W. W. Norton & Company, 2002), 264.
14 Jacques-Alain Miller, *Introduzione alla clinica lacaniana* (Rome: Astrolabio, 2012), 210.
15 Jacques Lacan, *Écrits*, 707.
16 Jacques Lacan, *Le Séminaire. Livre X. L'angoisse, 1962–63* (Paris: Seuil, 2004), 24.
17 Blaise Pascal, *Pensées and Other Writings* (Oxford: Oxford University Press, 2008), 148.

18 Matteo Bonazzi, 'L'*automaton* lacaniano', in *Automaton* (Napoli-Salerno: Orthotes, 2019).
19 Jacques Lacan, *The Seminar. Book XI*, 166.
20 *Méprise*, by which Lacan translates Freud's *Vergreifen*.
21 Jacques Lacan, *The Seminar. Book XI*, 180.
22 'Against the closure of this universe that will be One if it wishes, but that I am an extra o', Jacques Lacan, *Le Séminaire. Livre XVI*, 174.
23 Jacques Derrida, *Positions* (Paris: Les Éditions de Minuit, 1972).
24 Jacques Lacan, *The Seminar. Book VII. The ethics of psychoanalysis. 1959–60* (New York, London: W. W. Norton & Company, 1997), 183.
25 Jacques Lacan, *Le Séminaire. Livre XVI*, 249.
26 Jacques Lacan, *Le Séminaire. Livre XVIII*, 116.
27 Jacques Lacan, *Écrits*, 207.
28 Karl Marx, *Capital*, volume 1, in *Marx & Engels Collected Works, vol. 35* (London: Lawrence & Wishart, 2010), 196.
29 Ibid., 85.
30 'The object is a failure', Jacques Lacan, *The Seminar. Book XX*, 58.
31 Jacques Lacan, 'Télévision', 516.
32 Jacques Lacan, *Écrits*, 642.
33 Jean Delay, *La jeunesse d'André Gide* (Paris : Gallimard, 1956).
34 Jacques-Alain Miller, 'Il Gide di Lacan', in *Logiche della vita amorosa* (Rome : Astrolabio, 1997), 161.
35 Jacques Lacan, *Le Séminaire. Livre XVI*, 19.

Bibliography

Bonazzi Matteo. 'L'*automaton* lacaniano', in *Automaton*. Napoli-Salerno: Orthotes, 2019.
Delay Jean. *La jeunesse d'André Gide*. Paris: Gallimard, 1956.
Derrida Jacques. *Positions*. Paris: Les Éditions de Minuit, 1972.
Lacan Jacques. 'Della struttura come immistione di un'alterità preliminare', *La Psicoanalisi*. Rome: Astrolabio, 2016.
Lacan Jacques. *Autres écrits*. Paris: Seuil, 2001.
Lacan Jacques. *Écrits*. New York, London: W. W. Norton & Company, 2002.
Lacan Jacques. *Le Séminaire. Livre X. L'angoisse, 1962–63*. Paris: Seuil, 2004.
Lacan Jacques. *Le Séminaire. Livre XIV. The logic of the phantasm. 1966–67*, unpublished, 10 May 1967.
Lacan Jacques. *Le Séminaire. Livre XVI. D'un Autre à l'autre. 1968–69*. Paris: Seuil, 2006.
Lacan Jacques. *Le Séminaire. Livre XVIII. D'un discours qui ne serait pas du semblant. 1971*. Paris: Seuil, 2006.
Lacan Jacques. *Le Séminaire. Livre XXIII. Le sinthome. 1975–76*. Paris: Seuil, 2005.

Lacan Jacques. *The Seminar. Book VII. The ethics of psychoanalysis. 1959–60.* New York, London: W. W. Norton & Company, 1997.

Lacan Jacques. *The Seminar. Book XI. The four fundamental concepts of psychoanalysis.* New York, London: W. W. Norton & Company, 1981.

Lacan Jacques. *The Seminar. Book XX. Encore 1972–73.* New York, London: W. W. Norton & Company, 1998.

Marx, Karl. *Capital*, volume 1, in *Marx & Engels Collected Works, vol. 35*. London: Lawrence & Wishart, 2010.

Miller Jacques-Alain and Di Ciaccia Antonio. *L'uno-tutto-solo. L'orientamento lacaniano.* Rome: Astrolabio, 2018.

Miller Jacques-Alain. 'Il Gide di Lacan', in *Logiche della vita amorosa.* Rome: Astrolabio, 1997.

Miller Jacques-Alain. *Introduzione alla clinica lacaniana.* Rome: Astrolabio, 2012.

Miller Jacques-Alain. Laurent Eric, *L'Autre qui n'existe pas et ses Comités d'ethique*, Course held at the Department of Psychoanalysis at the University of Paris VIII in 1996–97, unpublished.

Pascal, Blaise. *Pensées and Other Writings.* Oxford: Oxford University Press, 2008.

Tomšič, Samo. *The Capitalist Unconscious: Marx and Lacan.* London: Verso, 2015.

Part Three

Capitalism

9

Jansenist Morality and the Compulsion of Capitalism

Samo Tomšič

Renunciation of life and surplus value

In Seminar XVI, Jacques Lacan stated: 'What the master lives from, is a life, but not his own, the slave's life. That is why, whenever a wager on life is at stake, it is the master speaking. Pascal is a master and, as everyone knows, a pioneer of capitalism. For reference, the calculating machine and then the bus.'[1] Do we really know that Pascal was a pioneer of capitalism? The connection is anything but evident, even though Lacan backs his claim with the reminder that Pascal invented the bus and the first mechanical calculator (*machine arythmétique*).[2] These technical inventions may suggest a certain compatibility of Pascal's scientific spirit with the proverbial innovativeness of the capitalist system, and yet they do not justify as strong a thesis as the one formulated by Lacan. Since the initial quote references not only Pascal's inventions, but also the notorious wager – Pascal's probabilistic argument for God's existence – one question imposes itself. Could Pascal be a pioneer of capitalism, not just in the innovative and thereby epistemological sense, but equally in the 'deeper' spiritual sense – in the very same sense in which ever since Max Weber one tends to envisage in the synchronic historical emergence of Protestantism and of the capitalist organization of social production more than mere chance? The Protestant work ethic sheds light on an essential aspect of the function of labour, understood as an ascetic process under capitalist socioeconomic conditions, and allows to recognize in capitalism not just a social mode of production, but moreover a spiritual attitude.[3] Therefore it turns out to be more relevant that Pascal, in addition to being an ingenious mathematician and inventor, was equally a passionate Christian, defending the controversial doctrine of Jansenism, a heretical view according to which only a small fraction of humanity was predestined for salvation, through an incalculable and radically contingent act of divine grace. Opposite to the calculating machine, there is the incalculable divine grace, the mysterious and unpredictable will of God, indeed a capricious God. This pessimistic worldview and its limitation of salvation to a select few (not even all devout believers will be saved automatically) could hardly be any further from universal happiness, at least in theory if not in practice – that universal happiness promised for centuries by the advocates of capitalism.[4] How, then, does Pascal, this ardent apologist of a radically pessimistic religious doctrine, in which at best a negative universalism (the universality of downfall) applies, fit into the familiar ideological self-promotion of capitalism as an economic order and a worldview defined by a hypocritical type of universalism, the promise of happiness for all?

First, some context. The initial quote appears in the final lecture of Lacan's *Seminar XVI, D'un Autre à l'autre*. In this crucial seminar, which in many ways responded to the political events of 1968 – first and foremost to the general, indeed universal strike in France – Pascal plays as prominent a role as Marx. In the first lesson of the seminar, Pascal, a passionate advocate of religion preaching universal downfall of humanity, and Marx, a passionate thinker of revolution pushing for universal emancipation of humanity, are nevertheless introduced as silent partners: as thinkers whose work, admittedly from opposite points of view, thematises an essential feature of what Lacan somewhat enigmatically calls 'modern morality'. In doing so Lacan unambiguously indicates that he, too, understands the capitalist mode of production above all as a moral order (hence, a symbolic order), and more specifically, a compulsive mode of production. It is this compulsive character that capitalism and religion have in common, hence the initial tandem 'Pascal *avec* Marx'. They both understood that the main feature of modern morality comes down to 'renunciation of enjoyment', which again seems to contradict the sensational exhibition of consumerist hedonism that dominates late capitalist societies. Or, behind this appearance of continuous 'enjoyment' there is an imposed renunciation, structurally linked to the social function of labour: 'Just as labour was nothing new in the production of commodities, so the renunciation of enjoyment, whose relation to labour I do not need to specify here, is nothing new. From the very beginning [...] it is precisely this renunciation that constitutes the master, who knows well how to make it the principle of his power.'[5]

The link between labour and renunciation of enjoyment is nothing new; it defines all historical (and concrete) forms of labour, as well as all the relations of domination and subjection. In this sense, the capitalist master – Marx calls him *monsieur le capital* – remains in perfect continuity with the premodern forms of mastery, while turning the master into a decentralised and dispersed abstraction. However, something other changes in modernity, when labour is turned into an abstraction.[6] Only now renunciation of enjoyment, which always-already underpinned relations of mastery, became universalized and, in the guise of abstract labour, swallowed individual and social life in its entirety. Labour now constitutes the central process, necessary for the social reproduction and moral justification of life under capitalism. In this life of labour, the modern subject is not simply deprived of enjoyment, but must, so to speak, actively renounce it. Again, in his initial quote Lacan suggests that this renunciation of enjoyment can, even *must* be understood as synonymous with renunciation of life. If the master lives from the lives of others, this means that he imposes renunciation of life onto them, subjecting them to a compulsive economic process that is labour; the capitalist master places them in a situation, in which they must voluntarily renounce their lives in order to live the master's life (whereby the master must again be understood as an abstraction, in the last instance as synonymous with capital), i.e., produce his enjoyment that Lacan in the seminar in question equates with surplus-value. Surplus-value is the vital 'substance' of the capitalist master and the Marxian name for systemic enjoyment.

At the same time, the labour process and the renunciation that goes along with it impose the incompatibility of life and enjoyment, the prohibition of enjoyment in life, since the latter supposedly implies wastefulness, as was last repeated during the European debt crisis, but also throughout the decades of neoliberal dismantling of the welfare state, public education, the health and university systems, etc. Privatization and, more generally, any intrusion of private capital into the public sphere – into the life of society or sociality – is supposed to ensure that life will not 'go to waste' and will continue to be organized in such a manner that the greatest possible amount of surplus value could be extracted. If we let life run its course, it is supposedly defined by excess, 'living beyond one's means'; at least that is the suspicion that the advocates of capitalism repeatedly address to society. It was this suspicion that motivated Margaret Thatcher's claim that 'there is no such thing as society' – or, to slightly adjust this controversial statement, there *must be* no such thing as society.

Thatcher formulates an ontological statement – the fundamental thesis of neoliberal political ontology on the inexistence of an entity called society. Thatcher does not say that society does not exist; she uses the strong negation: 'there is no'. By denying society every positive ontological status, and hence every participation on the order of being, Thatcher pointedly demonstrates Lacan's insistence on the commanding nature of ontology. Understood as concretization of the 'master's discourse', ontology assumes the right to decide, not simply what is and what is not, but moreover what ought to be and what must not be. Although it insists on the contrary, ontology never speaks of being in neutral manner; it commands and thus discursively produces being. The same goes for (political) non-being: what the master-ontologist (here, Thatcher) says that does not exist (or simply is not), in fact must not exist (must not be). The negative ontological statement is, in the last instance, a prohibition, a performative production of not-being. Society must not come into being, since such social being, such ontological enforcement of society and of sociality would, in the eyes of neoliberalism, mean as much as institutionalising laziness and wastefulness, pursuing a form of social life and social enjoyment, which would no longer be organised around the economic imperative of constant growth. As the expression suggests, the social welfare state reinforces (neoliberals would probably say 'forces' or 'imposes') the existence of society and thus restricts, if not actively undermines the unfolding of 'creative potentials' of economic ('social') competition and market deregulation.[7] Thatcher therefore did not bother concealing or mystifying that neoliberalism is fundamentally about building an anti-social state and reinforcing a system of organized anti-sociality (what capitalism in the last instance always was; the 'social market economy' is a *contradictio in adiecto*).

When Lacan argues that what constitutes the master is the renunciation of enjoyment, this clearly does not mean that it is the master who renounces enjoyment and through this act of renunciation becomes a master first and foremost. Instead, the master is constituted by an act in which renunciation is violently imposed onto the other. Renunciation comes as an imperative, to which every human being must submit. The latter is then placed in the position of subject, which, following the etymology of *subiectum*, denotes that which constitutes the ground, but also that which is subjected (*unterworfen* in German). Following this line, the subject is a person whose life is in the hands of the master, a person who is dispossessed of their status of person because they do not possess their body (and therefore do not possess 'their' life). Lacan mentions the slave, the paradigmatic example of the absolute dispossession of body and life. The slave is joined by the worker and the woman, who sum up two other dominant imposed renunciations and exemplify the way in which the subject, in capitalism and beyond, is dispossessed of its body in and through the labour process: forced labour (slave), wage labour (worker), reproductive labour (woman). The triangle of race, class and gender is not only at the heart of 'modern morality's' renunciation of enjoyment-life, but also the way premodern relations of domination persist throughout modernity and postmodernity.[8]

When Lacan speaks of the renunciation of enjoyment in the form of labour, he is of course thinking particularly of wage labour, the economic reduction of life to a valorized and quantified labour-power, a commodity that the worker is supposedly free to dispose of and invest in an act of economic exchange. Marx thoroughly exposed the radical asymmetry in this apparently symmetrical *quid pro quo* of commodity exchange (labour power in exchange for wages). In the last instance, the worker is paying for, or buying, the right to live, for the economic exchange takes place in a hostile symbolic universe, where the moral rule 'those who do not work shall not eat' applies. In other words, those who do not submit to the systemic valorisation of their being are in their very being equal to nothing, they *have no being* (to be understood again as imperative and imposed lack, *they must not be*). Of course, the work that is commanded is not just any activity, but only that which produces surplus value. Hence the implicit truth of the moral rule 'those who do not work shall not eat' is: 'those who do not produce surplus value do not work at all'. Given the devaluation of labour in capitalism and the systemic tendency to degrade working life,[9] *all* labour appears as unproductive and redundant, as labour that never lives up to its economic task and whose productivity is never convincing.

Moving on to the other side of the asymmetry in economic exchange – the act of purchase – Lacan suggests that it must be understood as repetition, which is not without consequences:

> The wealthy have property. They buy, they buy everything, in short – well, they buy a lot. But I would like you to meditate on this fact, which is that they do not pay for it. [...] Why is it that once he has become rich he can buy everything without paying for it? Because he will have nothing to do with jouissance. That is not what he repeats. He repeats his purchase. He buys everything again or, rather, whatever turns up, he buys.[10]

Lacan is of course talking about the modern (capitalist) affluent class, since the premodern affluent class did not buy everything. Behind the appearance of investing their financial means, there is the ongoing appropriation of other people's lives and the calculation, manipulation, gambling with other people's value.[11] The repetition of the act of buying, the headless buying or absolute valorisation, in short, constitutes the buyer first as the master over foreign life, and the seller as the subject of a presumably free and voluntary renunciation of life. As Marx writes: 'The capitalist has bought the labour-power at its daily value. The use-value of the labour-power belongs to him throughout one working day.'[12] The use-value of labour-power is ultimately the worker's body, and the capitalist has thus acquired the right to possess the other's body, or, more precisely, the master is a disembodied abstraction, and his body is, strictly speaking, the other: the slave, the serf, the worker, etc. Investing in production, repeating the act of purchase without paying (i.e., without an actual *quid pro quo* ever taking place) also comprises accumulation of working bodies, a way in which capital intensifies its corporeality. The latter is then not reducible only to 'dead labour' (the means of production), but comprises 'living labour' (labour power). Marx then continues with the famous lines that reduce the capitalist to the personification (not the embodiment) of capital, which 'has one sole driving force, the drive to valorize itself, to create surplus-value, to make its constant past, the means of production, absorb the greatest possible amount of surplus labour. Capital is dead labour which, vampire-like, lives only by sucking living labour, and lives the more, the more labour it sucks.'[13] Indeed, the master lives from the life of others, but this feature is not specific to capital and its social personifications; pre-capitalist masters – the feudal lord, the ancient slaveholder – were already figures of parasitic mastery. Capitalism introduced something else, for which the vampire is indeed a well-chosen metaphor: the *extractivist master* who transforms living labour through extraction into unpaid surplus labour, Marx's synonym for surplus value. Extractivism here obviously means more than the material extraction of raw materials from the natural environment; it denotes abstract extraction, or more precisely, the extraction of a specific abstraction (surplus value) from materials, bodies, society and the environment. The purpose of this continuous extraction is to sustain the modern form of life, as Marx clearly writes: capital lives all the *more*, the *more* labour it sucks. It is a life that does not simply reproduce itself and thus maintain itself in equilibrium or *status quo*, but rather grows – a surplus life that contains a tendency to growth. It is indeed a brilliant coincidence that Marx describes this tendency as 'life-drive' (*Lebenstrieb*), whereby it is almost impossible not to think of Freud's theory of the drives and the dualism between Eros and the death drive. Furthermore, Marx's metaphor of the vampire leaves no doubt that the condition of this capitalist Eros is precisely the ongoing production of death. The life-drive of capital is, in short, a life that is situated beyond the opposition between life and death – and that lives at the expense of other life – an 'eternal' life that sows death and devastation (from colonial violence via perpetual war to climate breakdown).[14] Such a life was unknown to the premodern, pre-capitalist master, even if he clearly based his power on the exploitation of labour and the expropriation of bodies (but in a system that knew no surplus value, hence no growth). Even if the link between work and the renunciation of enjoyment is nothing new, the consequences of this link are fundamentally altered by the introduction of labour-time as a universal measure and valorization of life.

If capitalism imposes renunciation of enjoyment, its economic priorities are underpinned by an ascetic demand that makes it an absolute moral order. It is questionable, however, whether this modern, capitalist morality can really be compared with the Protestant work ethic. Lacan's reference to Pascal certainly points in a different direction, suggesting that the spirit of capitalism may be Jansenist. This implies, among other things, that labour in a Jansenist context cannot be understood as a path to salvation, but rather appears as a meaningless, compulsive and redundant process. In the capitalist mode of production, labour is precisely the opposite of a guarantee of salvation: it becomes a universal 'road to hell' insofar as it supports a system that is generally hostile to the organization, preservation and reproduction of (natural and cultural) life. Pascal's Jansenism thus proves most useful for further contextualizing Marx's engagement with the destiny of life under the capitalist 'absolutization of the market',[15] within a symbolic order based on the imposed renunciation of any form of life that does not generate surplus value.

In the first three lectures of *Seminar XVI*, Lacan presents his by now familiar but still controversial homology between surplus-value (*plus-value*) and what he henceforth calls surplus-enjoyment (*plus-de-jouir*). If we accept this homology, we must also accept that surplus-enjoyment, or enjoyment understood as surplus, is a specifically capitalist mode of enjoyment and does not exist outside modernity. This thesis has its rather surprising anticipation in Freud, who at some point wrote:

> The most striking distinction between the love life of the old world and our own no doubt lies in the fact that the antiquity placed the accent on the drive itself, whereas we displace it to its object. The ancients celebrated the drive and were prepared to honour through it even an inferior (*minderwertig*) object, whereas we degrade (*geringschätzen*) the drive activity in itself, and find excuses for it only in the merits (*Vorzüge*) of the object.[16]

The words *minderwertig, geringschätzen* and *Vorzüge* directly address the question of value. When an object is *minderwertig* (of lower value), this means, among other things, that value is not considered the key feature that binds the drive to this object, or in other words, the drive is not fixated on and by the object's value. In Marx's terms, the object is not fetishized in a capitalist way, value does not constitute its essential quality. When in the capitalist scenario I see an object, I do not simply see in it something that is more than itself and transcends its sensuous materiality. I do not see mere embodiment of value, but more precisely I perceive movement of value, value as an excess over itself: I observe the 'more' (surplus) of value. In capitalist modernity, the object attracts the drive only because it makes growth possible, or more precisely, because it itself grows. The object *is* surplus, *mehr* (more) in *Mehrwert* (surplus value). It is noteworthy that Freud speaks of the ancient 'celebration of the drive', suggesting that the drive may have acted as a binding force of community or sociality. In modernity, so Freud argues, this is no longer the case. The drive's activity is degraded, while the object's status is elevated. Now it is the object's 'merits', and particularly its value, that legitimise the drive's activity. It is therefore, after all, not so peculiar that Marx uses the term 'drive' (*Trieb*) when he speaks of the dynamic of capital and other capitalist abstractions. As the drive's object, surplus value makes the capitalist drive acceptable. The apologetic view of capitalism openly admits this, but in the same move obscures – Marx would say, mystifies – the 'impure' origin of surplus-value in systemic violence, of which exploitation of labour is merely one exemplification.

The drive becomes object-fixated, but this object is inherently unstable. When the accent is on the drive, its objects can be exchanged, whereas in the modern degradation of the drive, the object remains the same, but contains movement and change. In antiquity, the drive reached satisfaction regardless of value, whereas in modernity it can only be satisfied by means of value, it is essentially a drive for value. The displacement goes from quality to quantity; hence the difference between premodern and modern libidinal economy lies in the objectification and valorization of this 'more' (growth) – and we know that constant growth, which also implies continuous dissatisfaction, is an essential feature of the capitalist organization of economic, social and subjective life. In the eyes of the advocates of capitalism, the economy never grows enough, there is no such thing as 'enough' growth, and therefore, to repeat, society must be rejected from the field of being, since the organization of social life would expose the insurmountable contradiction between the sociality that defines human beings and the capitalist anti-sociality, which obtains its expression in the fanatic pursuit of economic growth for the sake of growth. The fixation on value means that the drive of capital does not operate as a binding force of society, but as a force that disintegrates, dissolves and dismantles sociality. If premodern masters were already anti-social in their violence, exploitation and obscenity, the modern drive of capital is founded on the liberation of the 'creative potential' of anti-sociality, the production of surplus value from the organization of anti-sociality into an absolute system. Globalization thus stands for an ongoing and violent expansion of anti-sociality.

From this perspective, *Triebverzicht*, renunciation of the drive, which, according to Freud, is characteristic of the cultural condition in general, obtains an additional twist. In the context of modern (capitalist) morality, *Triebverzicht* marks, first and foremost, a change in the relation of the drive to the object and, consequently, to its own satisfaction. Renunciation does not mean that the drive is simply cut off from some presumably authentic and immediate satisfaction, but that its satisfaction becomes indistinguishable from dissatisfaction; that its demand for 'more' (surplus), on the one hand, makes satisfaction impossible, and on the other hand, constant.[17] What matters is the continuation of enjoyment – and it is this feature that unites the modern mode of enjoyment with the production of surplus value. Both are objective abstractions characterized by movement, and as such they fortify the identity of satisfaction and dissatisfaction. This does not mean, of course, that the drive does not relate to other objects; rather, it continuously extracts from them the 'value of enjoyment' (to recall Lacan's well-pointed formula). Thus, one could indeed say that the modern fixation of the drive on the surplus-object grounds an extractivist mode of enjoyment, just as it grounds an extractivist economy in the social context. Both imply that the sensuous object from which the surplus is to be extracted must be destroyed, and extraction is itself an activity marked with violence and aggressivity.

The renunciation of the drive also implies that modern capitalist and scientific culture is a culture of repression; this was the main thesis of Freud's persistent critique of the predominant 'cultural morality' and of its link with the 'modern nervous illness'.[18] Of course, this does not mean that pre-capitalist cultures knew only non-repressive satisfaction of the drive and, consequently, did not know repression at all. Still, Freud seems to suggest that the emphasis on the drive rather than the object allowed a mode of satisfaction that did not imply complete indistinctness from dissatisfaction. In Freud's vocabulary, the term sublimation marks such a difference between repressive and non-repressive mode of enjoyment. Along these lines, Marcuse's notion of 'repressive desublimation' targets the same transformation of the premodern drive into the modern one, a displacement from sublimation to repression and consequently oppression (sublimation would mean the sociality of the drive and of enjoyment). The key point is that Marcuse uses the term desublimation to pinpoint both a certain 'vulgarization' of enjoyment and a social rise in aggressiveness, the foundation of social bonds on unbound aggressivity.[19]

The emergence of faith from compulsion to repeat

After linking the notion of surplus value to the modern transformation of enjoyment, Lacan turns to Pascal and, in a series of sessions of *Seminar XVI*, focuses on one specific detail from Pascal's *Pensées*, the notorious wager, with which Pascal strives, on the one hand, to develop a probabilistic argument for God's existence and, on the other, to shed light on the mechanism of conversion, the transformation of the unbeliever into a believer. If anywhere, Pascal's link with capitalism is to be sought in this at first somewhat eccentric link between the question of the existence of a supreme being and play or gambling, in the structural function of the wager and the emergence of faith. The wager, in fact, stands for a sophisticated anti-philosophical shift in relation to the fundamental endeavour of systematic philosophy to provide solid proof of God's existence. Throughout its history, philosophy has invested much effort in this endeavour, but the results were poor; particularly with the advent of modern science, the certainty of God's existence has been increasingly undermined from within by atheist doubt.

In short, instead of subjecting God to proof, Pascal, contrary to the philosophical tradition, insists that one must wager on His existence and live with the consequences of the ontological decision imposed by the wager. The relationship between the subject (believer or non-believer) and God is here radically reversed: while in the philosophical proof God is, as it were, humiliated, degraded to the 'subject' of proof, in the wager the degradation affects the individual who is confronted with the question of God's existence. In other words, it depends on the ontological proof whether the individual will accept God as an effective or ineffective fiction and whether faith will be strengthened through the proof. But, as anticipated, the path of proof only expands the space for doubting God's existence and the ontological legitimacy of faith. It is not surprising, therefore, that Lacan at one point declared theologians to be the main atheists, since they dare to speak of God – they speak precisely along the path of hair-splitting scholastic proof, entangling faith in labyrinths of demonstrations and thus exposing both God and organized faith to risk. Theology, understood as 'science of God', does the most damage to the latter. Pascal knows this, which is why for him the existence of God is not a matter of knowledge but of risk. In contrast to Descartes' tendency to formulate a definitive and absolutely certain ontological proof of God's existence, Pascal links religion with gambling, thus effectively neutralizing the other risk to which religion exposes itself by the mere attempt to apply (scientific) demonstration to its own object.[20] In contrast to the 'metaphysical subtleties and theological niceties' (as Marx would say), Pascal's wager displaces the risk from God (and his institutional guardians) onto the subject. God here remains what religion claims him to be and is no less split between existence and non-existence. But the question that arises is what every subject should do with their life in the face of these two metaphysical possibilities concerning the Other; how they are to invest their life in the most profitable way; how they are to extract profit or surplus from their own, finite earthly life. If the subject wagers on God's inexistence, then there can be no surplus whatsoever – there is only life here and now. This life is characterised by its inevitable movement towards death – it is essentially life-toward-death (or as Heidegger would say, being-toward-death). Such life is always already nothing; its value equals zero – it is marked by no growth, no potential or actual increase, and that is why, according to Pascal, we can, indeed we must renounce it. It is only through this renunciation that we can ensure that a different movement from being-toward-death will emerge within life, and life-toward-death will be replaced by surplus life: a modern morality that deserves the label 'capitalist vitalism'.

And so, we find ourselves amid the economic valorization of life. When 'life in its totality is reduced to an element of value',[21] the possibility of a life beyond life emerges in life here and now; not simply a life beyond death, but a life without negativity, a life whose defining feature is, again, growth. Or, for the possibility of such life beyond life, the existence of God must be assumed and, in the same breath, the life that leads only toward death must be renounced. For this reason, Pascal insists that in betting on the existence of God we in fact renounce nothing, since we renounce a life which is always already nothing from the viewpoint of its finitude and mortality. Only with this renunciation, 'nothing' can become an essential element of the economic calculus, in relation to which loss and gain, debt and profit, minus and plus, are henceforth calculated. Only when invested in a moral system sustained by God can life be made to grow and expand, overcome its limits and, in doing so, convert them into mere boundaries to be continuously overcome.

This moral system indeed functions like a machine, which brings us back to that very notion in Pascal – not only the 'calculating machine', but moreover the mechanistic nature of the moral system itself. Not by chance, Pascal introduces and discusses the wager in a fragment of *Pensées* entitled precisely *Discours de la machine*. The formulation means both a 'treatise on the machine' and a 'discourse of the machine' (in a more Lacanian translation). We therefore arrive at the psychoanalytic link between discourse and compulsive repetition (automatism). Pascal writes the following:

> God is, or He is not. But to which side will we incline? Reason can determine nothing here. There is infinite chaos, which separates us. A game is being played, at the extremity of this infinite distance, where heads or tails will turn up: what will you bet? With reason you cannot do neither one nor the other, with reason you cannot defend none of the two.[22]

Again, Pascal's main concern is the act of conversion of non-believers, and the fragment continues with an imaginary dialogue between Pascal's apology of Christian faith and a hesitant libertine who questions the sense of renouncing life and its pleasures in favour of a life in accordance with restrictive religious morality. From the quote it becomes clear that reason necessarily remains split in the face of the alternative and cannot ground a definite decision. True conversion, conversion of the heart, cannot be accomplished based on the principle of sufficient reason or rational demonstration. Philosophical reasoning may convince reason but not the heart; in other words, according to Pascal philosophy cannot inspire passion.

A closer look shows that the wager is not a simple negation of proof, but a sophisticated anti-proof that not only shifts the focus from God to the subject, but moreover contains a performative aspect in which the activity of the discursive machine gradually transforms the unbeliever into a believer, and generates faith. To repeat, Pascal's argument is probabilistic, which means no less rational; it is certainly more scientific than Descartes' ontological proof in *Meditations*, not only because it is underpinned by mathematics (probability calculus), but also because it does not claim to prove God in the first place. Instead, it makes of God an economic order based on the speculation with the subject's life (and ultimately with political life). When the non-believer asks whether he is not wagering too much by investing his whole life, Pascal replies:

> Let us see. Since there is an equal chance of win and loss, if there were only two lives to win for one, you could still wager. But if there were three to win, you would have to play (since you are in necessity to play), and you would be foolish, when you are forced to play, not to risk your life to win three at a game, in which there is an equal chance of losing and winning. But there is an eternity of life and happiness. This being so, if there were an infinity of chances, and only one in your favor, you would still be right to wager one life in order to win two; and, being obliged to play, you would act wrong if you refused to stake one life against three in a game, in which, out of an infinity of chances, there is one in your favor, if there were an infinity of infinitely happy life to be won: but here there is an infinity of infinitely happy life to be won, one chance of winning against a finite number of chances of losing, and what you are staking is finite. All bets are off:

wherever there is infinite and wherever there is no infinity of chances of losing against the chance of winning, there is nothing to hesitate, one must give everything. And so, when you are forced to play, you have to renounce reason to preserve life, instead of risking it for an infinite gain, which is as likely as a loss of nothing.[23]

Of course, Pascal pushes the libertine to renounce life in earthly pleasures; more fundamentally still, he urges him to renounce a specific type of reasoning. This renunciation does not mean simple choice of the irrational against the rational or an affirmation of the irrationality of faith; the wager, as anticipated, is based on the valorization of life, which is a rational-mathematical procedure. Therefore, to wager against the existence of God would be tantamount to renouncing reason. At the same time, by sharpening the opposition between wager and proof, Pascal insists in an antiphilosophical manner that the essence of faith is not reason or thought, which would be separate from the body, but affect, the union of thought and body. The main aim of the wager is therefore to spark the passion of belief, to strengthen religion as an enduring affect in the body. In order to achieve this, the libertine's decision regarding the existence of God is insufficient; what is required is the internalisation of compulsion under which one *must* wager (and Pascal, as we shall see, insists on this point).

When Pascal advises the libertine to counter his doubt and hesitation, he writes the famous lines that Louis Althusser, and later Slavoj Žižek, used to illustrate the nature of ideology: 'Follow the manner in which [the believers] began: namely to act just as if they believed, by taking the holy water, by having masses said, etc. Naturally, this will make you believe and stupefy you.'[24] The wager must be supplemented and supported by senseless (stupid, or compulsive) repetition (Freud's *Wiederholungszwang*), which constitutes the structural 'bone' of spiritual practices and rituals. Commentators of Pascal's text stumbled over the term *abêtir*, which means 'to make stupid' and 'to make beastly'. Beast or animal (*bête*) here appears as the realization of automaton, reflecting the Cartesian view that animals and living bodies in general are driven by an automatic mechanism. Descartes reduced the body to pure geometric extension, thus exemplifying an operation characteristic of both modern science and economic valorization: 'reduction of material' (*reduction de materiel*).[25] Pascal's 'discourse on the machine' follows this line, concluding that 'life in its totality is reduced to an element of value' (to repeat Lacan's well-pointed formulation). Once the unbeliever stops reasoning, renouncing (Cartesian) doubt, and instead engages in repetition of religious rituals and practices, he gradually transforms into an automaton: the materiality of his body (its resistance, as well as the resistance of his thoughts) is reduced; moreover, the process of this religious automation, the becoming-automaton of the body leads away from Cartesian dualism: it blends thought and affect. The emergence of faith is an affective event, the materialisation of the automaton. Pascal thus antagonizes the subject by enforcing an epistemological conflict between two kinds of proofs: intellectual and affective, rational and passionate, demonstrative and experienced. Proof by the automaton is more effective because it is both corporeal and compulsive, it leads to a fusion of the symbolic and the somatic. Therefore, it is unsurprising that Pascal locates it in the heart, an organ that serves as a metaphor for affectivity and for the automatic pumping of blood through the organism.

Marx pursued a very similar issue in his analysis of the transformation of labour under capitalism. The labour process is equally based on the reduction of materiality, the quantification of bodily functions and their conversion into labour power, which is both a material force and the symbolic measure of life's value. In this process, an abstraction common to all concrete forms of labour is isolated, which Marx calls abstract labour (and which receives its commodified expression precisely in labour-power). The result of this process is that labour becomes the central compulsive process in the capitalist universe. But then a crucial political problem emerges, namely that – again in line with Pascal's insight – it is the compulsiveness of the labour-process that generates and reinforces the subject's faith in the capitalist economic system. Just like Pascal's non-believer ultimately works for religion by repeating senseless rituals, the capitalist transformation of living bodies into working bodies multiplies believers in an economic system, which is ultimately indifferent to the preservation of life and the construction of social bonds. Marx's proletariat is a paradigmatic example of Pascal's embodied automaton; through the production process the subject becomes a believer in the capitalist system. This has serious implications for the presumably revolutionary character of the working-class and partially answers the question as to why this social class today votes against its own political interests.[26] The compulsive nature of labour, which is directly linked to the modern imperative to renounce life, is thus an essential factor in generating faith in the system. Those who work always-already believe, and this belief is conditioned by the compulsive character of 'abstract labour', actualized in every concrete form of labour. The analysis of labour also shows that for the subject the only alternative to labour is death – and this alternative, either work or death, i.e., either renunciation of life or death, is equally at the heart of Pascal's valorization of life, which is profoundly capitalist in this very respect: from the perspective of the possibility of a surplus-life, the preservation of any other life is an economic absurdity and a moral scandal. Individuals and societies must abandon every hope, of inventing a form of life that is not organized around the production of surplus-life – which pertains less to these individuals and societies than it does to the expanding capitalist system.

Through automation, then, the body is invested in the gradual emergence of religion – this is what 'reduction of material' ultimately stands for, the programming of matter, or in Pascal's case, religious coding. Where the body goes, the mind follows – for with the emergence of religious passion, reason is equally transformed, so this transformation is marked by the already mentioned expression *abêtir*. An editorial note to the French edition of Pascal's *Pensées* comments on it as follows: 'This word, which shocked, merely points to the theory of "machine". One part of the human being is mechanic; and this "piece" of his being is an object of training [*dressage*]. The superiority of intelligence is that it knows and acknowledges this: intelligence can choose its habits, not escape them.'[27] *Abêtir* is a wordplay through which Pascal embraces the senseless core of religion and, moreover, highlights the birth of sense out of nonsense (or the extraction of sense as a form of enjoyment, which Lacan condensed in his neologism *joui-sens*, enjoyed sense). Habit is something that needs to be forced. But the reverse is equally true: once established, habit is a compulsion that takes on the appearance of spontaneity, refined compulsion whose forceful character remains unfelt, does not penetrate consciousness and operates silently in its background, in the nexus of the mental and the bodily (or the symbolic and the material). Pascal's machine is thus both the symbolic organisation of corporeality and corporeality itself, and it is precisely in this respect that the machine overlaps with Lacan's notion of discourse, a linguistic structure that operates both between bodies (as a social bond) and within bodies (as speech). In one of his Cartesian inspirations, which at the same time turns Descartes upside down, Pascal writes:

> For we should not misrecognize ourselves: we are as much automata, as we are spirit. Therefore, the instrument, by which persuasion is made, is not mere demonstration. How very few things are demonstrated! Proves convince only spirit; custom makes our proofs strongest and most believed: it persuades the automaton, which pulls [*entraine*] the spirit without it thinking about it.[28]

Entraîner is another word worth dwelling on. Pascal in fact speaks of religious training, which takes place independently of conscious reflexivity and intentionality, as compulsive repetition.[29] In these lines Pascal somewhat anticipates Kant's famous definition of the human being: 'The human is the only creature that must be raised [*erzogen*]. Under raising [*Erziehung*] we understand sustention (care, maintenance), discipline (fosterage) and instruction besides cultivation [*Bildung*].'[30] *Erziehen*, raising or education, explicitly addresses the dimension of compulsion in the verb *ziehen* (pull). But unlike Kant, who aims at education towards reason, Pascal targets education towards passion, which, again, is not opposed to reason, but is affective reason and, as such, source of a different kind of proof, which is anchored in the body and in the fusion of sense and enjoyment (thus generating what Lacan called *joui-sens*).[31]

Pascal and Kant nevertheless share the recognition that human beings need discipline, or as Kant puts it: 'human is an animal who, when living among others of his race, needs a master' who will 'break his will'.[32] Kant's suspicion was that human beings are fundamentally anti-social (a 'race of devils', as he writes elsewhere), their will being in contradiction to what he calls 'the general will under which everyone can be free'.[33] The kernel of both Kantian and Pascalian positions is that the human being is a 'compulsive animal', a being whose life is antagonised by the master who does not even need to be another fellow human being; on the contrary, as Pascal shows, the master is indeed an abstraction, precisely a form of automated or compulsive repetition. The source of this compulsion, in short, must not be located in another human being, but in the symbolic link between them. Pascal points this out when he confronts the unbeliever with the imperative character of a wager: 'Yes, but one must wager [*il faut parier*]. This is not voluntary, you're on board'.[34] *Vous êtes embarqué*, the unbeliever is always already 'on board'. When confronted with the imperative ('this is not voluntary'), he cannot choose not to wager. By seeking an argument for God's existence in probability, we evaluate the consequences that follow from the decision to invest our entire life in a wager for or against divine existence. Pascal was a pioneer of capitalism with his unique combination of mathematics (the core of modern scientific revolution) and the production of religious sense as surplus, which grows in and through compulsion. He made the beyond, whose existence is presupposed by religion, a matter of calculus. The beyond can be calculated and by making it calculable one integrates the beyond in the here and now. This integration ultimately produces the object with which modernity is obsessed: the surplus-object actualized by surplus-value.

Pascal's wager is a play, and the link between playing and enjoyment is most evident in French: *jouer* (play) is only a metonymic shift away from *jouir* (enjoy).[35] But in Pascal's scenario, one detail caught Lacan's eye, and that is the notion of happiness, projected into the future and presented as an 'infinity of infinitely happy life'. For Pascal, the libertine must wager because his future happiness is at stake, and only wagering on God opens the possibility of obtaining an endless life beyond life characterized by happiness. There is no happiness outside gambling; but this also implies that happiness is a lucky chance (for the lucky few). Moreover, in this game of chance one must work – submit oneself to the automaton, enter a compulsive labour-process – in other words one must work for happiness, which always remains a promise. That work leads to happiness is another essential component of modern morality, an ideological axiom of capitalist eudaimonia.

But as the libertine's hesitation shows, there is an asymmetry built into the wager; all the risks fall on the side of the one who wagers, and this is not unrelated to Pascal's function of the master, the one who exposes his addressee to risk:

> Pascal does not know what he says when he speaks of happy life, but we have its incarnation there. What else could be graspable under the term *heureux*, if not precisely the function that is incarnated in surplus-enjoyment? Also, must we not wager on a beyond in order to know what is at stake where surplus-enjoyment is unveiled in bare form. This has a name – it is called perversion.[36]

Perversion denotes a structure of the subject who, in the name of the Other (in Pascal's case, the Christian God), voluntarily reduces himself to the object in order to respond to the Other's demand. Or as psychoanalysis teaches us, the perverse subject offers itself to the Other as an object of enjoyment. What Pascal does not know is that this is the truth of what he calls happiness; in his passionate belief, he overlooks that he is championing systemic perversion, which consists in placing the non-believer in a position where the only possible choice is to let his life, and thus himself, be consumed by the Other. By wagering on God, we supposedly guarantee the *possibility* of acquiring a life that will be embedded in a process of constant growth, and so we choose to abandon a life whose limit is death. The object of the wager is that there is such a thing as life without negativity, and Pascal insists that by the mere renunciation of a life marked by emptiness, finitude and death, we have already gained a better, happier life, since life in accordance with morality remains more highly valued than fragmented life in pleasures, but also in despair and unhappiness. In the system of faith, surplus-life is not merely a promise, but is actively produced here and now; we merely must renounce a multitude of senseless and futile earthly pleasures. But there is a trick here, which Lacan addresses in the following manner:

> In short, you have heard about something that is in the wager and that sounds like this, *renounce pleasures*. This is said and repeated in plural. [...] it is the very principle, on which a certain morality that can be qualified as modern is

installed. [...] The *capitalist* enterprise, to name it properly, does not place the means of production in the service of pleasure.[37]

Modern morality is founded on a cut that does not merely involve the renunciation of pleasure, but replaces a multiplicity of pleasures with a single form of pleasure: compulsive surplus-enjoyment.[38] The term *plus-de-jouir*, with which Lacan captures the object of Pascal's wager, contains the ambiguity that, when pronounced, it means both 'more enjoyment' and 'no more enjoyment'. By means of the wager, then, we renounce enjoyment in the name of enjoyment, and in return we receive a promise of enjoyment, an enjoyment constantly torn between 'not yet' and 'no more', in short, empty enjoyment. The subject is divided between the feeling of having lost something and the feeling of gaining something, caught between the loss of nothing and the spectre of surplus which is ultimately mere promise. This, in short, is the paradox in which Pascal's libertine gets caught, and that Lacan points out in a most Marxian observation: that capitalism puts the means of production, not at the service of (subjective) pleasure, but at the service of (systemic) enjoyment, in which the subject is always at a loss.

The separation of the means of production from pleasure also means their separation from the satisfaction of vital needs. Renouncing pleasures ultimately means renouncing the basic conditions for the maintenance of life, and since capitalism requires its subjects to renounce precisely this vital aspect of the social organization of production (economy), it establishes itself as an anti-social project and as a systemically organised anti-sociality. With the solidification of modern morality, what is renounced is the social dimension of pleasure, or simply social pleasure. In return, an anti-social type of enjoyment is imposed, which as such does not pertain to the subject of renunciation, but to the capitalist system itself. The system rests on an imposed renunciation of life; it requires everyone to renounce the preservation and care of life – their own, that of others, and that of society. Along with life, any system of the common good and of society as the space in which this common good is practised, is excluded or prohibited. By this renunciation, the subject is 'invited' to allow itself being consumed by the system, i.e., being transformed into the systemic enjoyment which surplus-value is. To repeat Lacan's point, in this way a socio-economic order is established that reinforces the link between pleasure and perversion, in which the one who lives according to this morality accepts to be transformed into the Other's enjoyment. But instead of placing every subject in the position of perversion, modern morality establishes a compulsive regime in which the subject remains alienated and suspended in the position of renunciation, where labour ultimately finds its place. Pascal's fragment on the wager certainly pictures a situation where the act of conversion integrates the non-believer in an extractivist machine that sucks the life out of the subject and embeds it into systemic surplus-life. Again, the master is the one who lives from the lives of others, and in doing so he is the more alive the more life he extracts from the inexhaustible multiplicity of living bodies. If Pascal is a master, then he is so only insofar as he is not a subject, insofar as his perversion – Jansenism – makes him indifferent to whether he will be saved or not. By submitting to the machine, he has sacrificed himself to God without need or hope of reward. His happiness is the happiness of the system.

The anti-sociality of capitalism vs the sociality of analysis

In the initial quotation, Lacan evokes the Hegelian master-serf dialectics, in which the master is the one who wagers his existence in a struggle on life and death. Through this risk, he establishes himself as master not only of his own life, but also and moreover of the lives of others. By turning the opponent into his serf, the master simultaneously triumphs over death. But Pascal is not concerned with this Hegelian myth of the initial master's wager; indeed, he presents us with a more sophisticated and entirely modern figure of the master.[39] Pascal's master does not have to wager anything, because the commanded play delegates the risk onto the libertine, turning him into God's compulsive worker. Thus transformed, the former non-believer must henceforth work for a God who is radically indifferent to human sacrifice and whose will cannot be swayed by any human action. Indeed, this obscene God resembles more a demon or an evil spirit than the Christian God of love and mercy. Pascal's perversion comes entirely down to the invention of a moral order in which the subject must submit to a senseless renunciation of life that imposes useless work, since as a member of humanity he is already doomed. The libertine's work is misplaced, and, in this respect, it defines the fate of living labour under capitalism, its uselessness and redundancy. Labour does not serve to improve life, whether individual or social, but to maintain a system whose extractivist tendencies are hostile to life, society and subjectivity. The conditions of life on the planet are dismantled, humanity is doomed, human beings are already nothing and will remain nothing whether they sacrifice their nothingness to God or not – and if Pascal is declared a master, it is because he passionately affirms his nothingness and the nothingness of earthly life. In the game of wager, divine enjoyment is nevertheless produced: God feeds on lives that are doomed in advance, and these lives are doomed so that God can enjoy.[40] It is not insignificant that Pascal's fictional dialogue with the libertine fails to mention an essential part of the Jansenist doctrine, according to which divine grace is ultimately an arbitrary, senseless and contingent act. Surplus-life is a promise without guarantee, so behind the supposed win-win situation there is an a priori loss for the one who wagers.

Pascal's master is undoubtedly more intimate than the Hegelian one, since it denotes internalized compulsion rather than external violence. At the same time, the capitalist master is also more external, since the promise of an infinitely happy life remains forever out of reach. While the master lives from the lives of others, the subject is forbidden to live his life, and the reduction of life to an element of value, eventually to labour-power, reflects the expropriation of the subject for his life and body. Consequently, in the labour process, if we understand it as a specific case of Pascal's talk of 'automation', the body itself is turned against the subject. And just as in Pascal the body becomes the seat of religious faith (this is the function of habit), the automation of labour makes the body the seat of faith in capitalism – the faith that according to capitalism will gradually lead every individual and humanity as such to a better life and establish an economic heaven on earth.

Lacan's engagement with Pascal's wager is significant for another reason: it points to the complexity of scenarios that Pascal did not consider; on the contrary, he ruled them out in advance. After the two possibilities of wagering on either God's existence or inexistence, two additional scenarios emerge: one is to wager against God, knowing that he exists, and the other is to wager for God, knowing that he does not exist. The first scenario, in which one wagers against God even though one is certain of His existence, is particularly interesting. Dominiek Hoens comments on it as follows:

> The true wager consists of placing the nothing of one's life as something against the infinity of the Other. As one plays against God/Other, knowing he/it does exist, what one gets in return is hell. If this one case, out of the four possible cases, is indeed, as Lacan claims, what Pascal's wager is basically about [...], then it looks like the true Christian is not the one who wisely chooses for God, betting on an eternal heaven awaiting him in a life after this earthly life, but the one who knows that with regard to God he is nothing and yet a superfluous something that prevents this Other from being One.[41]

To wager against God is an act of separation from the Other, an act in which the subject assumes the status, perhaps not so much of object *a*, but of symptom, the point of inconsistency of the Other. It is worth remembering that Lacan defined the symptom as that which prevents the machine of discourse from running in circle –[42] thus introducing malfunctioning into the circulation that is supposedly the capitalist discourse (the fake 'fifth' discourse that Lacan introduced with great hesitation in 1972 and never returned to again). It is worth recalling that for Lacan it was Marx who invented the notion of the *social* symptom, thus detaching it from its medical signification and epistemological framework. The very idea of a social symptom points to the tension in the social bond where sociality and anti-sociality are negotiated and where existence or inexistence is therefore decided – not so much of God, but of the subject, of society and of life in general.

Taking a step back, Lacan's analysis of wagering points to the distinction between alienation and separation. Alienation is a situation that affects the Pascalian non-believer: he is always-already on board, embarked, as Pascal puts it, and forced to play a game which, behind the appearance of two (in reality, four) options, imposes only one possible choice. The wager is a forced choice, the aim of which is to introduce a modern form of alienation into the subject's life, or more precisely, to ground the production of 'enjoyment of the Other' (systemic enjoyment) on the link between alienation, valorization and exploitation. Capitalism makes alienation profitable, and this is what distinguishes it from premodern modes of production, where alienation was not a source of surplus-value (even though it was a source of 'surplus-power', intensifying and reproducing power relations). At the same time, the capitalization of alienation links capitalism to Pascal's analysis of religious mechanisms and their enforcement. As anticipated, for Pascal the religious conversion of the non-believer is a key problem, and it is also a key problem for capitalism: how to permanently ensure that people will not lose faith in a system that destroys the conditions of possibility of life and of sociality.

In separation, the subject takes on alienation in a slightly different way: not by 'choosing' the imposed option, but by choosing, within this option, his or her own nothingness, thereby rejecting the imposed renunciation of life and the embeddedness of this renunciation in the production of surplus-life. This displacement within necessity exposes the incompleteness and instability of the Other and shatters the system of life's exploitation. From alienation of the subject in the Other, we arrive at the alienation of the Other itself, and the renunciation of enjoyment morphs into the renunciation of the Other. However, one can only renounce an Other for which one assumes (some kind of) existence.[43] We can then ask ourselves what Lacan wants to do with Pascal in the first place:

> Lacan is in line with Pascal's Jansenist conception of the relation between God and human beings. They made the mistake to turn their back against their creator (cf. original sin, etc.), which makes that human beings *only* deserve hell. From the severe, Jansenist point of view, no one but a few will be saved, by an incalculable divine act of grace, for whom an exception will be made. In that sense, hell is our first and our natural condition, whereas heaven is the exception.[44]

Lacan is in line with Pascal only insofar as he takes the implications of his 'thought experiment' more seriously than it may seem to others, insofar as the alienation generated by the wager itself opens the possibility of separation from the imposed alienation. While behind the apparent renunciation of a life in pleasures Pascal is in fact preaching to 'choose life' – in the manner of contemporary religious fundamentalists, namely a life of conformism to the system – psychoanalysis offers the subject the option of choosing death. Of course, this death does not mean suicide; it stands for what Lacan occasionally calls 'the second death' – death in the exploitative symbolic order that consumes the subject's life. But this second – symbolic – death can occur in one way or another: it can stand for the exhaustion of the subject in the labour-process imposed by the existing mode of production, or it can mean the collapse of this mode of production itself, and thus the death of the Other. Unlike the Other, the subject does not require infinity but finitude, and in this respect the choice of death equals the destruction of infinity, or more precisely the destruction of the capitalist faith in its own immortality, which is pushing humanity into catastrophe. For this 'second death' to be actualized in the second sense – the collapse or death of the Other – organized work in a non-exploitative social bond is required, a political practice that mobilizes and binds political subjectivity. In short, what is required is shared labour on enforcing (communist) sociality against (capitalist) anti-sociality.

Pascal's concern was to examine the mechanism of conversion in order to reaffirm the primacy of the biblical God over the philosophical God and, consequently, of religion over philosophy and science. The scandal of the philosophical God, the God of knowledge, is that once introduced, it can also be missed; we can do without him, and this was ultimately the path of modern science. Meanwhile, Pascal's anti-philosophical agenda is the triumph of Christianity and, within Christianity, the triumph of Jansenism. In Pascal we could also recognise the first spiritual consultant, and in Jansenism a kind of religious version of reintegrative therapy. Yes, life is fragmented and full of despair (or as Lacan puts it, '[hell] is everyday life').[45] Since, according to the Jansenist doctrine, a major part of humanity, 'the 99%', is already doomed, it is not so much a question of ensuring salvation, since we cannot influence the will of God, but of making hell more bearable. This is possible if the suffering subjects touch the infinite, if only for a moment; they can only achieve this by offering their lives to God and accepting hell as the necessary, quasi-natural state of humanity. Conversion is the only change Pascal aims at; it is the only way to make life in hell bearable. This is also the element of perversion that links Pascal to Marquis de Sade, who is equally concerned with the conversion of victims – with the difference that in Sade's scenarios the victims are forced to recognise their own enjoyment in suffering. Sade is much more Catholic than he would be willing to admit, and Pascal much more sadistic, and it is this moment of sadism in his speculative Jansenism (speculative in the economic sense, as in financial speculation) that prompts Lacan to make the seemingly peripheral observation that Pascal does not know what he says when he talks about happiness. He talks precisely about hell as that which stands at the beginning, at the end and amid subjective and social life – and in doing so he overlooks his own perversion: Pascal *avec* Sade.

If Lacan recognized in Pascal the pioneer of capitalism, this means that capitalism is born out of the spirit of Jansenism, out of the radical Jansenist morality which demands that we sacrifice our lives to the Other (the system), even though we can hope for no mercy or absolution from this Other, because the Other despises us. It is the God of Abraham, Isaac and Jacob, obscene and capricious God, not the God of love or the God of knowledge. It is not so much the Protestant ethic and its linking asceticism and labour that reflects (the efficiency of) capitalism, but Jansenist morality – and this becomes most evident in our age of disaster capitalism, when systemic indifference to our sacrifices is omnipresent, and God-Capital promises only universal downfall in the form of climate collapse accompanied by the conditions of global civil war. Hell is everywhere, systemic compulsion holds us all hostage, and the capitalist system is overtly running amok. Humanity is not only lost; it is moreover redundant, and Marx called this redundancy of humanity in the eyes of capitalism surplus-population. Indeed, capitalism comprises an ongoing 'becoming-surplus-population' of humanity. To this we can add Lacan's occasional observation that God is unconscious (i.e., neither is nor is not) – this observation, when linked to Pascal, implies that God is the very structure of hell.[46]

Psychoanalysis evidently cannot follow the Pascalian path. It may indeed depart from the assumption that life is hell, and even the analysands sometimes experience the process of analysis as hell (hence the notorious problem of resistance against psychoanalysis). Insofar as it is both theory and practice, psychoanalysis promises neither heaven at the end of analysis, nor that the subject will, even if only for a moment, reach happiness. Instead, psychoanalysis involves its own training, which seeks to transform the symptom, to mobilize its sociality as a possible way out of everyday hell. Analysis may not offer the ultimate exit, but at least it accompanies the analysand to the door. This door does not point to an outside that would be heaven; it is also an exit from the fantasy of heaven (life without negativity, abolition of alienation, life without symptoms, etc.). Psychoanalysis is a working bond that is essentially social. That is why Lacan classified it among other social bonds, and it is important to stress the word *social*. Analysis must face the impossible and yet necessary task of striving for a way out of the capitalist anti-social bond, out of the globalized hell imposed and exacerbated by capitalism.

Lacan remarked at one point that the exit from capitalism will not be considered progress if it happens only for some. Unlike Pascal's Jansenism, which is indeed only for some, psychoanalysis does not leave salvation to divine caprice, but as a clinical practice takes matters into its own hands. Freud called this *Durcharbeiten*, working-through, relational and therefore always-already social work, which links subjects and aims at structural (social) change. Lacan opposed modern morality (renunciation of pleasures) with the ethics of psychoanalysis, which, rather than being a system of compulsions or constraint, is a process of forming life, and above all a process of transforming the damaged life produced by capitalist morality based on production, whose condition of possibility is the continuous dismantling of life, society and subjectivity. Psychoanalysis is a *social* bond precisely because it refuses to accept hell as something it calls life, and is here to stay until the end of life.

Notes

1 Jacques Lacan, *Le Séminaire, livre XVI, D'un Autre à l'autre* (Paris: Seuil, 2006), 396. All translations are by the author.
2 Interesting biographical detail: the young Pascal invented the calculator to help facilitate his father's work. Pascal's father was a supervisor of taxes in Normandy. Collection of debts and arithmetic, financialization and computation, father and

son: here Pascal's link to capitalism gets clearer, but not necessarily deeper. Even on the level of 'paternal metaphor', it remains superficial.

3   One cannot avoid mentioning Walter Benjamin's massively commented fragment on capitalism as a cult of indebting that knows no redemption and thus no act of grace (*sans merci*, writes Benjamin). Weber and Benjamin, of course, each in his own way, develop Marx's points regarding capitalist spiritualism (commodity fetishism, fictitious capital, understood as self-engendering value, 'automatic subject' etc.). See Walter Benjamin, 'Kapitalismus als Religion', in *Gesammelte Schriften*, Vol. VI (Frankfurt am Main: Suhrkamp Verlag, 1991), 100.

4   In our times of accelerated climate breakdown and the implosion of history, there is little to say about happiness; even neoliberals understood that talking about happiness became tantamount to obscenity. In turn, the advocates of neoliberalism no longer conceal their authoritarian face and push for a systemic transition to a neo-feudalism, in which international corporations and platforms are the new feudal lords, the new abstract, digital masters living from lives of others.

5   Lacan, *D'un Autre à l'autre*, 17.

6   Capitalism is characterized by the invention of what Marx called 'abstract labour', hence by successful quantification of all concrete forms of labour, to the extent that this quantification subsumes intellectual activities and processes as well; Freud also spoke of 'dream-work' and other types of abstract and impersonal unconscious labour.

7   Competition is understood here as a social bond and as the fundamental logical determination of our social being or our 'being-with-others' in the capitalist universe.

8   Of course, these imposed renunciations cannot be compared, and the question is not of comparing them, since this would reproduce the competitive relations that are in themselves an equally important component of capitalist morality, the way in which capitalism successfully disarms emancipatory movements that, despite their different historical experiences of systemic violence, politically speaking belong together (and it disarms them, among others, by recognizing them as separate identities that have to compete for rights and recognition on the political market).

9   The process goes back to the structural conditions of the capitalist mode of production and is only exacerbated by contemporary capitalism; Marx alludes to it very explicitly in his discussion of the so-called primitive accumulation, but this line would open a chapter too long for the present text.

10 Jacques Lacan, *Seminar, Book XVII, The Other Side of Psychoanalysis* (New York: Norton, 2006), 82.

11 When Jeff Bezos, this personification of capitalist antisociality, returned from his excursion into space, addressing Amazon's underpaid workers, and the users of Amazon's services and consumers, with a statement that was supposed to thank them – 'You guys paid for all this!' – he unknowingly demonstrated Marx's critical point: not only do workers pay for the anti-social adventures of the capitalists (the

trip into space was an anti-social, 'idiotic enjoyment', as Lacan would put it), but even more fundamentally, they constitute the material basis on which capitalist speculations with value take place. Working bodies are hostages of the system; Bezos' cynical remark admits this willingly.

12 Karl Marx, *Capital*, Vol. 1 (London: Penguin Books, 1990), 342. The sequel is not unimportant: Marx asks the highly philosophical question of what or how long the working day is, and answers that the capitalist has his own ideas about the length of the working day, about its limit, ideas which are of course compatible neither with the worker's nor with the capacity of the working body. The limit of the working day is, in the last instance, death, or at best burnout.

13 Marx, *Capital*, 343.

14 Of course, the condition of this eternity is the production of death – and just as a vampire lives 'eternally' only on condition that he drinks the blood of his victims, literally sucking the life out of them, so the drive of capital lives only by destroying the planetary conditions of life. The life-drive of capital is thus a figure of the death-drive (in a very literal sense: death as drive).

15 Lacan, *D'un Autre à l'autre*, 37.

16 Sigmund Freud, *Drei Abhandlungen zur Sexualtheorie*, in *Studienausgabe*, Vol. 3 (Frankfurt am Main: Fischer Verlag, 2000), 149, fn. 1.

17 Therefore, Freud calls the drive a 'constant force', but this constancy has completely different consequences when an object is invented that presumably continuously grows, and in which 'more' and 'no more', surplus and lack, are interchanging.

18 See Sigmund Freud, 'Die kulturelle Sexualmoral und die modern Nervosität', in *Studienausgabe*, Vol. IX (Frankfurt am Main: Fischer Verlag, 2000), 13–32. Today, we would probably prefer to speak of depression as the most widespread 'social symptom', a system-generated pathology.

19 One should therefore defend Freud's 'repressive hypothesis' against Foucault's criticism, which conflates repression and oppression. Even though the former grounds the latter (repression conditions aggressiveness) it also stands for the foundation of a mode of enjoyment rooted in the demand for more. To repeat, repression does not cut the drive off from some presumable direct satisfaction, but rather from the possibility of temporary satisfaction; it liberates the problematic potential of 'more' (*encore*), thus making dissatisfaction determine satisfaction. In the mechanism of repression, lack-of-enjoyment and surplus-enjoyment, dissatisfaction and satisfaction mutually condition each other, embedding the subject in a vicious circle. Furthermore, by inciting aggressivity in the perpetuation of dissatisfaction, the regime of repression enforces the antisocial character of the drive; hence, Freud's increasing preoccupation with the problem of aggressivity in his later work. There is one specific destiny of this aggressive turn of the drive: it turns upon and against its own person (*Wendung gegen die eigene Person*), its

psychological carrier, the subject and its body. Aggression, turned inward and outward, becomes then the main feature of the modern mode of enjoyment. One can link this with the problematic of *ressentiment*, the latter being the central affect of the capitalist extension of competition to all spheres of human praxis.

20 If we want to find a link to capitalism, it is right here – the link between religion, gambling and speculation is an essential feature of modern venture capital. The structure and function of Pascal's wager illustrate the foundation of the capitalist social bond on the necessity of renouncing life as well as sociality as the framework in which life is sustained. The 'other life' in which one must invest one's entire existence – the life of capital, the life of financial abstractions understood as continuous economic growth – becomes not only more valued but the only 'true' life.

21 Lacan, *D'un Autre à l'autre*, 18.

22 Blaise Pascal, *Pensées* (Paris: Classiques Garnier, 1991), 469.

23 Pascal, *Pensées*, 469.

24 Ibid., 471. See also Slavoj Žižek, *The Sublime Object of Ideology* (London: Verso, 1989), 38–9.

25 'Reduction of material means that logic begins at the precise moment in history when someone who knows these things replaced certain elements of language, which function in their natural syntax, with simple letters. And that is what grounded logic' (Lacan, *D'un Autre à l'autre*, 34). Another example of the reduction of material is the commodification of labour, which reduces all corporeality to a quantified and valorized labour-power measured in labour-time; the same reduction is encompassed in Pascal's wager, where all life is reduced to a minimal value (for Pascal, equal to 'zero'), which is invested (renounced) in the choice of divine existence.

26 As commentators have concluded in the wake of political events such as Brexit or the 2016 US elections. Of course, it should be immediately added that this interpretation was premature and in its own way reflected the contempt of the liberal 'elites' for the working class. Members of the working class who contributed their 'protest votes' in both cases were merely drawn into the broader reactionary revolt of the white middle-class and market fundamentalists. It is not only the working class who votes against its own interests; everyone who accepts the capitalist status quo as the sole game in town does too.

27 Pascal, *Pensées*, 471, fn. 7. The last remark could be extended to the notion of freedom: freedom is always relational, i.e., not merely restricted by the freedom of others, as is often repeated, but more fundamentally, embedded in a system of constraints that make it possible as freedom. Recursively speaking, freedom is the possibility of transformative work on the constraints of freedom. There is no freedom where the constraints of freedom cannot be altered, or more precisely,

where the struggle for a different constraint of freedom and thus for different freedom is made impossible. In this respect, capitalism is a system working on the total abolition of the conditions of possibility of freedom, despite all the liberal and neoliberal noise about 'freedom without boundaries', by which, of course, they mean first and foremost 'freedom of the market'. The condition of freedom for the deregulated market, that (neo)liberalism strives for, is the abolition of relational freedom, which is linked to at least two other elements, equality and solidarity ('fraternity').

28   Pascal, *Pensées*, 451.
29   According to Freud, compulsive repetition is common to religious practices and to obsessive neurosis – see Sigmund Freud, 'Zwangshandlungen und Religionsübungen', in *Studienausgabe*, Vol. 7 (Frankfurt am Main: Fischer Verlag, 2000), 21. At the core of both compulsive orders, neurosis as 'individual religiosity' and religion as 'universal obsessive neurosis', is precisely *Triebverzicht*, renunciation of the drive, which only constitutes the latter, and for this precise reason *Triebverzicht* should be understood as the renunciation built in the drive itself, i.e., as the drive's own renunciation of satisfaction constitutive for what Freud elsewhere calls *Triebleben*, the life of drive.
30   Immanuel Kant, *Über Pädagogik,* in *Werkausgabe*, Vol. XII (Frankfurt am Main: Suhrkamp Verlag, 1991), 697.
31   Pascal is here a figure of counter-Enlightenment *avant la lettre*; he even gives us an insight into the logic of conspiracy theories, where belief, proof and affect are equally fused into one.
32   Immanuel Kant, 'Idee zu einer allgemeinen Geschichte in weltbürgerlicher Absicht', in *Werkausgabe*, Vol. XI (Frankfurt am Main: Suhrkamp Verlag, 1991), 40.
33   Kant, 'Idee zu einer allgemeinen Geschichte', 40.
34   Pascal, *Pensées*, 469.
35   That enjoyment emerges in the process of play is illustrated in Freud's description of the *fort-da* game in *Beyond the Pleasure Principle*. According to Freud's interpretation, his grandson economizes an unpleasurable chance (his mother's departure) and thus transforms the disturbance of pleasure into a source of pleasure, the renunciation of satisfaction into a source of what Lacan occasionally calls 'other satisfaction' (by means of discourse, and thus through repetition in the symbolic order).
36   Lacan, *D'un Autre à l'autre*, 23.
37   Ibid., 109.
38   Pascal can be contrasted with another, more obvious pioneer of capitalism and founder of a different capitalist morality, Adam Smith, who, in contrast to Pascal, promises universal salvation here and now, guaranteed by market Providence. Thus, we have the scenario of (religious) wager and Grace on the one hand, and

(economic) knowledge and Providence on the other. Smith is at the origin of a tradition that assumes the internal stability, self-regulation and (rational) knowledge of the market; knowledge and morality coincide in Providence, which is a more important concept in Smith's writings than the notorious 'invisible hand'. With the notion of Providence, Smith assumes that markets are inherently social, that there is such a thing as a society of markets: the invisible hand or market Providence guarantees the just distribution of wealth by forcing the rich to social behaviour and economic justice.

39 In *Seminar VII* Lacan remarks that Hegel's philosophy (he means, of course, the *Phenomenology of Spirit*, filtered through Alexandre Kojève's reading) thought to the end the ancient figure of the master, who no longer has any place in the universe of modern science. Hence it is also Hegel who finally humiliates and devalues the premodern master by presenting him as a fraud (*dupe*). In the modern universe, the master becomes an abstraction, which, for Lacan, is more appropriately and subversively thought by utilitarianism, with Bentham at the front. In relation to these framings, *Seminar XVI* reads as a peculiar corrective, according to which Pascal must be added to utilitarianism, revealing the perverse nature of the modern master. Not to mention Marx's equation of the master with capital.

40 What Lacan calls 'enjoyment of the Other' is directly related to the subject's renunciation of his own life and future. The condition for the existence of God is the inexistence of the subject; God exists the more the subject loses its existence, and it is against the background of this loss that the subject is forced to work. Capitalism is a secular version of this scenario, a system whose logical goal is the downfall of humanity, which alone makes the production of surplus-value, the self-valorisation of capital and continuous economic growth possible.

41 Dominiek Hoens, 'Is Life but a Pascalian Dream? A Commentary on Lacan's Louvain Lecture,' in *Psychoanalytische Perspectieven*, 36:2, 2018, 181.

42 See Jacques Lacan, 'La troisième', in *La Cause freudienne*, 79, 2011, 17.

43 When Lacan in his later texts and seminars almost compulsively repeats, 'The Other does not exist', this does not mean that he 'chooses' the inexistence of the Other against its existence. His statement 'The Other does not exist' does not deny that this inexistence has real consequences. For this precise reason the remark is not to be interpreted as expressing naïve atheism which would simply dismiss God as an inefficient fiction or illusion.

44 Hoens, 'Is Life But a Pascalian Dream?', 182.

45 Lacan, *D'un Autre à l'autre*, 161.

46 It is worth recalling that the addressee in Pascal's fragment on the wager is a libertine who is confronted with the imperative of renouncing pleasure. Pascal is also in this respect the flipside of Sade, whose 'pornographic' literature served Lacan to make the point that the superego concerns the imperative of enjoyment. Like

Hegel's master, Sade's libertine is a figure of the *ancien régime*, while Pascal makes the libertine into a capitalist libertarian, a passionate gambler with the fate of other people's lives, which is why this libertarian cannot be recognised as anything other than a perverse subject. As today's unbound neoliberalism repeatedly demonstrates, no one believes in the system more fervently than libertarians, these Pascalian libertines transformed into economic fanatics, apologists of social renunciation in exchange for nothing. Fanaticism is indeed a characteristic that Marx explicitly links to the capitalist drive of accumulation and of self-valorization – systemic fanaticism that today expresses itself in the guise of disaster capitalism.

Bibliography

Benjamin, Walter, 'Kapitalismus als Religion', in *Gesammelte Schriften,* Vol. VI (Frankfurt am Main: Suhrkamp Verlag, 1991, 100–3.
Freud, Sigmund, 'Drei Abhandlungen zur Sexualtheorie', in *Studienausgabe,* Vol. 3, Frankfurt am Main: Fischer Verlag, 2000, 37–145.
Freud, Sigmund, 'Zwangshandlungen und Religionsübungen', in *Studienausgabe,* Vol. 7., Frankfurt am Main: Fischer Verlag, 2000, 11–22.
Freud, Sigmund, 'Die "kulturelle" Sexualmoral und die moderne Nervosität', in *Studienausgabe,* Vol. 9, Franfurt am Main: Fischer Verlag, 2000, 11–32.
Hoens, Dominiek, 'Is Life but a Pascalian Dream? A Commentary on Lacan's Louvain Lecture', in *Psychoanalytische Perspectieven,* 36:2, 2018, 169–85.
Kant, Immanuel, 'Idee zu einer allgemeinen Geschichte in weltbürgerlicher Absicht', in *Werkausgabe,* Vol. 11, Frankfurt am Main: Suhrkamp Verlag, 1991, 33–50.
Kant, Immanuel, 'Über Pädagogik', in *Werkausgabe,* Vol. 12, Frankfurt am Main: Suhrkamp Verlag, 1991.
Lacan, Jacques, *Le Séminaire, livre VII, L'éthique de la psychanalyse,* Paris: Seuil, 1986.
Lacan, Jacques, *Le Séminaire, livre XVI, D'un Autre à l'autre,* Paris: Seuil, 2006.
Lacan, Jacques, *Seminar, Book XVII, The Other Side of Psychoanalysis,* New York: Norton, 2006.
Lacan, Jacques, 'La troisième', in *La cause freudienne* 79, 2011, 11–33.
Marx, Karl, *Capital,* Vol. 1, London: Penguin Books, 1990.
Pascal, Blaise, *Pensées,* Paris: Classiques Garnier, 1991.
Žižek, Slavoj, *The Sublime Object of Ideology,* London: Verso, 1989.

10

Capitalism and Law: From Servitude to Freedom

Todd McGowan

Stating the case

Capitalist modernity introduces two competing forms of authority. One is the state with its legal apparatus that functions as the site of avowed authority. This is an authority that everyone can see, even if not everyone respects it as an authority. The state's dictates place restrictions on what people can do without incurring some form of punishment, which the state holds over them to keep them in line. Its authority is self-evident and unyielding. In contrast, the other form of authority does not appear to be an authority at all. Unlike the state, the capitalist economy doesn't issue any explicit orders that must be obeyed. Its authority appears in the form of an invisible hand that we don't even perceive as inherently authoritative.[1] We don't face immediate imprisonment for disobeying the demands of capitalism. Refusing to accumulate doesn't earn me the death penalty, at least not directly from the order of some master capitalist like Jeff Bezos. The capitalist economy provides an arena where people can do what they choose – invest where they want, sell what they want, buy what they want. All in all, it seems like a less rigorous authority than the state. It appears so uncoercive that most don't look on it as an authority at all.[2] But this appearance is entirely misleading. Capital functions as the fundamental authority in modernity, an authority all the more exacting because it appears in the form of liberation.

The capitalist economy is the site of servitude in the modern universe, while the state, despite its sheen of coerced obedience, is the site of potential freedom. Capitalist society's ability to reverse these valuations – to convince people that the capitalist economy is liberating and the state is oppressive – indicates the overall retreat from the possibility of freedom that occurs in modernity, despite the fact that freedom emerges as a genuine possibility for the first time in the modern universe. Modernity creates the possibility for political freedom by stripping authority of its substantial status and allowing people to see it as contingent rather than necessary. It thus facilitates revolutions against oppressive authorities, such as those that occur in France and in Haiti. But capitalism accompanies modernity and undermines its revolutionary dynamic, even though the champions of capitalism see it as unquestionably a locus of freedom.[3] The political alignment of the capitalist economy with freedom represents the fundamental barrier to recognizing the actual structure that freedom takes. It fools not just conservative defenders of the capitalist order but also many of its leftist opponents who recoil from any assertion of state power.[4] The liberal conception of freedom that provides the basis for the capitalist system includes an implicit slander against the state that leads to a widespread misperception of its function. In order to regain contact with the possibility for freedom inherent in the modern break, we must recognize the state as a vehicle for an emancipation that the capitalist economy vitiates.

It is Hegel who is the first to assert the state as the condition for freedom. Where earlier thinkers see a barrier to freedom, Hegel recognizes how the state allows freedom to become actual rather than just persisting as an ideal. This is the central conclusion of the *Philosophy of Right* and the reason for Hegel's embrace of the state as theoretically necessary. He writes, 'The state in and for itself is the ethical whole, and actualization of freedom, and it is the absolute end of reason that freedom should be actual.'[5] Through the form of its legal structure, the state constitutes the subject as free, giving it a terrain on which it can make this freedom actual through what it does.

Without the state structure, the subject would simply be at the whim of whatever natural or social conditions determined it. The state provides the subject with the opportunity to determine itself by uprooting itself from its determinants through recourse to the law. The limit of the law provides the paradigm for the subject's free self-limitation. In the act of limiting itself, the subject freely determines its field of action rather than simply following its inclinations or the givens of the society. In this way, the state gives the subject the opportunity to break from what conditions it. This possibility distinguishes the state from the capitalist economy, which induces the subject to give in to what conditions it, to follow what everyone else does. This emancipatory role of the state is what Hegel demonstrates in the *Philosophy of Right*, which is why he sees the state as a necessary corrective of the exigencies of capitalism (which he calls 'civil society' [*bürgerliche Gesellschaft*]).[6]

Although the state makes laws, it is the unwritten rules of the capitalist economy that have the most direct impact on the form that modern subjectivity takes. More than subjects of a specific state, we are capitalist subjects, no matter what state we reside in. But unlike state laws, capitalism's implicit rules don't present themselves as limitations on our subjectivity. They do not manifest themselves as oppressive restrictions. Instead, they appear as a panoply of possibilities for the subject that give it an open field in which to act. Capitalism's charge that I accumulate ceaselessly feels like a prompting to do what I most want to do, to amass a lot of things. I don't experience it as an onerous prohibition. The capitalist system seems to allow me to perform the work I'd like, to go where I'd like, to eat what I'd like, and, most importantly, to live how I'd like. But this semblance of freedom obscures a thoroughgoing coercion.

Capitalism controls through the pressure that it puts on everyone to invest themselves in and model themselves on the commodity form. The commodity form defines the capitalist system. It is a form that always promises more – more wealth, more commodities, more enjoyment. One invests oneself in the commodity form because it has within it the lure of magically growing this investment. The demand to commit oneself wholly to the commodity form is the sine qua non of capitalist society. One must always strive for more. To do otherwise is to find oneself without even the bare minimum for survival. Within capitalist society, one's survival depends on one's capitulation to the rule of the commodity form, on the acceptance of the commodity form as a model for one's subjectivity.

Through its deployment of the commodity, the capitalist economy seduces us into capitulation without ever making us aware of our freedom. We cede freedom to the authority of capitalism when we invest ourselves in the commodity form, which is a form of accumulation. Capitalism restricts freedom by channelling it through the promise of always acquiring something additional. Freedom becomes the freedom to constantly have more without any restrictions. The commodity form becomes the only conceivable form that subjectivity can take. It is a form that opens up possibilities while closing down freedom into the freedom to accumulate.

The first movement of the collective servitude that occurs within capitalism is the exchange of freedom to act for free choice among a series of commodities. Once we do this, we have already ceded our freedom to the fetishism of the commodity. Which commodities one chooses to invest in or purchase are unimportant. Even when I can choose among different commodities, this free choice marks the absence of freedom because I can no longer choose to act outside the logic of the commodity. Capitalist society appears as a free society because it allows subjects, provided they have enough money or are able to go into debt to obtain enough, to choose the commodities that they desire. Although there is some restriction on these commodities at the margins – one cannot legally purchase a murder, for instance – the limits do not emanate from the capitalist economy itself. The state is always the source of these limits. Within the economic realm, one has an unrestricted choice of commodities for investment and for purchase. The field of commodities accommodates a liberal conception of freedom, a freedom that brooks no limitation, save that of the freedom of others.

In capitalist society, I must sell my labour power – my active potential to create – as if it were just another commodity (because it is). There is no existence possible in capitalist society without the subject's self-commodification. This is why Marx contends that prostitution represents the basic form of capitalist subjectivity. As he puts it early on in his thinking, 'Prostitution is only a *specific* expression of the *general* prostitution of the *laborer*.'[7] The prostitute is not an exception within capitalist society but the paradigm for all wage labor, which requires everyone to invest in the commodity form.[8] Capitalism is a dictatorship of the commodity form that sells itself as a reign of freedom.

The basic problem with the authority perpetuated by capitalist economy is that we cannot confront it as an authority. Instead, capitalist society establishes the state as the explicit site of authority in order to obscure the primacy of capital in forming the social order. Of course, no one figure designs the social structure this way, which is why authority under capitalism is always mystified. One cannot see where the authority really lies because the question is never who is pulling the strings but what is doing so. However, the overt presence of the state renders it culpable in the thinking of most capitalist subjects, including the theorists of biopower such as Michel Foucault and Giorgio Agamben.

For these theorists, state power is the fundamental threat that confronts us today. As they see it, state power has become more dangerous than ever because it now takes the form of power over life itself, which they call biopower. In contrast to previous epochs of human history, it controls through determining how people must live rather than just threatening them with death if they disobey. Modern biopower represents an intensification of state control that Foucault originally identifies with the moment that the state begins to enforce its dominance productively instead of just punitively. While they devote multiple volumes to the state's overreach, the theorists of biopower pay scant attention to capitalism's dominance. For instance, at the beginning of his most influential work, *Homo Sacer*, Agamben announces the principal danger that confronts us as modern subjects. It's not the exigencies of capitalism but the expansion of state power. He writes: 'At the threshold of the modern era, natural life begins to be included in the mechanisms and calculations of State power, and politics turns into *biopolitics*.'[9] The revolution in the form of state power portends less space for people to operate outside the state's reach. Its entrails begin to invade every aspect of one's life and to enforce a regime of proper living on everyone: I must follow a healthy diet, exercise, and watch my cholesterol. The condition in which I keep my body becomes an affair of the state, no longer just my private concern. This regime replaces obeying the law as my social duty. It is more oppressive because it is more invasive.

Neither Foucault nor Agamben foregrounds the role of capitalism in the expansion of biopower.[10] Perhaps the problem is that Foucault died before the invention of the Apple Watch (although Agamben was here to witness it). For them, biopower is an affair of the state in which capitalism plays at most a secondary role. Most of the time in their analyses, capitalism does not even garner a mention. The absence of any discussion of capitalism in the analysis of biopower is intentional on the part of Foucault: he explicitly wants to break from the economic focus of a Marxist interpretation of history. But in doing so, he and the other theorists of biopower inadvertently perpetuate the basic mystification that capitalism itself advances. This is the idea that capitalism is not an authority, that it does not imprint itself on the form of subjectivity. It is able to pull off this con thanks to the sleight of hand that it propagates, a sleight of hand that manages to take in the theorists of biopower, who are fully onto the state's con.

Within capitalist society, the state plays the heavy. Even though capitalism uses the state to enact its system – to be clear, capitalism could not operate without it – the state functions as the organ that receives the brunt of the dissatisfaction that the capitalist economy requires in order to keep going. The state is capitalism's scapegoat. Subjects react to the state as if it is the source of all the oppressiveness of capitalist society, and the capitalist economy receives disproportionately less of people's disapprobation. This is a fundamental misdirection at work in how we conceive freedom in relation to capitalism. We perceive capitalist relations as a realm of freedom that contrast with the constraint that the state perpetuates. Since capitalism doesn't operate with explicit restrictions and the state does, one must interpret both structures in order to see that it is the state that is the site of freedom and capitalism that relegates us to servitude.

The state within capitalism places restrictions on the subject's freedom through the form of laws. Law stands in contrast to the commodity form in the relationship that each have to the subject's freedom. When we adopt the liberal conception of freedom that capitalism demands, state law cannot but appear as a limit on this freedom. But the limitations that the state's laws impose create an opportunity for the capitalist subject to recognize its freedom. The subject can recognize the state's laws as its condition of possibility, as a site for the assertion of freedom rather than its elimination. Their restrictiveness is an enabling limitation, a limitation that create possibilities. In contrast to the commodity form, state laws, when we pay attention to their structure, force subjects to recognize that their freedom emerges through the limit, not by surpassing all limits.

State and ideology

Due to the state's complicity with capitalist relations of production, most anticapitalist movements have had a profound suspicion of the state. Anarchism takes this suspicion to its end point and calls for the state's abolition. Although Marxism is politically distant from anarchism, it does see the state as a barrier to the achievement of communist society.[11] Not only does Marx believe that communist society will eventually do without the state, he sees the state here and now as complicit with capital's reign.

For Marx, the state is an effect of capitalism. It emerges with the capitalist epoch as the superstructural accompaniment to the capitalist infrastructure. In his celebrated essay on ideology, Louis Althusser describes the basic Marxist understanding of the state. He writes: 'The State is a "machine" of repression, which enables the ruling classes ... to ensure their domination over the working class.'[12] The state pretends to address a society of equals while actually providing covert support for the reigning relations of production. A seemingly neutral set of laws actually exist to protect the interests of the capitalist class. As Althusser and many other Marxists (inclusive of Marx himself) see it, the oppressiveness of the state occurs in its very structure, not just when police officers gun down unarmed Black victims. To fight against the dominance of the state, Marx doesn't think of it as independent from the class interest that it serves.[13] To consider the state as a force distinct from capitalism, for Marx, is to become a dupe of the basic form of capitalist ideology, to take the superstructure as independent of the infrastructure that determines it (even if only in the last instance).

This alignment between state law and the class interest of the bourgeoisie is easiest to see with laws against theft. Capitalist society outlaws theft in order to secure the property of those who own the means of production while obscuring the legal theft of surplus value that keeps these business owners in place. The law against theft prevents a revolutionary expropriation of the expropriators. Because most people in capitalist society respect this law, those who legally steal the surplus value of their labourers can sleep restfully at night. The cops keep guard over their legal theft: rather than prosecuting it, they protect it. One cannot divorce law, even the instances of law that seem most fundamental, from class interest.

Marx's suspicion of the state and its legal apparatus is for the most part justified. But what he misses is the contradiction that develops between law and capitalist economy, a contradiction that leads law to act as a barrier to capitalist production. Law becomes a barrier to the continual expansion of capitalism because it erects a limit, while capitalism has a profound allergy to all limits. It is through the limit that we should recognize the fundamental distinction between the state and capitalism. Capitalism's abhorrence of the limit subtends its allergy to freedom, while the state's recourse to the limit renders it a site for the expression of freedom.

Rather than accept any constitutive limit on the creation of value, capitalism treats every potential limit as a barrier that it must attempt to transcend. Marx himself makes this clear in the *Grundrisse*, where he notes, 'as a representative of the general form of wealth – money – capital is the endless and limitless drive to go beyond its limiting barrier.'[14] Despite the insight of this characterization of capitalism, what Marx doesn't see is that the refusal of any limit puts capitalism inevitably at odds with law, which is always limiting, even when the forces of capitalism construct the law to facilitate the production of capital. The state is not just a superstructural outgrowth of the capitalist economy. It is this, but it is also the site of a fundamental limit that represents an existential challenge to capitalism's imperative to drive beyond all limits.

The key anti-capitalist effect of the law consists in the psychic role that it has for the subject. Although particular laws, such as property laws, work hand-in-hand with capitalist accumulation, law as such erects a limit to this process. As the indication of an intractable limit, law as such commands subjects to give up the allure of an unlimited enjoyment for the sake of the possibility of living together. In this way, the law represents a challenge to the promise of the commodity, which is an implicit promise for future unlimited enjoyment. When confronted with the law, rather than do what I desire without restraint, I accept the limit that constitutes social existence. I sacrifice doing whatever I want in the same way that everyone does. We all collectively agree not to run down the street screaming in the middle of the night, even though this sounds like a lot of fun. By not disturbing the peace (or committing whatever crime), we take part in a joint sacrifice that constitutes the social order. The law as such demands this sacrifice, this abandonment of unrestrained enjoyment. In this sense, the sacrifice associated with the state runs counter to the dynamic that sustains the capitalist economy, which survives on the future promise of precisely the unrestrained enjoyment that the law requires me to give up.[15] Even while the state keeps capitalism going, it marks a point that challenges the imperative that underlies the capitalist economy, provided that we relate to the state's limiting function as a structural necessity rather than as a regrettable encumbrance.

The role of law in constituting the social order predates capitalism. Every social compact in history depends on some form of law, either written or unwritten. Law articulates a shared limitation that everyone who exists in the society must accept. Those who refuse to accept the limitation risk punishment, exile, or death. This limitation is a sacrifice of enjoyment without restraint. Life in the social order entails the acceptance of partial enjoyment.

But there is a deception at the heart of the law's imperative for sacrifice. By the fact of its constitution as a subject within a system of signification, the subject is condemned to partial enjoyment. Unlimited enjoyment is possible only in the imagination of those who speak. It is not attainable because signification necessarily produces divided subjects, subjects incapable of attaining self-completion or complete enjoyment. The subject is divided from the possibility of completion by virtue of being a subject.

As a result, law prohibits the impossible. It bars unrestricted enjoyment even though this is unattainable. Although particular laws prohibit what is certainly possible – it is possible to kidnap even though the law interdicts it – the law as such stands in for the prohibition of the impossible – complete enjoyment. The existence of the law tells me that I cannot do just as I please, that I must content myself with partial rather than unlimited enjoyment. This introduction of a fundamental limit has the effect of binding the inhabitants of the social order together through their shared sacrifice, even though they are sacrificing what it is impossible to attain. The bond functions all the better insofar as they sacrifice what they could never have in the first place.

Accepting the limitation of the law is also accepting the symbolic fiction that the law sustains. As a member of the social order, I believe that the law constrains what is possible, not what is impossible. The recognition that I could never have what the law prohibits changes my relation to the law and to the society. To be a member of the society, I must accept both the law's limitation and its lie.

The paradigmatic law is the incest prohibition, which stands in for ultimate enjoyment.[16] This prohibition places the privileged object off-limits for the subject, but the privileged object is already an impossible object before this prohibition. To take the traditional version of the incest prohibition, if one has direct sexual access to the mother, she ceases to be the mother and becomes just an ordinary sexual object. Or, as Joan Copjec puts it in *Read My Desire*, 'It is because the good object is *already* lost, desire has *already* been repressed, that the law forbids access to it.'[17] As a result, there is no way of accessing what the law bans. There is no path back from the law to the privileged object. Violating the incest prohibition would transform the incestuous object into an everyday one. If one had sex with one's mother, she would cease to be the figure of the mother and become just another object.[18] The prohibition has the effect of making the impossible appear possible, which is exactly what all law does. Law's prohibition creates the appearance of a complete enjoyment lurking just beyond its restriction, but without this restriction, this enjoyment would disappear.

By prohibiting the impossible, law possibilizes it. Through this structure, law creates the illusion of a shared sacrifice that binds a society together. We become bound together because we have collectively given up direct access to the privileged object. We have all sacrificed complete enjoyment. But this is an illusory sacrifice: we have given up what we could have had only insofar as we have given it up. The privileged object has its privilege only insofar as it remains impossible. The sacrifice that the law commands retroactively creates the privileged object that it asks us to abandon. In the wake of this sacrifice of nothing, for subjects of the law, access to the object comes through the signifier. Such subjects can find only a partial enjoyment from their indirect relation to the object. The law commands the subject to obtain its enjoyment through the indirection of the signifier.

But by making us aware of the limitation on our enjoyment, the law poses a fundamental challenge to capitalist freedom to accumulate. This freedom brooks no constitutive limit, but the law indicates just such a limit. When the subject confronts the law as an intractable and constitutive limit, it has the opportunity to change its servitude to the commodity form. The law provides an opening to a form of freedom that stands in contrast to liberal freedom.

Breaking the law

Every specific law serves as a synecdoche for law as such prohibiting complete or non-lacking enjoyment. Even when I follow an easily obeyed law, like the law against driving under the influence of alcohol or drugs, I accept a limit on my enjoyment. I forego the thrill that comes from driving thoughtlessly after I leave the bar. I give up the feeling of being unconstrained behind the wheel. This restriction on driving while impaired impairs my enjoyment, but I accept the limit so that I can live together with other subjects – or so that other subjects can live.

The law against driving while impaired is not the incest prohibition, but it stands in for it in the way that all laws do. It forces the subject to recognize a clear limit on its enjoyment. It limits the subject to a partial enjoyment. But at the same time, it retroactively creates the illusion of a complete enjoyment that doesn't actually exist – driving while drunk. In actuality, driving while drunk isn't all that. It's difficult and typically leaves one full of remorse for what (or whom) one has hit. But because of its interdiction, it gains the status of an illusory complete enjoyment, as if the law forces me not to enjoy to the fullest by driving drunk with impunity.

Laws against drunk driving don't directly block the accumulation of capital. They may even assist it insofar as they keep the roads clear of fatalities that might block the smooth transportation of commodities. But by explicitly restricting complete enjoyment, this law implicitly erects a barrier to the capitalist imperative to accumulate and to the liberal conception of freedom. The promise of complete enjoyment drives the accumulation of capital. Just as the consumer in capitalist society seeks the fulfilment of this promise in the purchase of each commodity, the producer creates new commodities in search of this same goal. Capitalism depends on subjects believing in the possibility of achieving what every manifestation of the law tells them is forbidden.

Every commodity promises transcending the limit that the law announces. As a result, capitalism constantly finds itself at odds with law as such. Capitalism demands that people view the law's limitations as contingent and not as constitutive. The emancipatory opposition to capitalism reverses this way of seeing: it recognizes the law as constitutive for the subject. Once one does this, one has already stepped outside capitalist subjectivity and taken the path to emancipation.

But as long as we relate to the law as liberal subjects, the challenge that the law poses to capitalism disappears. The liberal conception of freedom sees only external limits to its reach. From this perspective, laws become a series of limitations imposed on us by others. Laws are the restrictions that the state lays down that limit our freedom. This is not just a way of perceiving the law. It is a way of misperceiving it that keeps capitalist society functioning.

It is absolutely crucial that the capitalist subject not know what it does, every bit as much as those putting Christ to death. The capitalist subject must view itself in terms of liberal freedom – striving to accumulate more commodities and more wealth.[19] This subject must seek out an increasing amount of enjoyment in the commodity. It must view every limit that it encounters as an external barrier to its freedom to produce or to consume. Without this conception of freedom, capitalist society would grind to a halt.

What actually happens with the law is that the limit that the law erects, perceived by the subject as external, has the effect of fuelling the subject's own desire. The limits that the state poses on capital in whatever laws that it passes have the effect of nourishing the capitalist subject's desire by limiting it. All enjoyment is the enjoyment of a limit, even the enjoyment that occurs in capitalist society. But this structure keeps capitalism going only so long as the subject perceives the limit as external to its freedom.

The moment the subject recognizes the limit of the law as its own proper limit, as the result of its own act of positing of itself as part of the society, the subject breaks from the accumulative logic of the commodity form. Seeing oneself in one's limit is irreconcilable with capitalist subjectivity. This is the radical act necessary to break the hold that the capitalist system has on people. It is an act that can recapture the lost possibility for freedom that modernity announces. The subject that freely limits itself is no longer a capitalist subject.

By relating to the law as the product of subjectivity, one eliminates its ability to function as a driver to more and more accumulation. The law operates as capitalism's supplement only insofar as capitalist subjects view it as an external limit. This limit drives them to produce and consume more, to further their servitude to the commodity form. But this dynamic fundamentally changes when the subject sees its own act in the law. As such, the law no longer drives one to go beyond it. One comes to see the law as one's own internal limit rather than as an external barrier that one must attempt to transgress in order to be free. In this way, the subject attains an authentic freedom that runs contrary to the liberal freedom that keeps capitalism running.

Capitalist subjects, in order to remain capitalist subjects, must believe that the limit on enjoyment that the law announces doesn't apply to them. They will try whatever machinations to get around this limit. Perhaps they will build a rocket and fly into space to attempt to transcend the reach of the law's limit. Most, however, use more quotidian methods. One of the primary ways that ordinary capitalist subjects use to bypass the limit on enjoyment is by going to sales. The sale allows the subject to enjoy a commodity that someone else has sacrificed for.

The enjoyment of a sale relies on the dupe who one imagines paying full price. Whenever one purchases a commodity, the enjoyment of the commodity derives from the sacrifice that goes into it, including the sacrifice of money used to purchase it. But this sacrifice is painful for the subjects parting with their money. This is where the sale comes to the rescue. The sale enables one to enjoy the other sacrificing money for the commodity that one buys for less. This is why the sale provides a privileged path to enjoyment in capitalist society: it produces an enjoyment of sacrifice that someone else makes. The sale is a legal attempt to transcend the law's interdiction on complete enjoyment.

It is only thanks to events such as sales that hold within them the promise of enjoyment without restraint that capitalism keeps going. Without the lure of this possibility, people will not comport themselves like proper capitalist subjects. If they accept the law's fundamental interdiction of the possibility of enjoying themselves completely, they betray their historical mission and fail to act as proper capitalist subjects. To abandon the fantasy of complete enjoyment is to introduce a limit into a capitalist universe that cannot abide the limit.

The tendency of capitalist subjects to resort to illegal activity is not just a sign of individual failings or contingent excesses. The turn to illegality is an inevitable effect of capitalism's relationship to the law. The proper capitalist subject necessarily indulges in some form of illegality – or at least flirts with violating the law by fudging on taxes, cheating on an expense account, or taking a muffin without paying for it from the grocery store.[20] In the capitalist universe, subjects experience a moral compulsion to act illegally in order to increase their accumulation of capital. They experience the law as an inherent violation of the imperative to accumulate without limit. One accedes to the capitalist imperative by violating legal imperatives. Such is the bizarre moral situation that capitalist society engenders.

This dynamic manifests itself most overtly when companies simply resort to illegality to maximize their profits. For instance, companies may violate restrictions on product safety to sell more cheaply, exceed pollution limits to cut production costs, or disregard dumping ordinances to eliminate charges for waste disposal. In all these cases, breaking the law is the path to greater profitability.[21] Companies do it because profit has more value in the capitalist universe than legality or morality. If a company decides to act ethically, its leaders place the company's survival at grave risk. Ethical capitalism is not a sustainable position because no one else is acting ethically. The capitalist who acts ethically will not succeed as a capitalist, which is why we should never fall for the professions of ethical probity on the part of the wealthy. They accumulate wealth through a series of violations of the moral law and, almost inevitably, state law as well.[22]

In the capitalist universe, rather than producing lawful subjects, the feeling of guilt drives subjects to break the law. When one remains within the limits of the law, one experiences oneself as violating a moral imperative to accumulate without any restraint. Capitalist society is like a group of friends pressuring one to snort cocaine: to refuse is to give up sharing in the unrestrained enjoyment that everyone else appears to participate in. Those who aren't accumulating are stuck watching everyone else seeming to have a great time high on the cocaine of capital. Giving in to the law's restriction puts one at odds with the only duty that capitalism countenances.[23]

The capitalist subject paradoxically feels guilty for obeying laws and for not committing crimes for the sake of the accumulation of capital. Obeying the law leaves me feeling like a dupe, as I see everyone else prosper because they violated it. One attempts to appease the capitalist demand for more enjoyment by doing things like pirating movies online, stealthily eating grapes in the supermarket, and cheating on one's romantic partner. Capitalist anti-morality leads to little acts of theft that violate the law while obeying the capitalist imperative. The more that one obeys the law, the more one disobeys this imperative and thereby runs afoul of capitalist anti-morality and the imperative to accumulate.[24] One feels as if one has wrongly restrained one's own freedom by not disobeying the law.

But illegal activity does not necessarily in itself indicate the existence of a contradiction between capitalism and the law, since we can imagine individuals or companies content to more or less follow the law. The antagonism becomes apparent when we see law acting as a fundamental brake on capitalist development, not just on overtly criminal activity. The points where the law stops a capitalist enterprise from extracting as much value as it can from labour reveal the contradiction. The law always has the possibility to act as a fundamental brake on the accumulation of capital. At the same time, it can act as the site of an emancipatory limit that will free us from the dominance of the commodity form. But it can only do so insofar as we embrace its limit as our own, which is, unfortunately, not the prevailing tendency.

When Giorgio Agamben becomes whimsical, he imagines a future relation to the law in which we would do away with its restrictiveness while still retaining it in an impoverished form. This, he intimates, will precipitate a freer relation to the law. In *State of Exception*, he states, 'One day humanity will play with law just as children play with disused objects, not in order to restore them to their canonical use but to free them from it for good.'[25] In this utopian future where we play with the law rather than submit to its limit, Agamben imagines a freedom that transcends our imagining. But escaping the law's restrictiveness is not freedom. Under such conditions, we would be the servants of our social situation. It is only the limiting event of the law that contains within it the possibility for freedom.

Rather than dreaming of a world without the state or the law, we should embrace a state without capitalism. The constitutive limit that the state law articulates enables the anti-capitalist structure of freedom to become apparent. It emancipates us from our servitude to the capitalist imperative to accumulate, to the constant demand for more enjoyment. To see freedom in limitation rather than expansion is to participate in the constitution of a non-capitalist modernity.

Notes

1 The reference here is of course to Adam Smith, who, somewhat surprisingly, mentions the invisible hand only once in *The Wealth of Nations*. Smith says: 'By directing that industry in such a manner as its produce may be of the greatest value, he intends only his own gain; and he is in this, as in many other cases, led by an invisible hand to promote an end which was no part of his intention. Nor is it always the worse for the society that it was no part of it. By pursuing his own interest, he frequently promotes that of the society more effectually than when he really intends to promote it.' (Adam Smith, *An Inquiry into the Nature and Causes of the Wealth of Nations* (Hamburg: Management Laboratory Press, 2008), 345)

2 Libertarianism looks on state restrictions as anathema, but it remains suspiciously silent about the restrictions that the capitalist economy introduces into society. For the libertarian, these simply are not restrictions at all but effects of human nature. Anarchists are at least more consistent, inveighing against both forms of authority – that of the state and that of capitalism.

3 F. A. Hayek is one such champion of capitalism. In *The Road to Serfdom*, he states that 'the system of private property is the most important guaranty of freedom, not only for those who own property, but scarcely less for those who do not' (F. A. Hayek, *The Road to Serfdom* (Chicago: University of Chicago Press, 2007), 136). For Hayek, the bond between capitalism and freedom represents his point of departure. Any intrusion of the state on the accumulation of capital is simultaneously a setback for freedom.

4 Even a committed and thoughtful leftist like Alain Badiou sees the state as a false battleground, as a site where no authentic political intervention is possible. In *Being and Event*, he states that 'the State is precisely non-political, insofar as it cannot change, save hands, and it is well know that there is little strategic signification in

such a change' (Alain Badiou, *Being and Event*, trans. Oliver Feltham (New York: Continuum, 2005), 110). As Badiou sees it, because the state is confines to the realm of representation, it can never accommodate emancipation. But this is to undersell the emancipatory potential of both representation and the state. It is precisely the formal structure of the state and not its content that aligns it with freedom.

5 G. W. F. Hegel, *Elements of the Philosophy of Right*, trans. H. B. Nisbet, ed. Allen W. Wood (Cambridge: Cambridge University Press, 1991), 279.

6 Incidentally, this is the same term ('*bürgerliche Gesellschaft*') that Marx uses to describe capitalism in his early writings. Its English translation as 'civil society' in Hegel's works and as 'bourgeois society' in Marx's helps to mystify Hegel's critique of capitalism and his proximity to Marx.

7 Karl Marx, *The Economic and Philosophic Manuscripts of 1844*, trans. Martin Milligan (New York: International Publishers, 1964), 133.

8 Nowhere does this Marxist idea of the generalization of prostitution through the ubiquity of the commodity form find a better expression than in Jean-Luc Godard's *Deux ou trois choses que je sais d'elle* (*Two or Three Things That I Know About Her*) (1967). The film depicts Juliette Jeanson (Marina Vlady) as a middle-class mother who takes up prostitution. By turning herself into the commodity form, Jeanson does literally what everyone else in the film does metaphorically, which is why the film ends with a shot of several everyday commodities (such as laundry detergent, cigarettes, and pasta) laid out on the grass. Rather than end the film with any of the characters, Godard concludes with a depiction of the commodity form that they have taken on.

9 Giorgio Agamben, *Homo Sacer: Sovereign Power and Bare Life*, trans. Daniel Heller-Roazen (Stanford: Stanford University Press, 1998), 3.

10 In *Creation and Anarchy*, Agamben devotes an essay to analysing capitalism's pseudo-anarchism, but even here he does not focus on it as a structure of biopower. See Giorgio Agamben, *Creation and Anarchy: The Work of Art and the Religion of Capitalism*, trans. Adam Kotsko (Stanford: Stanford University Press, 2019).

11 When he distinguishes himself from the anarchism of Bakunin, Marx and Engels specifically point out that the communist movement will result in the disappearance of the state. They claim that 'once the aim of the proletarian movement, i.e., abolition of classes, is attained, the power of the State, which serves to keep the great majority of producers in bondage to a very small exploiter minority, disappears, and the functions of government become simple administrative functions' (Karl Marx and Friedrich Engels, 'Fictitious Splits in the International,' in *Collected Works*, vol. 23 (New York: International Publishers, 1988), 121).

12 Louis Althusser, 'Ideology and Ideological State Apparatuses,' in *Lenin and Philosophy and Other Essays*, trans. Ben Brewster (New York: Monthly Review Press, 1971), 137.

13 State law is not an ahistorical tool. Its role in class domination has a relatively recent origin, as Marx sees it. Law takes the place of more direct oppression. In *The Holy Family*, Marx and Engels describe the movement from aristocratic privilege to capitalist law as a shift in ideological justifications rather than as an emancipatory turn in human history. They write that under capitalism '*Law* has ... taken the place of *privilege*' (Karl Marx and Frederick Engels, *The Holy Family, or Critique of Critical Criticism* (Moscow: Progress Publishers, 1975), 145). Law is class warfare by other means. It is a privileged form of class warfare in the capitalist epoch.
14 Karl Marx, *Grundrisse*, trans. Martin Nicolaus (New York: Penguin, 1993), 334.
15 The most vociferous proponents of capitalist accumulation argue against any state restrictions at all. For them, these restrictions represent an intolerable encroachment on their right to accumulate without limit. Any form of shared sacrifice indicates the existence of a social bond, which calls into question the purported isolation of the capitalist subject. Once this subject acknowledges a social bond, it has left the terrain of capitalist ideology.
16 Claude Lévi-Strauss is the first to theorize the limitation on enjoyment that the social order requires as the prohibition of incest. According to Lévi-Strauss, while this prohibition takes dramatically different forms, it is the one universal that no society can go without. Barring incest creates a social order by introducing a limit around which the social order can form.
17 Joan Copjec, *Read My Desire: Lacan Against the Historicists* (Cambridge: MIT Press, 1994), 94.
18 Proof of this is evident in David O. Russell's *Spanking the Monkey* (1994), a film that does depict a son having incestuous sex with his mother. When it happens, she becomes just another object rather than the object of unrestrained enjoyment.
19 Even in states that allow limited or no political freedom, such as contemporary China, the liberal conception of freedom continues to operate within the capitalist economy. This situation gives the lie to Milton Friedman's wager that (liberal) economic freedom inherently leads to political freedom.
20 None of these forms of theft occur because the culprit cannot afford to act legally. The transgression offers the promise of an enjoyment that comes from transgressing all limitation. But the moment one accomplishes this act, one realizes that one has missed the promised complete enjoyment.
21 Some of the greatest anti-capitalist films focus on companies that put profitability over even the law against murder. They corporations see the law as a mere impediment to ensuring more accumulation. Perhaps the masterpiece of this genre is Tony Gilroy's *Michael Clayton* (2008), which shows a corporation, U-North, that has produced a toxic pesticide. Rather than take the product off the market, U-North continues to sell it while knowing it causes cancer because to stop doing so would be to accept a limit on accumulation. The corporation doesn't just kill people with its weed-killer, but it

uses assassins to cover the mass death that results from its product. The film correctly presents this case not as an ethical failing on the part of the company's leaders but as the inevitable end point of the logic of capitalist accumulation. It is only thwarted when the eponymous Michael Clayton (George Clooney) gives up all his own possibility for accumulating and accepts his symbolic death – loss of career, loss of money, loss of status, even loss of his wallet and watch – in order to expose the corporation's malfeasance to the police.

22 Because Immanuel Kant wrote before the full development of capitalism, he didn't see the inherent anti-capitalist ramifications of his articulation of the moral law. According to his second formulation of this law, the subject must never use others merely as means but also as ends. This formulation directly rules out almost all capitalist activity, since the capitalist who doesn't treat workers and competitors as pure means will inevitably fail as a capitalist. Even actions that seem to treat workers as ends in themselves, like throwing a birthday party for one of them, always have an increase in productivity and profitability as their end goal, thus disallowing them as moral acts in Kant's accounting.

23 As capitalism develops, morality becomes increasingly naive. The idea that someone might act for moral reasons runs completely contrary to the prevailing imperatives of capitalist society.

24 The logic of *The Godfather Part 2* (Francis Ford Coppola, 1974) is that there is no distinction between the organized crime boss and the capitalist. Although Michael Corleone (Al Pacino) appears more bloodthirsty than the capitalists in the film, everyone seeks a path around the law in order to make more money.

25 Giorgio Agamben, *State of Exception*, trans. Kevin Attell (Chicago: University of Chicago Press, 2005), 64.

Bibliography

Agamben, Giorgio. *Homo Sacer: Sovereign Power and Bare Life*. Stanford: Stanford University Press, 1998.

Agamben, Giorgio. *State of Exception*. Chicago: University of Chicago Press, 2005.

Agamben, Giorgio. *Creation and Anarchy: The Work of Art and the Religion of Capitalism*. Stanford: Stanford University Press, 2019.

Althusser, Louis. *Lenin and Philosophy and Other Essays*. New York: Monthly Review Press, 1971.

Badiou, Alain. *Being and Event*. New York: Continuum, 2005.

Copjec, Joan. *Read My Desire: Lacan Against the Historicists*. Cambridge: MIT Press, 1994.

Hayek, F. A. *The Road to Serfdom*. Chicago: University of Chicago Press, 2007.

Hegel, G. W. F. *Elements of the Philosophy of Right*. Cambridge: Cambridge University Press, 1991.
Marx, Karl. *The Economic and Philosophic Manuscripts of 1844*. New York: International Publishers, 1964.
Marx, Karl. *Grundrisse*. New York: Penguin, 1993.
Marx, Karl, and Friedrich Engels. *The Holy Family, or Critique of Critical Criticism*. Moscow: Progress Publishers, 1975.
Marx, Karl, and Friedrich Engels. *Karl Marx and Friedrich Engels Collected Works*, vol. 23. New York: International Publishers, 1988.
Smith, Adam. *An Inquiry into the Nature and Causes of the Wealth of Nations*. Hamburg: Management Laboratory Press, 2008.

11

Matrix Resurrections, or *Jouissance* as a Political Factor[1]

Slavoj Žižek

To prevent the excessive use of exploding firecrackers in the holidays period, on 23 December 2021 the Slovene ministry of defence posted a tweet entitled 'Become a soldier!' which says: 'DON'T THROW FIRECRACKERS!!! Become a volunteer soldier, ignite an explosive, throw a bomb!' The pragmatic reason is clear: Slovenia does not have mandatory military service and lacks soldiers, plus throwing firecrackers can occasionally cause some damage. However, the brutal irony of this tweet cannot but strike the eye. The common wisdom is that, in order to avoid actual violence, we should channel our need for it into its more sublimated forms like competitive sport events such as boxing. We read a lot about potentially harmful consequences of children playing violent video games of killing opponents – the debate is: do such games incite real violence or do they allow player to act out their destructive impulses in a harmless way and thus prevent real violence? But the case of the Slovene ministry tweet is almost the opposite: In order to avoid throwing firecrackers (which is, in spite of the dangers, a minimally sublimated form of violence), become a soldier and train for real violence of wounding and killing people! This perverted logic is the hidden truth of many of today's complaints that we live in a fake virtual world and that we should return to real life, whatever the risks. Far from being opposed to the fascination with fictions, the escape into the Real is its immanent other side – both extremes characterize what was once called postmodernism, and the problem with *Matrix Resurrections* is that it proposes a postmodern solution in an era which has left postmodernism behind.

What is postmodernism reduced to its minimum? In the opening scene of the TV version of Agatha Christie's *Hickory Dickory Dock*, a mouse scurries through the walls of a boarding house in London searching for morsels of food. Having made his way to a bedroom in the upstairs, he pauses and twitches his whiskers: the crumbs from a bedtime cookie are lying on a saucer, but something strange is happening and he dare not advance to the plate of crumbs – one of the humans is killing the nice young girl who always eats cookies at bedtime.[2] The mouse knows the murderer's identity but the police are confused until Poirot enters the scene. From time to time, the mouse is shown in a close-up crawling in the background; it is noticed by humans only at the very end, after Poirot explains the case – at that very moment, the mouse appears on the bookshelf behind Poirot, Poirot's secretary Ms Lemon notices it and emits a terrified scream. So, Poirot finally puts into words what the mouse knew all the time. But already this reading of the presence of the mouse in contrast to the narrative line is too much; it ignores the stupid meaningless presence of the mouse as a little bit of the real totally indifferent to human concerns – this is how postmodernism works. And my first reaction to *Matrix Resurrections* was that it has too many characters who, although officially part of the narrative, are effectively nothing but mice running around. There was much praise for the 'complexity' of the story, as if the blurring of clear choices somehow makes the movie psychologically more 'realist'. In a properly postmodern way, this complexity is inscribed into the narrative form itself as a wealth of self-reflexive moments: 'quotes' from the preceding *Matrix* trilogy, bits of dialogue which evoke theories about the *Matrix* series or theories which served as its foundation (especially Baudrillard's) – as Rightist rednecks like to say about intellectuals, Lana Wachowski is often too bright for her own good.

The first thing that strikes the eye in the multitude of reviews of *Matrix Resurrections* is how easily the movie's plot (especially its ending) was interpreted as a metaphor for our socio-economic situation. Radical Leftist pessimists read it as an insight into how, to put it bluntly, there is no hope for humanity: we cannot survive outside the Matrix (the network of corporate capital that controls us), freedom is impossible.[3] Then there are social-democratic pragmatic 'realists' who see in the movie a vision of some kind of progressive alliance between humans and machines: sixty years after the destructive Machine Wars, 'the human survivors have allied with some of the machines to fight an anomaly that jeopardizes the whole Matrix. Scarcity among the Machines led to a civil war that saw a faction of Machines and programs defect and join human society.'[4] Humans also change: Io (a human city in reality outside the Matrix led by General Niobe) is a much better place to live than Zion, their previous city in reality (there are clear hints of destructive revolutionary fanaticism in Zion in previous Matrix movies).

At this point, we need to introduce a key factor and a new figure. Scarcity among the Machines refers not just to the devastating effects of the war but above all to the lack of energy produced by humans for the matrix. Remember the basic premise of the *Matrix* series: what we experience as the reality we live in is an artificial virtual reality generated by the 'Matrix', the mega-computer directly attached to all our minds; it is in place so that we can be effectively reduced to a passive state of living batteries providing the Matrix with the necessary energy. However, the unique impact of the film resides not so much in this premise but in its central image of the millions of human beings leading a claustrophobic life in water-filled cradles, kept alive in order to generate the energy for the Matrix. So, when (some of the) people 'awaken' from their immersion into the Matrix-controlled virtual reality, this awakening is not the opening into the wide space of the external reality, but first the horrible realization of this enclosure, where each of us is effectively just a foetus-like organism, immersed in the pre-natal fluid. This utter passivity is the foreclosed fantasy that sustains our conscious experience as active, self-positing subjects – it is the ultimate *perverse* fantasy, the notion that we are *instruments* of the Other's (Matrix's) *jouissance*, sucked out of our life-substance like batteries.[5] Therein resides the true libidinal enigma of this dispositif: *why* does the Matrix need human energy? The purely energetic solution is, of course, meaningless: the Matrix could have easily found another, more reliable, source of energy which would have not demanded the extremely complex arrangement of the virtual reality coordinated for millions of human units. The only consistent answer is: the Matrix feeds on human *jouissance* – so we are back to the fundamental Lacanian thesis that the big Other itself, far from being an anonymous machine, needs the constant influx of *jouissance*. This is how we should turn around the state of things presented by the film: what the film renders as the scene of our awakening into our true situation, is effectively its exact opposite, the very fundamental fantasy that sustains our being. But how does the Matrix react to the fact that humans produce less energy? Here a new figure called the Analyst enters: he discovers that if the Matrix manipulates fears and desires of humans, they produce more energy that can be sucked by the machines:

> The Analyst is the new Architect, the manager of this new version of the Matrix. But where the Architect sought to control human minds through cold, hard math and facts, the Analyst likes to take a more personal approach, manipulating feelings to create fictions that keep the blue-pills in line. (He observes that humans will 'believe the craziest shit', which really isn't very far off from the truth if you've ever spent any time on Facebook.) The Analyst says that his approach has made humans produce more energy to feed the Machines than ever before, all while keeping them from wanting to escape the simulation.

With a little bit of irony, we could say that the Analyst corrects the falling rate of profit connected with using humans as energy batteries: he realizes that just stealing enjoyment from humans is not productive enough, and that we (the Matrix) should also manipulate the experience of humans that serve as batteries so that they will experience more enjoyment. Victims themselves have to enjoy: the more humans enjoy, the more surplus-enjoyment can be drawn from them – Lacan's parallel between surplus-value and surplus-enjoyment is again confirmed here. The problem here is just that, although the new regulator of the Matrix is called Analyst (with an obvious reference to the psychoanalyst), he does not act as a Freudian analyst but as a rather primitive utilitarian following the maxim of avoiding pain and fear and getting pleasure. Here there is no pleasure-in-pain, no 'beyond the pleasure principle', no death-drive, in contrast to the first film in which Smith, the agent of the Matrix, gives a different, much more Freudian explanation:

> Did you know that the first Matrix was designed to be a perfect human world? Where none suffered, where everyone would be happy? It was a disaster. No one would accept the program. Entire crops /of the humans serving as batteries/ were lost. Some believed we lacked the programming language to describe your perfect world. But I believe that, as a species, human beings define their reality through suffering and misery. The perfect world was a dream that your primitive cerebrum kept trying to wake up from. Which is why the Matrix was re-designed to this: the peak of your civilization.

One could effectively claim that Smith (let us not forget: not a human being as others but a virtual embodiment of the Matrix – the big Other – itself) is the stand-in for the figure of the analyst within the universe of the film much more than the Analyst. This regression of the last film is confirmed by another archaic feature: the affirmation of the productive force of sexual relationship:

> Analyst explains that after Neo and Trinity died, he resurrected them to study them, and found they overpowered the system when they worked together, but if they are kept close to each other without making contact, the other humans within the Matrix would produce more energy for the machines.[6]

In many media *Matrix Resurrections* was hailed as less 'binary', as more open towards the 'rainbow' of transgender experiences – but, as we can see, the old Hollywood formula of the production of the couple here returns again: 'Neo himself has no interest in anything except rekindling his relationship with Trinity.'[7]

This brings us back to the basic point: what does the Matrix Machine stand for if we read it not as a direct description of our reality but as a metaphor of our actual situation? It stands for two big Others, two alienated substances that control us: *capital* and *the symbolic order*, the order of symbolic fictions that structures our reality. In both cases, the danger to avoid is that of a paranoiac reading – as if capital is represented by corporate bosses or bank managers who control the game, or as if the symbolic universe is programmed by a Matrix-like machine.

There is a fundamental difference between subject's alienation in the symbolic order and the worker's alienation in capitalist social relation. We have to avoid the two symmetrical traps which open up if we insist on the homology between the two alienations: the idea that capitalist social alienation is irreducible since the signifying alienation is constitutive of subjectivity, as well as the opposite idea that the signifying alienation could be abolished in the same way Marx imagined the overcoming of capitalist alienation. The point is not just that the signifying alienation is more fundamental and will persist even if we abolish the capitalist alienation – it is a more refined one. The very figure of a subject that would overcome the signifying alienation and become a free agent who is master of the symbolic universe, i.e., who is no longer embedded in a symbolic substance, can only arise within the space of capitalist alienation, the space in which free individuals interact.

The lesson is thus that we should reject any reference to positive Life as the ground which is perverted in alienation (as Marx often does): there is no actual life external to alienation, which serves as its positive foundation. The true fetish is not the fetishist reversal of the 'natural' hierarchy (instead of actual productive life serving as the foundation of the spectral life of capital, actual life itself is reduced to a subordinate moment of the mad dance of speculative capital); *the true fetish is the very notion of direct positive life preceding alienation, an organic life whose balance was destroyed by capitalist alienation.* Such a notion is a fetish since it disavows the antagonisms that traverse the very heart of actual life.

The best-known scene in the first *Matrix* occurs when Morpheus offers Neo the choice between Blue Pill and Red Pill. But this choice is a strange no-choice: when we are immersed in virtual reality we did not take any pill, so the only choice is 'Take the red pill or do nothing.' The blue pill is a placebo, it changes nothing. Plus, we don't have only virtual reality regulated by the Matrix (accessible if we choose the blue pill) and external 'real reality' (the devastated real world full of ruins accessible if we choose the red pill); we have the Machine itself which constructs and regulates our experience. (This, the flow of digital formulas and not the ruins, is what Morpheus refers to when he says to Neo 'Welcome to the desert of the real.') This Machine is (in the film's universe) an object present in 'real reality': gigantic computers constructed by humans which hold us prisoners and regulate our experiences.

The choice between the blue pill and the red pill in the first *Matrix* movie is false, but this does not mean that all reality is just in our brain: we do interact in the real world, but through our fantasies, which are imposed on us by the symbolic universe in which we live. The symbolic universe is "transcendental", and the idea that there is an agent controlling it as an object is a paranoiac dream – the symbolic universe is no object in the world; rather, it provides the very frame through which we approach objects. In this sense, there is nothing outside the symbolic Matrix since we (subjects) *cannot step out of ourselves*, i.e., we, as it were, stand on our shoulders and draw a clear line of distinction between what only appears to us and what belongs to 'things in themselves'. The Machine, in the sense of the symbolic big Other, is Kant's transcendental frame which structures our approach to reality. 'Transcendental' does not signal the superiority of the subject but precisely its limitation: everything we experience, interact with, appears within a horizon of meaning or symbolic space into which we are 'thrown', as Heidegger would have put it. When Heidegger characterizes a human being as 'being-in-the-world', this does not mean that we are an object in the world; it means that, because of our limitation, we can never fully self-objectivize ourselves: we cannot perceive and analyse ourselves as just another object in the world precisely because we are always-already *in* the world.

Does this mean that the symbolic universe as the transcendental horizon that regulates our approach to reality is our ultimate point of reference, something behind or beneath which we cannot reach? What eludes reality (constructed/mediated by the big Other) is the Real in the Lacanian sense, something that resists symbolization.[8] David Chalmers argues that virtual reality is genuine reality:[9] virtual worlds are not second-class worlds, we can live a meaningful life in virtual reality – we may even be in a virtual world already. The difference between ordinary 'real' reality and virtual reality is secondary and will gradually, with the further development of digital media, become irrelevant since humans will be able to pass from one to another reality, each offering a space into which we will be able to totally immerse. While I accept that our access to 'real' reality is always-already virtualized and mediated by some symbolic network, I don't think this simple multiplication of realities works: what makes 'real' reality different from virtual realities is not that it is in itself more 'real' but that it is traversed by an immanent impossibility, that it stumbles upon something that eludes it, while digital/virtual realities are constrained only by the immanent rules of their construction. I propose here to read Chalmers's title 'reality+' in the same way one should read 'LGBT+': is '+' just a stand-in for the missing positions (like 'and others'), or can one be directly a '+'? The properly dialectical answer is: yes, the subject is inscribed into a series of its possible identities precisely as a +, as an excess that eludes every identification. What this means is that the subject is a + and simultaneously a −, a lack in the signifying chain: it is the excess itself which functions as a lack. And the same goes for reality: there are not simply 'many realities' but many 'realities+', and this excess is inscribed into 'real reality' as a minus, as its constitutive lack.

Now we come to the key point: Lacan's key name for the Real is *jouissance*, and this is why the Matrix needs humans: to appropriate from them *jouissance* by means of which it can fill in (or, rather, cover up) its inconsistencies and antagonisms.[10] Today, however, we are getting closer and closer to manufactured machines which promise to provide a virtual universe into which we can enter (or which controls us against our will). China's Academy of Military Medical Sciences pursues what it calls the 'intelligentization' of warfare: 'War has started to shift from the pursuit of destroying bodies to paralyzing and controlling the opponent.'[11] We can be sure that the West is doing the same – the only difference will be (maybe) that if it goes public about it, there will be a humanitarian twist ('we are not killing humans, just for a brief time diverting their minds').

One of the names of 'taking the blue pill' is Zuckerberg's project of 'metaverse': we take the blue pill by registering in the meta-verse in which the limitations, tensions and frustrations of ordinary reality are magically left behind – but we have to pay a big price for it: 'Mark Zuckerberg "has unilateral control over 3 billion people" due to his unassailable position at the top of Facebook, the whistleblower Frances Haugen told to the British MPs as she called for urgent external regulation to rein in the tech company's management and reduce the harm being done to society.'[12] The big achievement of modernity, the public space, is thus disappearing. Days after the Haugen revelations, Zuckerberg announced that his company will change its name from 'Facebook' to 'Meta', and outlined his vision of 'metaverse' in a speech that is a true *neo-feudal manifesto*:

> Zuckerberg wants the metaverse to ultimately encompass the rest of our reality – connecting bits of real space here to real space there, while totally

subsuming what we think of as the real world. In the virtual and augmented future Facebook has planned for us, it's not that Zuckerberg's simulations will rise to the level of reality, it's that our behaviors and interactions will become so standardized and mechanical that it won't even matter. Instead of making human facial expressions, our avatars can make iconic thumbs-up gestures. Instead of sharing air and space together, we can collaborate on a digital document. We learn to downgrade our experience of being together with another human being to seeing their projection overlaid into the room like an augmented reality Pokemon figure.[13]

Metaverse will act as a virtual space beyond (meta) our fractured and hurtful reality, in which we will smoothly interact through our avatars, with elements of augmented reality (that is, reality overlaid with digital signs). It will thus be nothing less than meta-physics actualized: a meta-physical space fully subsuming reality, which is allowed to enter it in a fragmented form only insofar as it is overlaid with digital guidelines manipulating our perception and intervention. And the catch is that we will get a commons which is privately owned, with a private feudal Lord overseeing and regulating our interaction.

This brings us back to the beginning of the movie where Neo visits a therapist (Analyst) in recovery from a suicide attempt. The source of his suffering is that he has no way of verifying the reality of his confused thoughts, so he is afraid of losing his mind. In the course of the film we learn that 'the therapist is the least trustworthy source that Neo could have turned to. The therapist is not just part of a fantasy that might be a reality, and vice versa [...] He is just one more layer of fantasy-as-reality, and reality-as-fantasy, a mess of whims, and desires, and dreams that exists in two states at once.' Is, then, Neo's suspicion which drove him into suicide not just confirmed?

The film's end brings hope by merely giving the opposite spin to this insight: yes, our world is composed just of layers of 'fantasy-as-reality, and reality-as-fantasy, a mess of whims, and desires,' i.e. there is no Archimedean point which eludes the deceitful layers of fake realities. However, this very fact opens up a new space of freedom – the freedom to intervene and rewrite fictions that dominate us. Since our world is composed just of layers of 'fantasy-as-reality, and reality-as-fantasy, a mess of whims, and desires,' this means that the Matrix is also a mess: the paranoiac version is wrong, there is no hidden agent (Architect or Analyst) who controls it all and secretly pulls the strings. The lesson is that 'we should learn to fully embrace the power of the stories that we spin for ourselves, whether they be video games or complex narratives about our own pasts [...] we might rewrite *everything*. We can make of fear and desire as we wish; we can alter and shape the people who we love, and we dream of.' The movie thus ends with a rather boring version of the postmodern notion that there is no ultimate 'real reality', just an interplay of the multitude of digital fictions:

> Neo and Trinity have given up on the search of epistemic foundations. They do not kill the therapist who has kept them in the bondage of The Matrix. Instead, they thank him. After all, through his work, they have discovered the great power of re-description, the freedom that comes when we stop our search for truth, whatever that nebulous concept might mean, and strive forever for new ways of understanding ourselves. And then, arm in arm, they take off, flying through a world that is theirs to make of.[14]

The movie's premise that machines need humans is thus correct – they need us not for our intelligence and conscious planning but at a more elementary level of libidinal economy. The idea that machines could reproduce without humans is similar to the dream of market economy reproducing itself without humans wrong. Some analysts recently proposed the idea that, with the explosive growth of robotization of production and of artificial intelligence, which will more and more play the managerial role of organizing production, capitalism will gradually morph into a self-reproducing monster, a network of digital and production machines with less and less need for humans. Property and stocks will remain, but competition will be carried out automatically, just to optimize profit and productivity. So, for whom or what will things be produced? Will humans not remain as consumers? Ideally, we can even imagine machines just feeding each other, producing machine parts, energy and so on. Perversely attractive as it is, this prospect is an ideological fantasy: capital is not an objective fact like a mountain or a machine which will remain even if all people around it disappear. Rather, it exists only as a virtual Other of the social, a 'reified' form of social relation, in the same way that the value of stocks is the outcome of the interaction of thousands of individuals but appear to each of them as something objectively given.

Lacan is fully aware that *jouissance* is a political factor: 'the intrusion into the political can only be made by recognizing that the only discourse there is [...] is the discourse of *jouissance*.'[15] In short, ideology and politics can be explained neither by crude reference to actual class interests nor by a discourse-analysis that focuses on the competitive game for discursive hegemony, for which ideology will provide the dominant cognitive mapping of the situation. Even a brief look at racism and sexism suffices to see how, for an ideology to really take hold of us, it has to mobilize the dimension of *jouissance*. Oppression of women is sustained by the fear that, if not controlled, women will explode in excessive pleasures. Racism envies the Other's enjoyments in that it perceives this Other as a threat to forms of enjoyment that constitute our way of life. All such passionate ideological investments are traversed by sadism, masochism and all their perverted combinations, like enjoying one's own humiliation.

The extreme case of *jouissance* today is, of course, the prospect of apocalypse in all its versions (pandemic, ecological catastrophes, nuclear war, dissolution of social order) inclusive of total knowledge itself: wouldn't it be properly apocalyptic to gain a direct access another's stream of thoughts? Lorenzo Chiesa deftly points out that this desire is 'manifestly witnessed by our current fascination with virological, ecological, and technological figures of the Apocalypse. Adopting the terminology of *Seminar XX*, we could also call it a desire to be One in order to absolutely enjoy through and in (sexual) knowledge, a desire which instead leads to maximal entropy.'[16] Just think about snuff movies (pornographic films that shows the actual torture and murder of one of the performers during the sexual interaction) – really, as Lacan put it in a concise way, 'everyone is dying to know what would happen if things went really bad'.[17] This is why we are so fascinated by the precise features of a dystopian reality, from *Handmaid's Tale* and stories about European daily life if Hitler had won the war up to the future life on a devastated earth. 'Dying to know' should be taken here in its ambiguity: it means that I would really like to know it and that this knowledge would bring me to death.

What the notion of 'fully knowing a catastrophe' misses is the fact that, when we get too close to a catastrophe, the distance necessary for knowledge breaks down. We cannot combine the real of a full catastrophe with the safe distance of knowledge (like the idea of entering the sun or a black hole and registering what goes on down there). The lesson of Hegel's absolute knowing is exactly the opposite: it is a knowing which includes its own incompleteness. Knowledge is non-all in the Lacanian sense: it is not that something a priori eludes it, there is nothing that eludes it, but for this very reason it cannot be totalized. G. K. Chesterton wrote that that Christianity acknowledges one big mystery (God) as the exception which allows a Christian to perceive and understand all other reality as completely rational and knowable. For a materialist, the situation is exactly the opposite: there is no exception, which is why all reality is full of mysteries (just think of the mysteries of quantum physics). We can say that, in the same sense that anti-semitism is the stupid man's anti-capitalism, the full knowledge of an apocalypse is stupid man's version of Hegel's absolute knowing.

Notes

1. This is a revised version of a short piece published in *The Philosophical Salon* on 10 January 2022 with the title of 'A Muddle of a Movie'.
2. Description taken from Amazon.com: Customer reviews: Poirot - Hickory Dickory Dock.
3. https://gossipchimp.com/what-the-matrix-resurrections-is-telling-us-there-is-no-hope-for-humanity/
4. https://www.denofgeek.com/movies/the-matrix-resurrections-ending-spoilers/
5. I refer here to my reading of the first *Matrix* movie available online at https://www.lacan.com/Žižek-matrix.htm.
6. Every reader will have noticed that, in my description of the movie, I rely heavily on a multitude of reviews which I extensively quote. The reason is now clear: in spite of its occasional brilliance, the film is ultimately not worth seeing – which is why I also wrote this review without seeing it. The editorial that appeared in *Pravda* on 28 January 1936 brutally dismissed Shostakovich's opera *Lady Macbeth of the Mtsensk District* as 'Muddle Instead of Music' (the text's title). Although *Matrix Resurrections* is very intelligently made and full of admirable effects, it ultimately remains a muddle instead of a movie. *Resurrections* is the fourth film in the *Matrix* series, so let us just hope that Lana's next movie will be what the fifth symphony was for Shostakovich: an American artist's creative response to justified criticism.
7. https://www.theverge.com/2021/12/21/22841582/matrix-resurrections-lana-wachowski-keanu-reeves-carrie-anne-moss-review
8. I have written about this extensively in my previous books.
9. See David Chalmers, *Reality+: Virtual Worlds and the Problems of Philosophy* (London: Allen Lane, 2022).
10. I have dealt with the notion of the Real in most of my philosophical books – see, for example, *Absolute Recoil* (London: Verso Books 2015).
11. https://www.washingtontimes.com/news/2021/dec/29/pla-brain-control-warfare-work-revealed/
12. https://www.theguardian.com/technology/2021/oct/25/facebook-whistleblower-frances-haugen-calls-for-urgent-external-regulation
13. https://edition.cnn.com/2021/10/28/opinions/zuckerberg-facebook-meta-rushkoff/index.html
14. https://ethics.org.au/nothing-but-a-brain-the-philosophy-of-the-matrix-resurrections/

15 Jacques Lacan, *The Other Side of Psychoanalysis. The Seminar of Jacques Lacan, Book XVII* (New York: Norton 2007), 78.
16 Lorenzo Chiesa, '*Anthropie*: Beside the Pleasure Principle', in *Continental Thought and Theory* 3, no. 2 (2021), 151.
17 Jacques Lacan, *The Other Side of* Psychoanalysis, 176–7.

Bibliography

Chalmers, David. *Reality+: Virtual Worlds and the Problems of Philosophy*. London: Allen Lane, 2022.

Chiesa, Lorenzo. '*Anthropie*: Beside the Pleasure Principle'. *Continental Thought and Theory* 3, no. 2 (2021), 141–53.

Lacan, Jacques. *The Other Side of Psychoanalysis. The Seminar of Jacques Lacan, Book XVII*. New York: Norton 2007.

The Perfect Crime? Baudrillard, Covid-19 and Capitalist Virulence

Fabio Vighi

Introduction

When he first introduced the notion of *simulation* in the early 1970s,[1] Jean Baudrillard was acutely aware that modernity was being replaced by postmodernity. For him, this shift meant that social relations were no longer grounded in *production* but in the serial *reproduction* of reality's signs. With the rise of post-industrial consumer capitalism, in other words, referents are gradually substituted by the potentially endless reduplication of their signs: 'the annihilation of any goal as regards the contents of production allows the latter to function as a code' and therefore 'to escape into infinite speculation, beyond all reference to a real of production, or even to a gold-standard'.[2] In such a regime, society is organized around pre-arranged models where real conflicts and contradictions are neutralized by the principle of indifference and commutability ('of the beautiful and the ugly in fashion, of the left and the right in politics, of the true and the false in every media message').[3]

Crucially, for Baudrillard the coding of reality is imposed on societies in the form of a *gift* that blackmails everyone into obedience. Contemporary capitalism retains the exclusivity of gift-giving, which it uses to exert real domination. In this respect, Baudrillard effectively developed a radicalised version of Marcel Mauss's theory of the gift by conceiving the latter not as a type of generous exchange that predates or exceeds political economy,[4] but as the ideological core of modern capitalist societies. In contemporary capitalism, gift-giving is correlative to absolute symbolic power. As such, it materializes not only as the reward of wage labour, but especially as ubiquitous network of media information, virtual interactivity, and the normativity of 'protection agency, security, gratification, and the solicitation of the social from which nothing is any longer permitted to escape'.[5] As capitalist gifts become increasingly oppressive and unilateral, strategies of refusal – which Baudrillard invokes through the mobilization of 'counter-gifts'[6] – turn out to be impracticable. Simulation today would seem to denote the intrinsically totalitarian transfiguration of the real into the virtual code, which, in dramatically accelerating the elimination of referentiality (i.e., of its ontological ambiguity), consigns the social to its viral reproduction.

Since the 1970s, then, Baudrillard had lamented the abandonment of 'the referential base of the sign, with its singularity and the opacity of its signified in the real, its very powerful affect and its minimal commutability'. The 'hot phase' of the sign, which was still attached to symbolically authoritative signifiers, was being replaced by its 'cool phase', characterized by 'the pure play of the values of discourse [...] the omnipotence of operational simulation'.[7] In the new millennium, this epochal shift threatens 'the glaciation of meaning',[8] for the increasing fascination with hyper-mediatized signs is proportional to a growing disaffection with negativity, critical thinking, political struggle and subversion. In what follows, I attempt to correlate Baudrillard's reflections on simulation with both the implosion of contemporary capitalism and the ideological character of the Covid-19 crisis. By ideology I do not mean a lie that conceals the truth or distorts reality, but reality itself as the space of our social norms and interactions, which today is increasingly perceived as global, limitless and unregulated. My central assumption is that, far from being the 'guru of postmodernism',[9] as he was often labelled, Baudrillard provides one of the most acute critiques of our postmodern condition.

Viral simulations

Baudrillard's theory of simulation does not merely amount to another version of Marshall McLuhan's well-known claim that real contents and referents are neutralized by the medium ('the medium is the message').[10] Rather, it implies that the medium itself, insofar as it becomes hegemonic through an operational code, generates its own 'integral reality', which Baudrillard called *hyperreality*:

> The real is produced from miniaturized units, from matrices, memory banks and command models – and with these, it can be reproduced an indefinite number of times. It no longer has to be rational, since it is no longer measured against some ideal or negative instance. It is nothing more than operational. In fact, since it is no longer enveloped by an imaginary, it is no longer real at all. It

is hyperreal, the product of an irradiating synthesis of combinatory models in a hyperspace without atmosphere.[11]

For Baudrillard, the 'disappearance of reality' is akin to 'a perfect crime',[12] since the real evaporates before our eyes without leaving traces of its former configuration. All we are left with is a gigantic machinery of simulation, which increasingly signals the impossibility of critical intervention either through content or form. Every attempt to intervene is defused in advance by the very process of simulation, where vacuous transparency replaces the opacity of the real. Alienation itself can no longer be grasped because ideological manipulation now comes in the form of 'social control by means of prediction, simulation, programmed anticipation and indeterminate mutation', which takes us '[f]rom a capitalist productivist society to a neo-capitalist cybernetic order, aiming this time at absolute control'.[13] As a consequence, our enslavement to the virtual matrix of contemporary capitalism and its numbing utopia (a dimensionless, non-representational space-time where countless agents meet to share and create their 'realities') radically undermines our capacity to build relations based on symbolic exchange. Thus, society ends up buried beneath the simulation of the real, just as sexuality is buried beneath pornography:[14]

> This is really what we are seeing today: the disintegration of the whole idea of the social, the consumption and involution of the social, the breakdown of the social simulacrum, a genuine defiance of the constructive and productive approach to the social which dominates us. All quite suddenly, as if the social had never existed. A breakdown which has all the features of a catastrophe, not an evolution or revolution.[15]

The dissolution of the social bond is offset by the triumph of *simulated sociality*, which is assembled around 'the lowest form of social energy: that of an environmental, behavioral utility. Such is the face of the social for us – its entropic form – the other face of its death'.[16] While Baudrillard shared the Freudian postulate that all human communities depend on a degree of illusion, repression and alienation, he argued that, with the advent of viral simulation, the possibility of perceiving the alienating substance of the social tends to vanish. The more we are denied the experience of the gap between the real and its organisation into a socio-symbolic structure, the more alienation gets naturalized, thus morphing into hyperreality. When the sign loses its symbolic anchoring in the real, it begins to free-float, proliferating in metastatic fashion, while meanings turn commutable and superfluous. The rational exercise of thought is thus interdicted, as reality is replaced by self-reproducing simulacra.

In Baudrillard's view, the endless flow of information, the entropic virulence of what today we should call the 'corporate-owned mainstream media metaverse', has far more ideological traction than any kind of physical surveillance, since the media behave like a genetic code that ceaselessly defuse any spark of critical awareness and political contestation: 'Everywhere socialization is measured according to exposure through media messages. Those who are under-exposed to the media are virtually asocial or desocialized.'[17] Especially with the advent of digitality, we enter a flat social ontology without breaks or ruptures, a spurious discourse of pure operationality where the subject is progressively obliterated. We are only free to slot into a pre-packaged binary feedback system where 'differential poles implode into each other'.[18] Thus, 'the cool universe of digitality', which 'has absorbed the world of metaphor and metonymy',[19] turns ubiquitous communication and connectedness into repressive banality (or, to say it with Marcuse, into 'repressive desublimation').[20] Media virality, then, imposes itself with the force of a magnetic field made of largely insignificant diffractions and polarizations, whose only role is to reaffirm a code based on the universal principle of equivalence and exchangeability.

The above insights are reflected in Baudrillard's early 1980s remarks on New York's World Trade Centre as the architectural embodiment of the binary code of hyperreality:

> Why are there *two* towers at New York's World Trade Center? All of Manhattan's great buildings were always happy enough to affront each other in a competitive verticality, the result of which is an architectural panorama in the image of the capitalist system: a pyramidal jungle, all the buildings attacking each other. [...] This image has completely changed in the past few years. [...] Buildings are no longer obelisks, but lean one upon the other, no longer suspicious one of the other, like columns in a statistical graph. This new architecture incarnates a system that is no longer competitive, but compatible, and where competition has disappeared for the benefit of correlations. [...] This architectural graphism is that of the monopoly; the two W.T.C. towers, perfect parallelepipeds a ¼-mile high on a square base, perfectly balanced and blind communicating vessels. The fact that there are two of them *signifies* the end of competition, the end of all original reference. [...] There is a particular fascination in this reduplication. As high as they are, higher than all the others, the two towers signify nevertheless the end of verticality.[21]

Here, the 'end of verticality' informs a fake social bond where the subject is *foreclosed*, as Jacques Lacan had put it in his discussions of the 'capitalist discourse.'[22] In the digital system, reality is hyper-realized and simultaneously de-realized into pure operationality. No wonder that *The Matrix* (Wachowski brothers, 1999) was inspired by Baudrillard's notion of simulation – even though Baudrillard later remarked that the film was too Platonic: 'The Matrix is the kind of film about the matrix that the matrix would have been able to produce.'[23]

With simulation, then, the *irreducible ambivalence of the real* is wiped out by the dogma of the infinite reproducibility of reality's virtualized signs. In this respect, the significance of Andy Warhol, who for Baudrillard was the last great modern artist, lies precisely in *dramatizing* the operational principle of seriality that lies at the heart of global capitalism, exemplified today by the purely speculative play of financial signifiers. An example of this simulation can be found in Warhol's famous grids of Marilyn Monroe, Campbell's soup and his other replicas. What we witness here is the potentially infinite virtual reproduction of the same image (i.e., the same commodified sign) through minimal differences that are integral to the master code. With digitality, the potential for serial simulation reaches its apex, for all reality can now be coded in a virtual reproductive flow. And all that matters is that it continues to flow, to feign some kind of existence. As anticipated, the financialization of the economy provides a perfect illustration of this logic. Our economies are increasingly replete with enormous masses of fictitious capital that, to avoid collapse, blindly continue to follow their generative flows, while condemning large parts of the world to immiseration and destruction. Contemporary capitalism increasingly resembles an enormous dump of rotting nominal values (as in the balance sheets of central banks) replicating themselves in a parallel orbit with respect to the human suffering on the ground – an insanity which the International Monetary Fund and the *Financial Times* today elegantly call 'The Great Disconnect'.[24] In 1988, Baudrillard had captured this criminal decoupling with the following provocation:

> But can we still speak of the 'economy'? Or, indeed, of political economy (the logic of capital)? Certainly not. At the very least, the striking prominence of the economy at the moment has not at all the same meaning it had in the classical or Marxist analysis. For it is no longer in any sense driven by the infrastructure of material production, nor indeed by the superstructure. The engine of the economy is the destructuring of value, the destabilizing of markets and real economies, the triumph of an economy relieved of ideologies, social sciences, history and political economy and yielded up to pure speculation; it is the triumph of a virtual economy relieved of real economies (not really, of course, but virtually: yet it is not reality which holds sway today but virtuality); *the triumph of a viral economy which connects up in this way with all the other viral*

processes. It is as an arena of special effects, of unpredictable (almost meteorological) happenings – as the destruction and exacerbation of its own logic – that it is becoming once again a kind of exemplary theatre of current events.[25]

In partial disagreement with Baudrillard, I contend that within an economy driven by the self-referential logic of its financial industry, capital in fact returns to itself, i.e., it emerges for what it always was: a cold, anonymous, and merciless mechanism of self-reproduction. Today we are reminded that the inhuman face of capital was always its true face. As its socio-symbolic mask (value-productive labour) evaporates under the blows of technological automation, we have a chance to appreciate capital in its elementary form, which is the measure of both its freedom and undoing. Capital, in other words, becomes identical with the unbroken accumulation of self-cloning fetish-signs. And dancing to the rhythm of its virtual melody, it turns into what it always-already was: a purely immanent phenomenon, indifferent to human suffering and destined to self-destruction. But how can a global system that has expunged all externality – a system that coincides with its own operational code of endless simulation – manage to support itself?

The conspiracy of the Good

To answer the above question, let us quickly revisit a short polemical piece by Baudrillard published in *Libération* on 5 May 1997, titled 'La conjuration des imbéciles' (The Conspiracy of Imbeciles).[26] In this text the author lashes out against the insignificance of contemporary art and, especially, the conformist moralism of the democratic Left in confronting the political success, in France, of Jean-Marie Le Pen's *Front National*. As he had put it in *The Conspiracy of Art* (1996), contemporary art is merely an expression of hyperreality, and therefore cannot ignite any meaningful critique of the status quo:

> Nothing differentiates it [contemporary art] from technical, advertising, media, financial and digital operations. There is no more transcendence, no more divergence, nothing from another scene: it is a reflective game with the contemporary world as it happens. This is why contemporary art is null and void: it and the world form a zero-sum equation.[27]

Similarly, contemporary politics is engaged in 'reproducing itself in an endogamous confusion of all persuasions – the incestuous alliance of Right and Left producing an entire pathology and degeneracy characteristic of inbreeding.'[28]

Going back to Baudrillard's piece for *Libération*, two questions there strike at the heart of our present: 'Is it possible today to utter anything unusual, insolent, heterodox or paradoxical without being labelled a far-right extremist? [...] Why has everything that is moral, compliant and conformist, which was traditionally on the right, now moved to the left?' Summarizing an argument that he had repeatedly developed from the 1980s onward, Baudrillard contends that the left, 'by stripping itself of all political energy,' has become 'a purely moral jurisdiction, embodiment of universal values, champion of the kingdom of Virtue and guardian of the museum values of Good and Truth; a jurisdiction that can hold everyone accountable without having to answer to anyone.' Given this context, 'repressed political energy necessarily crystallizes elsewhere – in the enemy's camp. The left, therefore, by embodying the reign of Virtue, which is also the reign of the greatest hypocrisy, can only feed Evil.'

Baudrillard's point is that the fluid and non-referential 'values' of present-day ideology affirm themselves through a mythopoeic of evil and misfortune, whose role is to set up the moralistic horizon upon which capital continues to function. This is one of the reasons why today's fixation with emergencies is capital's perfect alibi. As argued in *Simulations*: 'Capital, which is immoral and unscrupulous, can only function behind a moral superstructure, and whoever regenerates this public morality (by indignation, denunciation, etc.), spontaneously furthers the order of capital.'[29] This claim is particularly useful if we are to grasp our post-political epoch's ideological obsession with morality – an obsession which necessitates the relentless production of crises and 'ethical deficits'. Our precarious membership in the neoliberal galaxy needs constant support from evil narratives, whose function is to consolidate the illusion that capitalism, which identifies us socially and psychologically, is morally grounded. Such an illusion is imperative for a world that has eliminated all external referents, starting from its own labour substance. A global economic system that has reached saturation – i.e., that can no longer extract sufficient surplus-value from labour-power for its own reproduction – cannot stand on its own feet. Rather, it becomes hostage to a perverse logic based on the creation of ferocious enemies who are ready to annihilate us:

> In a society which seeks – by prophylactic measures, by annihilating its own natural referents, by whitewashing violence, by exterminating all germs and all of the accursed share, by performing cosmetic surgery on the negative – to concern itself solely with quantified management and with the discourse of the Good, in a society where it is no longer possible to speak Evil, Evil has metamorphosed into all the viral and terroristic forms that obsess us.[30]

These 'viral and terroristic forms' can now be regarded as consubstantial with contemporary subjectivity, which is why the default position of today's liberal subject is that of the narcissistic victim obsessed with their own safety and devoted to the Bible of political correctness. In Baudrillard's words, contemporary ideology thrives on a supremely disingenuous 'culture of misfortune':[31] an aristocratic egalitarianism based on the dogma of victimhood, a form of reverse elitism that a priori reduces the subject to a fragile human being threatened by malignant forces. The paradox is that the more we perceive ourselves as intrinsically exposed to harassment and injury (from the gaze of a potential stalker to the contagion of a killer-virus), the more we respond by avowing the cynical 'rationality' of capitalist accumulation, now increasingly supplemented by state authoritarianism. In other words, reducing the subject to the status of a victim at the mercy of hostile forces intrinsically validates two ideological pillars of contemporary capitalism: the belief in 'universal rights' insofar as they allow us to continue to pursue egotistic self-interest; and the projection of victimhood on 'less fortunate' others (i.e., immigrants), which keeps them into a state of passivity, preventing them from acting against the very conditions that cause their 'misfortune'. As Baudrillard put it in one of his later works: 'Compassion [...] is useless and perverse: it merely adds to the inferiority of the victim.'[32] Within this line of thinking, the construction of 'evil narratives' – intended as narratives of misfortune, states of emergency, and a generalised ethical deficit – becomes the essential ideological ingredient for capitalist accumulation in the age of its virtualisation (or de-substantialization). Differently put: the flow of financial capital, supported by the creation of enormous masses of insubstantial money central banks, hinges on its cross-fertilization with mythologies of evil, whose purpose is to shelter us from the 'primal scene' of the 'incomprehensible ferocity' and 'fundamental immorality' of capital.[33]

It is revealing that, in the social scene set up by contemporary ideology, evil emerges as an obscene populist mob, that 'basket of deplorables' (Hillary Clinton) whom all liberals love to hate.[34] However, today's liberal moralists conveniently forget how the humanity they want to protect has already been plundered, crushed, and at best sold off to the highest bidder precisely by the knights of the liberal apocalypse. There is a simple claim in Baudrillard's *Libération* text that perfectly captures the hypocrisy I am referring to: 'Le Pen is criticized for rejecting and excluding immigrants, *but this is nothing compared to the processes of social exclusion that take place everywhere.*' Why limit yourself to fighting the racism of those who reject immigrants, when social discrimination is everywhere, in the form of exclusion, ghettoization, slave-like exploitation and war? Why persist in seeing only the populist walls, when globalization itself is patently criminal in the ways it promotes the interests of capital? Ultimately, perhaps, the answer is simple: by blaming the bad guy, we protect ourselves from our intimate collusion with systemic violence, upon which our identities (and privileges) are based. As shown by Domenico Losurdo,[35] the civil conquests of liberalism were established in symbiosis with the modern tragedies of slavery, deportation, and genocide.

Bereft of political energy, the postmodern left was always eager to play the morality game, to the extent that 'capitalism with a human face' suddenly became its only slogan. Investing in capital's social responsibility – i.e., choosing to disavow the fact that '[c]apital doesn't give a damn about the [social] contract' since 'it is a monstrous unprincipled undertaking, nothing more'[36] – was, for Baudrillard, the left's cardinal sin, the sign of its capitulation to the theatre of post-political simulations. By trading in class struggle and a radical critique of capital for moral immunity, the postmodern left has now become overtly reactionary. Its fixation on political correctness and identity politics is, fundamentally, a hypocritical gesture whose purpose is to conceal the catastrophic decision to abandon, and even sabotage, any expression of political antagonism. The result is that, by supporting the global destructiveness of capital through ethical and humanitarian pretences, the left does the job of the right more efficiently than the right itself.

Hypnotic deterrence

Drawing on the main theme of Roberto Esposito's philosophy,[37] today's 'humanitarian' obsession with vaccines mandates should also be read as an *immunological* metaphor that accurately depicts our *zeitgeist*. While Covid-19 mass vaccination (or, more precisely, mass genetic treatment) responds in large part to the logic of profit-making, it also captures the functioning of a global power apparatus that self-inoculates 'evil pathogens' to secure its own reproduction. From Le Pen to Trump, from Saddam Hussein's weapons of mass destruction to Islamic terrorism, from Iran's nuclear program to Putin's war, we are looking at a series of immunological operations whose function is to legitimize an implosive socio-economic model by unloading its murderous madness on 'flavour-of-the-month' villains. In this respect, Max Horkheimer's old admonition is more relevant than ever: 'Whoever is not willing to talk about capitalism should also keep quiet about fascism. [...] The totalitarian order differs from its bourgeois predecessor only in that it has lost its inhibitions.'[38]

Consider the semantic continuity between 'virus' and 'information'. Every virus carries information, and the 'viral load' has to do with the pathogen's ability to penetrate our line of defence, our immune system, or, figuratively, our subjectivity.[39] In Baudrillard's terms, the virus is also a metaphor for the power of the information system, which is particularly pervasive in the age of digitality. Let us take the example of the 6 January 2021 events in Washington, DC, where a group of Donald Trump supporters stormed the Capitol. The first thing to notice here is the speed with which the news was universally codified and circulated ('memed') by the media as a 'Coup d'état'. The irresistible viral force with which the message of the 'attack on democracy' flooded mainstream media highlighted a spatiotemporal paradox that we are increasingly exposed to in our daily lives: the news we are given for consumption precedes the actual facts, shaping their content in advance. For months, the corporate-owned media had prepared us for the likelihood of a 'Trump coup' in the event of his defeat at the presidential elections. So when the plebs entered the sacred temple of Western politics, we had a perfect demonstration of how information today travels faster than facts. Put differently: referential reality is increasingly vanishing into the virtual form of its coded simulation, where it resurrects as hyperreal.

This para-religious capacity to generate reality before reality happens is truly hypnotic; it corresponds to what Baudrillard called the 'ecstasy of communication'.[40] We should therefore insist that, in our age of endemic simulation,

> Facts no longer have any trajectory of their own, they arise at the intersection of the models; [...] This anticipation, this precession, this short-circuit, this confusion of the fact with its model (no more divergence of meaning, no more dialectical polarity, no more negative electricity or implosion of power) is what each time allows for all the possible interpretations, even the most contradictory – all are true, in the sense that their truth is exchangeable, in the image of the models from which they proceed, in a generalized cycle.[41]

The ideological significance of simulation for the post-political management of capital's terminal crisis – the valorization crisis exploded in the 1970s with the Third Industrial Revolution – cannot be underestimated. Our implosive socioeconomic order thrives on *political hyperrealism*, a regulated game of false binary oppositions that is now completely detached from our social substance, just as the financial sector is detached from the real economy. The exercise of bipartite alternation in our 'democratic systems' is a perfect illustration of what

Baudrillard meant by simulation: 'simulation of opposition between two parties, absorption of their respective objectives, reversibility of the entire discourse one into the other'. This implies 'a *tactical doubling of monopoly*', since 'any unitary system, if it wishes to survive, must acquire a *binary regulation*'. Thus, 'power is absolute only if it is capable of diffraction into various equivalents' – all responding to a binary matrix whose functioning prevents real antagonism from emerging.[42]

In this respect, the only conspiracy we should denounce here is the one concerning the accelerated dispossession of our lives by the hyper-mediatized operational system of contemporary capitalism. It is capital itself, through its self-regulated corporatocracy, that wages a total war on dissent and contradiction, attempting to neutralize in advance any radically critical intervention into its *modus operandi*. The only narratives we are left with are pathetic binary duplications of each other that are cynically peddled as constitutive of our 'healthy democratic systems'. Let us remind ourselves that the true aim of simulation is to collapse the difference between the (inherently ambiguous) real and its (socially effective) illusion, so that the real vanishes and the illusion morphs into unassailable hyperreality. The goal is to eliminate any remnant of the ontologically divisive and conflictual real, so that reality, insofar as it is mediated by the capitalist mode of production, appears as indisputable and factual as the very existence of the sky above our heads. What is at stake, then, is the reproduction of a socio-economic order that, having destroyed its substance (value-productive wage labour), condemns itself to faking its existence by simulating its conditions of possibility (real economic growth). Since the 2007–08 economic crisis, the monetary simulation of real growth, with attendant currency devaluation, has turned into the absolutely necessary precondition of capitalist accumulation. Hence we could argue, with Baudrillard, that we increasingly live in a single totalizing conspiracy, which as such 'has no author' since we are all 'caught up in a certain form of shameful complicity with the system itself'.[43] The proliferation of preformatted and propagandized pseudo-events is symptomatic of the totalizing ideological *dispositif* that mediates our existence globally. Today the illusion of growth, which is the very essence of capitalism, is replaced by an all-encompassing hyperreality where growth is made to coincide with its monetary simulation. And capitalist hyperreality is now turning openly totalitarian. In order to conceal an increasingly volatile and unmanageable dynamic of social reproduction, it has no choice but to embrace its tyrannical vocation.

The totalitarian spirit of contemporary capitalism is demonstrated by our helplessness vis-à-vis an ideology that no longer merely obscures or manipulates evidence but rather hides it in plain sight. Systemic contradictions and inconsistencies are perfectly available for our scrutiny, and yet we remain blind to them. As such, the hyperreal bubble we live in resembles a 'perfect crime', as masterfully narrated by Edgar Allan Poe in his 1844 short story 'The Purloined Letter'. It is a crime against reality that resides in silencing reality *through reality itself*. The ideology of simulation is predicated upon the propagation of signs that remove reality by reproducing it serially, not by hiding it. The Covid-19 narrative is a perfect exemplification of this logic: strictly speaking, the pandemic does not originate in the spreading of a lethal virus, but in the viral reduplication of its countless signs (statistics, lockdowns, prediction models etc.), which produce the 'fear matrix' that frames us. The Covid-19 world was locked up in a structure of pure repetition, the magnitude of which had never been experienced before.

Knowing that the coronavirus narrative is deeply unreliable does not in itself undermine its ideological effectiveness. While we might doubt the basic reasoning behind pandemic restrictions, our critical resistance is a priori demolished by the repetition of apocalyptic memoranda of the pathogen's deadliness. In pre-pandemic times, satirist C. J. Hopkins effectively summed up this strategy:

> [A]ll the ruling classes have to do is make up an emotionally-loaded narrative with a halfway-believable official enemy and have their 'authoritative media sources' repeat it, over, and over, and over, in a thousand different iterations, each repetition reifying the others, until the narrative becomes the axiomatic 'truth', which no respectable, normal person would ever think of wanting to question.[44]

What makes the pandemic narrative such a powerful ideological tool is precisely its viral character, which has nothing to do with the virus as real referent. The Covid pandemic, in other words, is the product of its naming, and as such it is supported by a relentless campaign of fear-inducing signifiers that reduplicate automatically. Fundamentally, it is an exercise in semantic simulation. The exploitation of fear is maximized by the fact that our brains have long been wired to respond to simple binary inputs such as negative/positive, healthy/sick, true/false, democratic/fascist, Good/Evil, scarcity/abundance and so on. We live in a 'testing culture' that has replaced the complexity of reality (the context) with its hyperreal caricature, which is why we readily translate a positive test as sickness and contagion. The real object of the test no longer matters, since testing produces its own hyperreal 'truth'. Whatever its result may be, the test is framed in advance by the ideology of testing, which, as Ivan Illich had illustrated,[45] is implanted into our brains from the first years of schooling. In a context of endemic simulation, our lives are ruled by an 'economy of the sign' structured around a binary logic:

> The entire system of communication has passed from that of a syntactically complex language structure to a binary system of question/answer – of perpetual *test*. Now tests and referenda are, we know, perfect forms of simulation: the answer is called forth by the question, it is design-ated in advance.[46]

In a culture saturated with preformatted answers to one-dimensional questions, manipulation turns absolute. Statistics, graphs, and algorithmically cloned media messages produce contagion everywhere, while Covid-19 acquires the status of hyperreality. Should the simulation stop, the fear of the virus would immediately vanish.

It is politically depressing to note that the elites and the left speak with one voice against pseudo-events. The acceleration of the valorization crisis of contemporary capitalism generates the most formidable 'TINA (There Is No Alternative) moment' ever experienced by humanity. Through a seemingly endless series of morality tales, we are being hooked into a matrix with immense totalitarian potential and appetite. We are in the cloud of capitalism's operational system. Subjectively, the result is widespread resignation coupled with misology; objectively, unstoppable implosion: 'a generalised deterrence of every chance, of every accident, of every transversality, of every finality, of every contradiction, rupture or complexity in a sociality illuminated by the norm and doomed to the transparency of detail radiated by data-collecting mechanisms.'[47]

Needless to say, the implosion of our societies is itself marketed as an opportunity for its resetting, which is designed to produce a fairer, safer, and more resilient world, cloaked in green energy for all. This is clearly stated on the website of the World Economic Forum (WEF), which meets every year in Davos.[48] There, the wealthiest and more powerful people of the planet come together to make history. Their idea of resetting the world entails building a 'platform economy' capable of 'unlocking prosperity for billions of workers'. It also involves the commitment of '*corporate activists*: companies that take concrete action on the most prominent challenges that we are facing' such as 'the climate crisis, the increasing disconnection of urban and rural communities, or even the current global pandemic'. Our corporate 'pioneers of change' also know that, while spinning their narratives, they must reinvent faith, which is why they rely on decidedly Franciscan slogans like 'Believe in something, even if it means sacrificing everything.'[49]

Neo-feudal capitalism

'Welcome to 2030. I own nothing, have no privacy, and life has never been better.' This is not a cruel parody, but the title of a short piece by Ida Auken (former Minister for the Environment and currently member of the Danish 'Folketing for the Social Democrats' party) which appeared on the WEF website in 2016.[50] Essentially, Auken tells us that in the near future we will live in model cities where 'I don't own a car. I don't own a house. I don't own any appliances or any clothes.' (Our private property will truly be abolished!). And yet, despite not owning anything, we will finally find happiness, because in the city of digitized services, freed from traffic and pollution, 'we have access to transportation, accommodation, food and all the things we need in our daily lives'. There will be no need to 'pay the rent' either, because when we are out cycling, or picking daisies, 'someone else is using our free space'. Shopping will be a distant memory, as 'the algorithm will do it for me since it knows my taste better than I do by now'. With robotics in full swing, work will have morphed into a pleasant activity: 'thinking-time, creation-time and development-time'. Although Auken is genuinely concerned about the people 'who do not want to live in our city, those we lost on the way, who have perhaps formed little self-supplying communities, or stayed in the empty and abandoned houses in small 19th century villages'; and although, she writes, 'once in a while I get annoyed about the fact that I have no real privacy', since 'somewhere, everything I do, think and dream of is recorded'; despite these small complications, life will be 'much better, because we will have defeated all these terrible things happening: lifestyle diseases, climate change, the refugee crisis, environmental degradation, completely congested cities, water pollution, air pollution, social unrest and unemployment'.

It takes only a small leap of the imagination to grasp that this utopian fairytale is, in truth, a dystopian nightmare. The reason for our dispossession is that, after disciplining the have-nots and impoverishing the middle classes, the world elite will truly own it all. In respect of this vision, the recent pandemic psychodrama appears to be the first step of a longer plan whose overarching goal is the controlled demolition of what remains of the real economy (based on labour-power). If this is true, then Covid-19 was the icebreaker: the inauguration of the accelerated collapse of labour-based society. The latter would lead to the stipulation of a new Leviathanic social contract in which our own survival depends on the 'charitable' intervention of central banks and other supranational monetary institutions. In this context, the 'new normal' is the reshaping of humanity so that it accepts Capitalism 4.0, based on the fourth industrial revolution. Gaining full control over the money supply through central bank digital currencies (CBDCs) appears to be crucial for the reproduction of capitalism, whether in a unipolar or multipolar configuration. To achieve this, the steady devaluation of our hyper-indebted fiat money system, currently dominated by the US dollar, is both necessary and inevitable. Inflation, in other words, would seem to be 'baked into the Covid cake', as well as into overlapping emergencies like the Ukrainian war started in February 2022. The devaluation of money capital means that the impoverished masses will be tied to the new-fangled, highly centralized digital currency infrastructure. It is in this sense that Covid-19 and its variants were deployed to manage an epochal shift to what looks increasingly like a neo-feudal type of senescent capitalist order ruled by monetary seigniorage, whose longevity may well exceed any optimistic expectation for radical transformation.

The media hype around the pandemic had an easy time injecting the virus of fear into today's anaemic social body, which is as hyperactive as psychically empty, and therefore helplessly delivered to manipulation. Technology, mainstream media and the state are but extensions of the economy's global domination. They are entirely subordinate to the power of capital, which requires populations to be docile and meek (that is, isolated, insecure, and scared) vis-à-vis its authoritarian acceleration. Following Baudrillard, we should insist that the implosive trajectory of today's hyper-financialized, debt-based system continues to be concealed by moralistic deterrence coupled with the coding of reality into hyperreal simulation. The apocalyptic Covid-19 narrative allowed the economic, social, political and biological spheres to meet in a hyperreal bubble of lies. Global governance in the field of bio-security is perhaps the most evident manifestation of this predicament, which finds its ideal economic expression in so-called 'stakeholder capitalism': while gobbling up huge stock market profits, managers and shareholders of large multinationals also control a powerful political and media-friendly front driven by philanthropic sensitivity. After all, the WEF defines itself as an 'International Organization for Public-Private Cooperation',[51] and no doubt it is one, since it promotes the private interests of the wealthiest as they co-opt social and environmental (i.e., public) issues, peddling the ideological fantasy that we are all stakeholders, all sharing the same challenges and dividends. As Baudrillard intimated, this strategy works, for any voice of dissent vis-à-vis irresistibly compassionate fantasies is a priori re-coded as right-wing extremism. As French journalist Olivier Malnuit put it in 2006,[52] and as was later popularized by Slavoj Žižek,[53] we should think of the Davos billionaires as 'liberal communists', an ironic oxymoron that captures nicely the ruse at the heart of the public-private cooperation narrative.

The bottom line is that, by instituting a near-ontological state of meta-emergency, the capitalist Moloch aims to silence and subjugate the whole planet. Behind the mask of *Homo Pandemicus* lies the cynical grin of *Homo Economicus*, who desperately tries to manage its own increasingly unmanageable contradiction by pushing for paradigm change. Covid, then, is the latest form of capitalist realism, for lockdowns and the global suspension of economic transactions allowed the Federal Reserve (US Central Bank) to flood the ailing financial markets (which in September 2019 were again on the verge of a catastrophic crash) with trillions of freshly printed dollars, thereby avoiding the risk of sudden hyperinflation and ensuing social chaos. Simultaneously, the Covid scenario acted as the ideal 'window of opportunity' not only for the introduction of the digital infrastructure (vaccine passports) as a pillar of the incipient neo-feudal regime of capitalist accumulation; but also for the controlled demolition of liberal democratic societies through the gradual devaluation of their fiat currencies.[54] The destruction of large sectors of the real economy and, at the same time, the draconian biopolitical measures of social control imposed through the emergency mantras, are integral to the 'insane rationality' of capital, which by nature is indifferent to those who are crushed or left behind. As Marx had noted, the capitalist mode of production is so blind in its lust for profit that it even destroys the very sources of value, i.e. wage-earners on the one hand, and land and natural resources on the other.

Conclusion

By applying some of Baudrillard's key categories, I have argued that the coronavirus crisis that hit the world in 2020 was the apotheosis of a formal model of coding no longer built around the socio-symbolic production of reality, or even its ideological fabrication. Rather, it is based on the tyranny of a closed operational circuit that, in defining our relationship with the world, a priori excludes the ontological ambivalence of the real, recreating objectivity as reified hyperreality. This model functions through an emergency loop: the simulated reproduction of crises and conflicts that are vastly disproportionate in respect of their actual threat. The ideological violence of today's mode of societal reproduction lies in the magnetic field it generates through its coding. The advent of virtuality and digitality has made the totalitarian nightmare possible by hooking humanity into the 'capitalist cloud'. What we are left with is a self-totalizing matrix that generates a hypnotic reality-effect through ubiquitous networks of preformatted news, data, statistics, differentials and so on. Today, hyperreality is a self-fulfilling prophecy impeccably realised in the info-sphere. As such, it knows no transcendence, only the immanence of a molecular code that unifies the world under a single reproductive principle. While production is increasingly dependent on labour-shedding technology, capital replicates itself through the virtual signs of finance, whose debt-fuelled orbital loop is now decoupled from real growth in the 'work society'. In this respect, financial simulation can be seen as the sublimated truth, and nemesis, of the founding capitalist fiction it compensates for, namely the one based on the spurious equivalence between money and labour-time.[55]

When global capitalism is increasingly threatened by its own incontinence (a debt hyper-bubble it is no longer able to manage), it has no choice but gamble on the therapeutic power of emergencies,[56] upping the stakes on what was always a favourite weapon. Today, this means exploiting formidable 'narratives of guilt and misfortune'. Never before were humans reduced to such mute obedience. We are therefore witnessing the accelerated and at the same time *controlled* demolition of liberal consumer capitalism, which is now obsolete. Global financial and geopolitical interests will be secured by mass data harvesting, blockchain ledgers, and digital apps peddled as empowering innovation. At the heart of our predicament lies the ruthless evolutionary logic of a socioeconomic system that, to survive, is ready to sacrifice its democratic framework and embrace a monetary regime supported by corporate-owned science and technology, media propaganda and disaster narratives accompanied by pseudo-humanitarian philanthropy.

Again, this is capitalist realism at its most cynical. Breaking with today's implosive authoritarian dynamic is increasingly urgent. Repeating Antonio Gramsci, however, it would seem that a long 'interregnum awaits us, where the old is dying and the new cannot be born, and a great variety of morbid symptoms appear'.[57] And yet, when no head-on resistance seems to have any chance of succeeding; when integral virality infiltrates every nook and cranny of our lives; when all negativity is absorbed into systemic entropy; then, perhaps our best chance is to bet on the system's inconsistency, which alone leaves open the possibility for new singularities to emerge. Baudrillard defined singularity as that 'which doesn't resist, but constitutes itself as another universe with another set of rules, which may conceivably get exterminated, but which, at a particular moment, represent an insuperable obstacle for the system itself'.[58] As William

Pawlett put it, quoting from *Symbolic Exchange and Death*, 'Baudrillard's conviction is that people will never acquiesce to the system and resign themselves to being merely "the capitalist of their own lives".'[59]

Baudrillard once intimated that in any perfect crime, the crime is perfection: it coincides with the attempt to set up a watertight totalitarian structure where all accidents are either pre-empted or defused and eliminated.[60] Today this crime lies in the capitalist will to cleanse the world of what cannot be brought under total control. Yet we must insist that domination cannot totalise itself. Inevitably, something will give, for the simple reason that those who are in charge of the matrix are themselves under its influence. Dupers always end up duped by their own duping strategy. The distinctive feature of our global ideological order is that it functions through the automatic proliferation of its effects, while causes are obliterated and disappear into oblivion. In simulated hyperreality, nobody cares for causes any longer. But a world propelled by the reduplication of its destructive effects will struggle to hide its implosion, and with it the emptiness of its cause. It is in connection with the impossibility of achieving complete systemic closure that the strength of our desire to unmask our dystopian narrative will be measured. If we fail, it will mean that we have compromised on our desire, and by implication that our will has also been done.

Notes

1. See Jean Baudrillard, *The Mirror of Production*, trans. by Mark Poster (New York: Telos Press, 1975 [1973]), 114–15.
2. Jean Baudrillard, *Symbolic Exchange and Death* (revised edition), trans. by Iain Hamilton Grant (Los Angeles and London: SAGE, 2017 [1976]), 29.
3. Ibid., 30.
4. See Marcel Mauss, *The Gift. The Form and Reason of Exchange in Archaic Societies* (London: Routledge, 1990 [1925]).
5. Baudrillard, *Symbolic Exchange and Death*, 58. See also Jean Baudrillard, *For a Critique of the Political Economy of the Sign* (New York: Telos Press, 1981 [1972]), 164–84.
6. For Baudrillard, the counter-gift haunts the system as the agent of its potential destruction or destabilization. This may come in various forms (potlach, expenditure, refusal, sacrifice, suicide, inertia, hyper-conformity, etc.), all of which would seem to bear some elementary structural resemblance with the Freudian 'return of the repressed': a disruptive violence that necessarily accompanies all symbolic systems. While Baudrillard sees the counter-gift as a subjective challenge

to existing power relations, his definition of what a counter-gift might entail changes with the progression of his work, making its politicization problematic.

7   Ibid., 44.
8   Jean Baudrillard, *In the Shadow of the Silent Majorities, or the End of the Social and Other Essays*, trans. by Paul Foss, Paul Patton and John Johnston (New York: Semiotext(e), 1983), 35.
9   In Richard Smith's words: 'Rather than a "postmodernist", Baudrillard was, in fact, a trenchant critic of many of the taken-for-granted features of advanced capitalism and western culture – consumerism, the postmodern celebration of pluralism and 'diversity', globalization, capitalism, modernity, mass communication and the information economy – as destroyers of the act and social relation of symbolic exchange' (Richard Smith, 'Introduction: the words of Jean Baudrillard', in *The Baudrillard Dictionary*, edited by R. Smith, Edinburgh, Edinburgh University Press, 2010, 1).
10 See Marshall McLuhan, *Understanding Media: the Extensions of Man* (Abingdon: Routledge, 2001 [1964]).
11 Baudrillard, *Simulations*, trans. by Paul Foss, Paul Patton and Philip Beitchman (New York: Semiotext(e), 1983), 3.
12 Jean Baudrillard, *The Perfect Crime*, trans. by Chris Turner (London and New York: Verso 2008 [1995]).
13 Baudrillard, *Symbolic Exchange and Death*, 81.
14 Jean Baudrillard, *Seduction*, trans. by Brian Singer (London: Macmillan, 1990 [1979]).
15 Baudrillard, *In the Shadow of the Silent Majorities*, 71.
16 Ibid., 77.
17 Ibid., 96.
18 Baudrillard, *Simulations*, 70.
19 Ibid., 152.
20 Herbert Marcuse, *One-Dimensional Man* (Abingdon: Routledge, 2002), 59–86.
21 Ibid., 135–7.
22 See Jacques Lacan, 'Du discours psychanalytique', in *Lacan in Italia 1953–1978 / Lacan en Italie*, edited by G. B. Contri (Milan: La Salamandra), 32–55; and Jacques Lacan, *Television*, in *October* 40, 1987, 6–50.
23 Jean Baudrillard, *The Conspiracy of Art*, trans. by Ames Hodges (New York, Semiotext(e), 2005 [1996]), 202.
24 See https://www.ft.com/content/00b4937c-d47b-11e4-8be8-00144feab7de and https://www.imf.org/-/media/Files/Publications/covid19-special-notes/en-special-series-on-covid-19-the-disconnect-between-financial-markets-and-the-real-economy.ashx
25 Jean Baudrillard, *Screened Out*, trans. by Chris Turner (London and New York: Verso, 2002 [2000]), 31–2 (my italics).

26 See https://www.liberation.fr/tribune/1997/05/07/opposer-a-le-pen-la-vituperation-morale-c-est-lui-laisser-le-privilege-de-l-insolence-la-conjuration_206413, all translations are mine. The article has also been published with the title 'Exorcism in Politics or the Conspiracy of Imbeciles' in Baudrillard, *Screened Out*, 203–8.
27 Baudrillard, *The Conspiracy of Art*, 89.
28 Baudrillard, *Screened Out*, 79.
29 Baudrillard, *Simulations*, 27.
30 Jean Baudrillard, *The Transparency of Evil*, trans. by James Benedict (London and New York: Verso, 1993 [1990]), 81.
31 Jean Baudrillard, *Fragments. Conversations with Françoise L'Yvonnet*, trans. by Chris Turner (London: Routledge, 2004 [2001]), 59. 'Ideologized misfortune has become a kind of emblem today, and a mode of action. There's a whole "actionalism" of the deficit and the handicap, of legal action and seeking damages. The whole of the social order now rests on this kind of trading on misfortune, from which secondary gains may be derived' (Ibid.).
32 Jean Baudrillard, *The Intelligence of Evil of the Lucidity Pact*, trans. by Chris Turner (Oxford: Berg, 2005 [2004]), 171.
33 Baudrillard, *Simulations*, 28–9.
34 See https://time.com/4486502/hillary-clinton-basket-of-deplorables-transcript/
35 See Domenico Losurdo, *Liberalism: a Counter-History*, trans. by Gregory Elliot (London and New York: Verso, 2011).
36 Baudrillard, *Simulations*, 29.
37 See Roberto Esposito, *Immunitas: The Protection and Negation of Life*, trans. by Zakiya Hanafi (London: Polity Press, 2011 [2002]).
38 Max Horkheimer, 'The Jews and Europe', in E. Bronner and D. Kellner (eds), *Critical Theory and Society. A Reader* (London and New York: Routledge, 1989), 77–94 (78).
39 Baudrillard distinguished four modes of attack and defence embodied by different life forms: wolves, rats, cockroaches and viruses. The latter are considered the most dangerous because of their invisibility. See Baudrillard, *Fragments*, 71–2.
40 See Jean Baudrillard, *The Ecstasy of Communication*, trans. by Bernard and Caroline Schutze (New York: Semiotext(e), 1988).
41 Baudrillard, *Simulation*, 32.
42 Ibid., 133–4.
43 Baudrillard, *The Conspiracy of Art*, 66 and 69.
44 C. J. Hopkins, *The War on Populism. Consent Factory Essays Vol. II (2018–2019)* (Consent Factory Publishing, 2020), 28.
45 Ivan Illich, *Deschooling Society* (New York: Harper, 1970).
46 Baudrillard, *Simulations*, 116–17.
47 Baudrillard, *Simulations*, 64.
48 See https://www.weforum.org/agenda/2020/11/digitalization-platform-economy-covid-recovery/

49 See https://www.managementtoday.co.uk/modern-leaders-need-powerful-narrative/reputation-matters/article/1498184
50 The piece was reproduced here: https://www.forbes.com/sites/worldeconomicforum/2016/11/10/shopping-i-cant-really-remember-what-that-is-or-how-differently-well-live-in-2030/?sh=400cd76b1735
51 See https://www.weforum.org/about/world-economic-forum
52 See the French magazine *Technikart* (no. 99, 25 January 2006).
53 See https://www.lrb.co.uk/the-paper/v28/n07/slavoj-Žižek/nobody-has-to-be-vile
54 I have argued these points in detail in the following pieces: 'A Self-Fulfilling Prophecy: Systemic Collapse and Pandemic Simulation', *The Philosophical Salon*, 16 August 2021; 'The Central Bankers' Long Covid: An Incurable Condition', *The Philosophical Salon*, 18 October 2021; 'Variants, Inflation, and the Controlled Demolition of Society', *The Philosophical Salon*, 3 January 2022.
55 I have developed this theme in *Unworkable. Delusions of an Imploding Civilization* (New York: SUNY Press, 2022).
56 'When it is threatened today, by simulation (the threat of vanishing in the play of signs), power risks the real, risks crisis, it gambles on remanufacturing artificial, economic, political stakes. This is a question of life and death for it. But it is too late.' (Baudrillard, *Simulations*, 44).
57 Antonio Gramsci, *Selections from the Prison Notebooks* (New York: International Publishers 1971 [1947]), 275–6.
58 Baudrillard, *Fragments*, 71.
59 William Pawlett, *Jean Baudrillard* (London and New York: Routledge 2007), 66.
60 See Baudrillard, *Fragments*, 64.

Bibliography

Baudrillard, Jean. *The Mirror of Production*. New York: Telos Press, 1975.
Baudrillard, Jean. *For a Critique of the Political Economy of the Sign*. New York: Telos Press, 1981.
Baudrillard, Jean. *Simulations*. New York: Semiotext(e), 1983.
Baudrillard, Jean. *In the Shadow of the Silent Majorities, or the End of the Social and Other Essays*. New York: Semiotext(e), 1983.
Baudrillard, Jean. *The Ecstasy of Communication*. New York: Semiotext(e), 1988.
Baudrillard, Jean. *Seduction*. London: Macmillan, 1990.
Baudrillard, Jean. *The Transparency of Evil*. London and New York: Verso, 1993.
Baudrillard, Jean. *Screened Out*. London and New York: Verso, 2002.
Baudrillard, Jean. *Fragments. Conversations with Françoise L'Yvonnet*. London: Routledge, 2004.
Baudrillard, Jean. *The Intelligence of Evil of the Lucidity Pact*. Oxford: Berg, 2005.

Baudrillard, Jean. *The Conspiracy of Art*. New York, Semiotext(e), 2005.
Baudrillard, Jean. *The Perfect Crime*. London and New York: Verso 2008.
Baudrillard, Jean. *Symbolic Exchange and Death*. Los Angeles and London: SAGE, 2017.
Esposito, Roberto. *Immunitas: The Protection and Negation of Life*. London: Polity Press, 2011.
Gramsci, Antonio. *Selections from the Prison Notebooks*. New York: International Publishers 1971.
Hopkins, C. J. *The War on Populism. Consent Factory Essays Vol. II (2018–2019)*. Consent Factory Publishing, 2020.
Horkheimer, Max. 'The Jews and Europe', in E. Bronner and D. Kellner (eds), *Critical Theory and Society. A Reader*. London and New York: Routledge, 1989, 77–94.
Illich, Ivan. *Deschooling Society*. New York: Harper, 1970.
Lacan, Jacques. 'Du discours psychanalytique', in *Lacan in Italia 1953–1978 / Lacan en Italie*, edited by G. B. Contri. Milan: La Salamandra, 1978, 32–55.
Lacan, Jacques. *Television*, in *October* 40, 1987, 6–50.
Losurdo, Domenico. *Liberalism: A Counter-History*. London and New York: Verso, 2011.
Marcuse, Herbert. *One-Dimensional Man*. Abingdon: Routledge, 2002.
Mauss, Marcel *The Gift. The Form and Reason of Exchange in Archaic Societies*. London: Routledge, 1990.
McLuhan, Marshall. *Understanding Media: The Extensions of Man*. Abingdon: Routledge, 2001.
Pawlett, William. *Jean Baudrillard*. London and New York: Routledge, 2007.
Smith, Richard. 'Introduction: the words of Jean Baudrillard', in *The Baudrillard Dictionary*, edited by R. Smith, Edinburgh: Edinburgh University Press, 2010.
Vighi, Fabio. *Unworkable. Delusions of an Imploding Civilization*. New York: SUNY Press, 2022.

Index

Althusser, Louis 32, 99–101, 103n, 147, 170
Agamben Giorgio 2, 3, 5, 107, 168–9, 177
Arendt, Hannah 9, 36, 47–50
Aristotle 120
Auken, Ida 208
Austin, John Langshaw 98

Badiou, Alain 178n.
Barthes, Roland 41
Bakunin, Mikhail Alexandrovich 78, 179n.
Baudrillard, Jean 5, 184, 195–214
Beck, Ulrich 113
Benjamin, Walter 94–5, 159n.
Benveniste, Émile 89
Bergson, Henri 39
Bezos, Jeff 159n, 165
Bion, Wilfred 28
Blair, Tony 113
Boas, George 52
Bordieu, Pierre 74
Brecht, Bertolt 92

Castells, Manuel 66
Celan, Paul 37
Char, René 36
Chiesa, Lorenzo 192
Christie, Agatha 183
Clinton, Hillary 202
Copjec, Joan 173
Coppola, Francis Ford 181n.

Davis, Mike 81
Debord, Guy 77
Deleuze, Gilles 3, 30, 36–9, 41, 82
Derrida, Jacques 3, 82n.
Descartes, René 146
Dyer, Joe 65–6

Esposito, Roberto 203
Ewald, François 114

Foucault, Michel 3, 12, 73–5, 78, 105–14, 160n, 168–9
Frank, André Gunder 76
Freud, Sigmund 4, 32, 100, 120, 143, 160n, 162n.
Friedman, Milton 180n.

Gehlen, Arnold 12
Geiger, Theodor 3, 76, 83n.
Giddens, Anthony 113
Gide, André 129
Gilroy, Tony 180n.
Gramsci, Antonio 211
Guolo, Renzo 116n.

Habermas, Jürgen 48–50
Hayek, Friedrich August von 178n.
Heidegger, Martin 36–7, 145, 188
Hegel, Georg Wilhelm Friedrich, 3, 5, 51, 67–73, 75–6, 78–0, 82n, 88, 93, 100–1, 163n, 166, 179n, 192–3
Hitler, Adolf 60
Hopkins, Christopher J. 206
Horkheimer, Max 203–4
Hussein, Saddam 203

Illich, Ivan 207

Kafka, Franz 42
Kant, Immanuel 67–8, 74, 75–8, 150, 181n, 188
King, Stephen 55
Kojève, Alexander 88, 163n.

Lacan, Jacques, 1, 2, 4, 21–33, 40, 43, 54–7, 81, 88–90, 101, 119–25, 128–9, 135–9, 141–2, 144, 149, 151–8, 161n, 163n, 188–9, 191–2, 198
Lasch, Christopher 66
Le Bon, Gustav 32
Le Carrè, John 115n.
Lefort, Claude 43

Le Pen, Jean-Marie 200, 202, 203
Lévi-Strauss, Claude 180n.
Losurdo, Domenico 203

Machiavelli, Niccolò 15, 81
Marcuse, Herbert 12, 143, 198
Marx, Karl 4, 5, 60–70, 81, 105–14, 119, 120, 126–7, 136–3, 148, 155, 157, 159n, 160n, 168, 170–1, 179n, 180n, 187
Mauss, Marcel 195
McLuhan, Marshall 50–1, 196
Melville, Herman 42
Merleau-Ponty, Maurice 43
Miller Jacques-Alain 90, 122,
Monroe, Marilyn 199
Mussolini, Benito 60

Nancy, Jean-Luc 27

Pascal, Blaise 4, 119, 123–4, 135–7, 141, 144–58, 161n, 163n.
Pasolini, Pier Paolo 78
Pawlett, William 212
Plato 88, 95, 103n, 121, 130
Poe, Edgar Allan 206
Polybius 80
Proust, Marcel 38–9, 42
Putin, Vladimir 203

Quadagno, Jill 113, 116n.

Racine, Jean 90, 99
Ranciere, Jacques 73
Redi, Carlo Alberto 115n.
Russell, David O. 180n.

Sade, Donatien Alphonse François (Marquis de) 163n, 164n.
Saussure, Ferdinand de 89
Schmitt, Carl 12, 36
Shakespeare, William 41
Simoniti, Jure 103n.
Smith, Adam 71, 162n, 178n.
Smith, Richard 213

Thatcher, Margaret 137–8
Thompson, J. Lee 87
Trump, Donald 203

Wachowski (Lana & Lilly) 184, 199
Walby, Sylvia 113
Warhol, Andy 199
Weber, Max 4, 135

Žižek, Slavoj 3, 5, 87–103, 147, 209
Zuckerberg, Mark 189–90

www.ingramcontent.com/pod-product-compliance
Lightning Source LLC
Chambersburg PA
CBHW062221300426

44115CB00012BA/2165